Contents

PART 5: And They All Lived Happily Ever After . . .

Foreword

Too often we tend to think of folklore, legend and myth as distinct from religion and history, and less important in historical terms. In actual fact, history and folklore have been almost indistinguishable from each other for millennia, just as myths were once the religions of great and fallen empires.

Nowadays, we tend to make a hard distinction between fact and fantasy, legend and faith. But fantasy is not merely a collection of meaningless dreams and fairy tales. Dreams have all kinds of meaning, for those prepared to look for them. Like fairy stories, they show us the truth through the lens of fantasy. Magic is sacred or profane, depending on the practitioner. The relationship between simple faith and simple suspension of disbelief is in the eye of the believer. The common thread that links them all is *story*, and its relationship with power.

History is the account of events as recorded by those in power.

Religion is often the tool of that power, used to enforce its authority.

But *folklore* is the story of the common people, their hopes and dreams, or their desires and fears, passed from mouth to mouth, often in defiance of those in authority, for generations. And because over the centuries, the common people have not had the same access to education and literacy as those who write the history books, this common lore has always been on the margins of history, fragmented; half-forgotten; eclipsed by the tyranny of the printed word, the history we think we know.

What better place, then, now, to find those marginalised by society? We are living in a time of increasing intolerance for those who defy society's norms. The word 'queer', which entered the English language sometime in the sixteenth century, derives from a number of sources, notably from the

Latin *torquere*, 'to twist', and until the nineteenth century, where it began to imply sexual deviancy, meant 'odd, wrong, peculiar'. Nowadays it has been reclaimed as a term to describe those who are neither *heterosexual* nor *cisgender*, both words that entered our language relatively recently, much to the disapproval of those who wish to control its story and prevent its evolution.

Because language, too, is a narrative. Like myth, like religion, it comes from many sources – some official, some unofficial. According to the narrative that most of us are familiar with, queerness is a modern phenomenon, and the modern, alarming queerness of mermaids or unicorns is a recent deviation from the norm, subverting the innocence of our childhood fairy tales and making them into something dangerous.

Nothing could be further than the truth. Much of the folklore, myth and legend we remember from childhood comes to us through the distorting lens of colonialism and Christianity. The Victorians not only reinvented the concept of fairy stories, but also imposed their morality on them, bowdlerising them, erasing any trace of a past that did not conform to their standards. And yet, even a casual glance into the world of folklore shows that it has *always* been dangerous; always subversive; always sexual; always queer.

Stories tell us *who* we are. Folklore tries to tell us *why*. Queerness – and sex – exist as a thread that runs through world mythology. From Africa to China, to India, to South America, to ancient Egypt and all over Europe, gods and folkloric heroes change sex, fall in love with beings of the same sex, become hermaphrodite, transform into beings of a different sex, or sometimes assume an asexual aspect. From *The Epic of Gilgamesh* to *The Iliad*, queer relationships abound. Lives, identities and experiences that we would categorise as trans are often historically portrayed as especially sacred.

In folklore and legend throughout the world, queerness is alive and well, and if, as Jung maintains, all these are part of a larger, collective unconscious, then queerness has been part of our collective story since the existence of story itself; sometimes hidden, sometimes repressed, sometimes even forbidden, but always heartfelt, vibrant, alive; speaking truth to power.

Joanne Harris

Author Notes: Mind Your She's and Q's

Queerness, or anything that relates to lesbian, gay, bisexual, transgender and asexual people as well as a host of other identities, is a fascinating but thorny concept. The very word 'queer', which appears in the title and throughout the book, is still perceived as divisive, even repellent by some, and the LGBTQ+ community don't necessarily share all the same opinions on its applicability.

When I was at school, in the late nineties and early 2000s, 'queer' was a slur, something that might accompany a punch in the face, but it was also on the poster for the very first gay social event I ever went to. For me, the meaning of this word has therefore always had a duality, but it has evolved, from something dirty, to something cold and academic, then slowly into something I now use freely and easily. It is for me an umbrella that can encompass anyone within the lesbian, gay, bisexual, transgender, asexual and intersex spectrum of identities who wishes to shelter under it. It is a term that acknowledges the complex political history of people like us, and it is a word that spits in the face of that which would shame us. But if you personally don't like the word, I understand.

THE LIBRARY IS OPEN

What is folklore? I have taken the idea of folklore in its very broadest and least 'academic' sense by simply breaking it into its two constituent parts: 'folk' and 'lore'.

In this book folklore is any lore (meaning story) that folk (meaning people) tell. While some argue that 'true' folklore must be spread by spoken word, rather than recorded or written down, I do not make this distinction. Therefore, a book, a children's nursery rhyme, an oral tradition, a legend, a song and a myth are, for the purposes of this book, all receptacles of folklore. More controversially I also count films, video games, gossip, pop music, newspaper cartoons, erotic doodles and fashion trends as kinds of folklore, at least where they are relevant to people and the stories we tell.

A 'myth' has certain specific connotations; it is a story that explains something about the world or its origins, for example where the sun comes from, or why people fall in love. A 'legend' also has particular meaning; it is normally a story that includes an element of a fabricated or partially fictionalised history, such as the legendary adventures of King Arthur. These semantic distinctions will often be glossed over. In this book, all these ways of telling stories will be treated equally as sources, whether they are fairy tales, ancient texts, or popular culture tropes.

THE LION, THE WITCH AND THE PRONOUN

A pronoun in English is used to denote the gender or sex of a person: he, she, they, etc. Their use has been largely uncontroversial until we come to talk about transgender people, who may wish to use pronouns that strangers may believe to be 'wrong' or 'different', but which accurately express and reflect their lived identity. Transgender women will on the whole use 'she', just like their cisgender* counterparts. Transgender men will largely use 'he', and nonbinary people may use a gender-neutral pronoun, 'they/them', or what is termed a 'neopronoun', such as 'xe/ze'. When talking about living people I will always use the pronouns that they identify with.

Now, the clever reader may have spotted an issue. This is a book of folklore that blends historical and anthropological accounts, and

---

* Cisgender simply means anyone that is not transgender. For example, people who like myself who are assigned a gender at birth and continue to identify with that gender. I was born and assigned male, today I am a man, therefore I am a cisgender man.

therefore doesn't always deal with a living person who might speak for themselves. Additionally, it often explores mythical beings. How does one gender a long-dead person, let alone a legendary spirit? Where possible I will use the pronoun most commonly used by the individual when talking about themselves. Failing that, I will use the pronoun associated with them in their lifetime, as long as this is done in a way that respects their identity. Where there is a person who does not express a particular pronoun for use, and there are clear indicators that this person actively cultivated an identity that blurred lines of the gender binary, I will go for a gender-neutral 'they'. In cases where a person was living their life as a woman or a man, and there is evidence that they wanted to be perceived as such, I will use the corresponding pronoun irrespective of how regressive historical sources might describe them. When it comes to mythical, literary or supernatural beings, I will treat them as if they were people and use similar rules as above, but with particular emphasis on their authors, source communities and how they were spoken about.*

I will add that history is a living beast. Over time, as more research appears, the way we talk about particular people, their genders and sexualities in particular, might change after further evidence is uncovered. I would hope to update the use of gender markers (and other terminology) in this book when and if this happens.

---

* One area where I have made a decision that some readers may not agree with is around the gendering of so-called 'eunuch' or 'gallus' priests. Modern historians often write about these ancient castes of religious devotees as simply being 'feminine men' who have been castrated.

In source texts there are examples of them being described using both male and female pronouns, depending on the writer and the situation. By looking at the cultural role that these people fulfilled, how they were treated and perceived, I have chosen to use a gender-neutral pronoun to describe them or a feminine one. I also occasionally refer to them as priestesses rather than priests. It is true that any number of contemporary interpretations of these people's gender presentation could be argued to be valid or correct, as we have very few sources from the people themselves as to how they chose to identify.

FAIRY IN A BOTTLE

Among LGBTQ+ people there is a real hunger for representation. Queer history as a specific, organised and continuous area of enquiry, outside individual interest, has only existed for roughly fifty years. Therefore gay, lesbian, bisexual, transgender, asexual and queer people are all looking for missing representation in the past that speaks to their lives today. I understand this need – it was one of the things that drove me to write this book. But within this need, things can get unpleasantly territorial.

A person who died 600 years ago becomes a person to fight over – were they gay, or bisexual? Did she marry a man out of true desire, or was she a lesbian trapped in a loveless marriage? Is this person simply a cross-dressing feminine man, or a trans woman lacking the vocabulary of contemporary gender expression?

Rarely, if we go back more than a hundred years, do we find people who match contemporary queer identities exactly. There are women who love women, men who love men, and people whose sense of gender did not fit a rigid binary.* But these people were largely not using terms like 'gay', 'bisexual', 'lesbian' or 'trans', which only go back a century or so. Therefore what I aim to do is describe a person's life as openly and respectfully as possible, and to show the similarities with contemporary queer people's lives, without firmly labelling them. I may use contemporary terms anecdotally, simply for the sake of understanding for a contemporary audience, but in most cases I can acknowledge that these words or concepts would not have been fully understood by the people being discussed.

I hope, in doing this, to do a fair job of reflecting the past for what it

---

* Gender nonconformity and gender fluidity are complex ideas when it comes to talking about queer people. Just because a man or woman did not conform to rigid gender archetypes does not necessarily make them queer. There is controversy around mislabelling those who played with gender but still identified as men or women. That being said, throughout history gender nonconformity has also been a way for the LGBTQ+ community to express their identities, and can signify a gender identity outside or beyond the binary.

was, not just exploiting it as a mirror for today. I also hope to push away from this infighting around ownership of LGBTQ+ historical figures, so we can share our icons, heroes and idols. Because of the sheer complexity, I believe no particular identity should claim sole ownership of any person's life.

This even goes for mythical beings. Is a mermaid a feminist symbol or is she a queer symbol, or do merfolk say something about race, or disability? Ownership of people and symbols by minority groups, both within and outside the queer umbrella, is obviously a powerful and meaningful thing. I will endeavour to treat this with respect.

FLOWERS IN THE DARK

Historically ideas like age of consent, healthy relationships and equality have also changed enormously. Using homoeroticism in ancient Greece as an example: the kind of relationships these men were having with other men were not always the kind we should be celebrating today as ideal. Sex with underage boys, and abusive, incestuous or unbalanced relationships between men were not uncommon, and in some contexts were even celebrated. History doesn't care for our modern sensibilities, our desire to have flattering or affirming representations; it is its own beast. What I will assert is that these stories that make us deeply uncomfortable as queer people today are no less bad than the stories of men who loved women, or women who loved men.

As tempting as it might be to sand off the edges and present queer history in its best light (and, understandably, out of fear of how it can be used by those who wish to cause us harm today), I think we need to look at history warts and all. We are no worse than cisgender heterosexual people, but we are definitely no better either.

Another important point to make is that throughout history queer life was often challenging, and to some extent lived in secret. Even in so-called golden eras of same-sex love or gender nonconformity, eras I would argue are often looked at through very rose-tinted spectacles by our community, there was a shadow of prejudice, hatred and danger. People who live hard lives, who love in secret and struggle with their own identities may also make for less than perfect icons. This should come as no surprise. If you grow a flower in a dark cupboard, with only a small shaft of light, the plant may grow strange, or crooked, its leaves pale or shrivelled. Queer history is full of incredible fighters, and individuals persevering against unbelievable odds, but not all of these people come out undamaged. For people living like this, we do not need to condone their behaviour when it is harmful, abusive or unpleasant, but at least we can understand some of its origins.

OF SHAMANS AND SKINWALKERS

Waawaate Fobister in their play *Nanabush A Trickster*:

> Homo, that word cracks me up. There are many words used for two-spirited people in the Indian languages: lhamana from the Zuni, Gatxan from the Tlingit, Nadleeh the Navajo, Mohave the Alyahas, Winkte the Lakota Sioux, Mexoga the Omaha. Oh I can go on and on and on and on, but my favourite, my absolute favourite of them all, is the Anishnaabe word – Agokwe. Agokwe![1]

Perhaps the biggest monster under the bed in any study of history is colonialism, and its ongoing impact on people around the world. When talking about witches, fairies and vampires, much of my readership will picture the creatures born out of the folkloric traditions and popular culture of Europe and what we call the global north. As a white boy growing up in London, these were the examples I was exposed to. But they are obviously not the only examples. And here we come to a question: in including folklore from beyond my own culture, should I really draw parallels? Are Native American beliefs of shapeshifting skinwalkers and werewolves in any way aligned, or does that comparison whitewash and homogenise a set of beliefs with their own entirely separate history and symbolism? Worse still, it may entirely conflate living indigenous spirituality with 'movie monsters' or 'fairy tales'; this isn't just incorrect, it would be deeply offensive.

In this book as a whole I will mostly be focusing on categories of folklore with which I grew up and identified, so the chapters here are largely clustered and themed around the traditions of white and European settlers. I nonetheless want to include examples from other world cultures and indigenous belief systems, but with the full knowledge that these are systems I have never been immersed in, and cannot speak for. When I draw parallels, I do so from a frame of reference that humans the world over have told stories that follow certain beats, and themes, but are not the same.

As an example, in the chapters on ghosts, werewolves and witches I have explored elements of what is often termed 'shamanism' from different cultures. The term itself is a messy one, originating from the word 'samān' from a Tungusic language in Russia possibly describing Buddhist monks, but used throughout anthropology to describe practices of mostly indigenous people from North America as well as African and Asian countries. The very words used in anthropology and history can be inherently colonial, constructing a false 'us' (developed people) versus 'them' (indigenous people) hierarchy of culture.

The same also goes for LGBTQ+ identities. While we are a minority in the global north, queer people are not above enacting colonial ideas upon indigenous beliefs. Within Native American people there are concepts such as the third gender or two-spiritedness that it can be tempting to make synonymous with ideas of transgender identity. Similarly in the Pacific, ideas like 'takatāpui' of the Maori people might seem to overlap with certain LGBT identities. Many living people from these communities may even resonate with both sets of identities, but that does not mean they are the same. I hope that by their inclusion I am showing a sense of shared humanity, and not claiming ownership, or any deep-lived understanding.

I have asked for input from some indigenous individuals but the responsibility for good representation is not down to them. Therefore if I have misused a term, misrepresented an identity or a culture due to my ignorance, I apologise.

Introduction: Monsters in the Closet

Transport yourself to a Pride parade in any major city in the world. Consider the costumes you might see. Among the glitter and feathers, tank tops and hoodies, tiaras and Doc Martens, certain themes might recur. Whether in Paris, Rio, Tokyo or Sydney you will see papier-mâché unicorn heads trailing sequins, drag queens wearing mermaid tails, and more fairy wings and cat ears than you can shake a trident at.

To be clear, having a love for magic, mythical creatures and folklore is not something unique or specific to the LGBTQ+ community. Still, I would argue that the extent and depth of this goes beyond the status quo. From the language we use, both flattering and derogatory – 'fairy', 'bear', 'wolf', 'unicorn' – to the iconography used by LGBTQ+ charities and groups, there is something going on here. More than meets the eye.

This book was written to explore this, unpack this, and to make a statement. That statement is that we haven't just borrowed these symbols or co-opted them: we are woven into them. The bedtime stories of mermaids, vampires and fairies that many of us grew up loving were often created – or contain monsters and characters that were inspired – by people who had similar lives and loves to the lesbian, gay, bisexual and transgender people living today. These are stories that echo back hundreds and even thousands of years. The monsters and heroes we dress up as, the designs we tattoo our bodies with and the niche areas of academia we tend to throw ourselves into are no accident or mere quirk. In fact, to truly understand who queer people are today involves an adventure into the fantastical stories of our past.

As a museum worker, for me this started with artefacts: collections and paintings from museums and galleries around the world. But it soon took me away to some bizarre and surprising places: ancient temples of Syria, the HIV crisis in New York, the origin stories of superheroes, alien abductions, demonology textbooks and the satanic panic of the 1980s, just to name a few. This is going to be a wild ride through the night; monster by monster, myth by myth. There will be tales of bloodthirsty fairies, Victorian melodrama, burned love letters and flamboyant drag queens.

It's not always a happy place; if you know anything about LGBTQ+ history this will come as no surprise. These are too often stories of unfair and cruel treatment, unspoken love, unseen people, occasionally even death and torture. The histories contained within this book hold a lot of power and often tackle subjects that are sensitive and complex. Rather than adding content warnings for individual chapters, which may detract from the words or serve as unnecessary labels, I would like to ask readers to be conscious that some content may be hard to read and potentially distressing. This includes some references to assault, abuse, underage or non-consensual sex and sexual violence. But despite this, for the most part these are stories of people just getting on with their lives, showing remarkable resilience, wit, creativity and joy in places that might seem otherwise unforgiving. It is a deeply human story, despite focusing largely on inhuman monsters. I hope that non-LGBTQ+ people find a sense of meaning here also. You are welcome here. Queer history is everyone's history.

Once upon a time . . .

PART 1

Queer Be Dragons

(Magical creatures)

Come away, O human child!
To the waters and the wild.
With a faery, hand in hand,
For the world's more full of weeping than you can understand.

From 'The Stolen Child' by W. B. Yeats

A Twist in the Tail

I can picture myself at seven years old, sitting down in front of the small television in my parents' cigarette-stained living room on a Saturday morning, remote in hand. I was watching, rewinding and rewatching a particular section of my well-worn VHS tape of Disney's *The Little Mermaid*.

Although this was my favourite Disney film, starring Ariel as the titular mermaid, the particular scene that enthralled seven-year-old me featured Ursula, the large and vivacious cecaelia. Years later I would learn that a cecaelia is a half-human, half-octopus hybrid; it is a mermaid spin-off. The sea witch of the original fairy tale was written as a traditional mermaid with a fishtail, but the Disney writers and animators wanted Ursula to be something more sinister and visually different from Ariel. Ursula therefore appears as an enormous spiky-haired woman with six curling black tentacles instead of human legs. Eight legs would be normal for an octopus, but Disney animators baulked at the idea of having to animate so many limbs. Still, the cecaelia is more or less an entirely 2000s take on the classical mermaid. While terrifying seafood-hybrid monstrosities like the ancient Greek Echidna and Phorcys or medieval drawings of sea monks might come close, true octopus people appear mostly in contemporary fantasy writing and art. Urusula is a mermaid with a camp gothic twist; a mermaid in drag.

The scene I watched over and over again depicts Ursula as she gloats about stealing Ariel's voice in exchange for granting the mermaid legs. Ursula belts out 'Poor Unfortunate Souls' with feigned empathy to mock all the lives that she, shrewd businesswoman that she is, has ripped off and destroyed. This one musical sequence had such a strange impact on me, watching it to the extent that the tape began to stretch, so that while playing the tape back in 1994, lines of black and white static would occasionally cut through the footage and the sound would warp and burble.

In my early twenties I would go to my first live drag show at the currently closed Black Cap bar in London's Camden Town. In this intimate venue, a six-foot-tall drag queen, bedecked in silver sequins and fake pearls, performed on the small beer-soaked stage. To a sweaty room full of drunk gay and bisexual men, she gave an impassioned baritone rendition of 'Proud Mary': a song covered by Tina Turner. The sweat flying from her wig sparkled in the stage lights. It was only then that I realised this vision of gender-ambiguous confidence and glamour reminded me of something else. Of some*one* else, in fact. This drag queen was a powerful figure clutching a feather boa to her heaving rubber bosom, with the very same feel and stage presence as the sea witch in the Disney film.

In the film Ursula uses her two eel sidekicks as boas, thrusting and gyrating as she sings suggestively about 'the power of body language'. Also, she is far from the frail old crone depicted in many European fairy tales, from the likes of the Brothers Grimm. Hans Christian Andersen, who wrote the original story, gave no specific description of the witch beyond her ugly laugh and hideous dwelling made out of the bones of drowned sailors (although Andersen has his very own place later in this story). Original sketches by Disney show that the concept for Ursula was of a wizened, frail, fishtailed hag, and this was later changed due to the animators deciding on a very different direction for her. Instead, Ursula is a full-bodied, unapologetic and commanding figure. Her lipstick is bold cherry-red and her eyelids a rich and vibrant purple. Earlier in the scene we watch her put her makeup on in a large ornate mirror, not unlike watching a drag performer put on their face. Much of this sequence is more Dorian Corey, 1980s drag queen from the New York 'Ball Room' scene featured in the documentary *Paris Is Burning*, than children's bedtime story. Although this is a Disney film created primarily for children and based on one of *the* classic fairy tales of all time, sequences such as Ursula's can be directly compared to a drag show.

Moving beyond Disney, some of the recent cinematic representations of mermaid-inspired folklore have also developed a strong queer fanbase.

Both the Pixar animation *Luca*, about two sea monsters who transform into boys on land, and *The Shape of Water*, Guillermo Del Toro's retelling of 'The Little Mermaid' with a romance between a mute human and amphibious monster, have been heralded as deeply empowering by the queer community. Even after *Luca*'s director explicitly denied any intentional queer coding, saying, 'We were quite aware that we wanted to talk about that time in life before boyfriends and girlfriends. So there's an innocence and a focus on the friendship side', he still confessed, 'We thought a lot about having to "show your sea monster" as embracing your own difference, and as a metaphor for anything'.[1]

Authorial intent aside, the community continues to claim ownership; for many of us the symbolism of certain fantasy tropes as an LGBTQ+ herald is just too baked in. Queerness is so instilled in the very blood of the mermaid, that however she is presented she will always be deeply connected to us.

Recently, depictions of mermaids have appeared on the worldwide television reality-show sensation *RuPaul's Drag Race*. In season ten, an entire runway fashion challenge, 'The Mermaid Fantasy', was devoted to mermaids, inspired in part by Bette Midler and her performance as 'the Divine Miss M', a mermaid in a wheelchair. In an episode of Holland's *Drag Race*, Ivy-Elise arrives dressed as a hybrid of Ariel and Ursula, quoting, 'You poor unfortunate souls!' in her entrance. Ivy-Elise and two other contestants, Miss Abby OMG and season-two winner Envy Peru, all belong to the Mermaid Mansion, a 'house', or collective of drag queens.

Mermaids are a universal symbol that contemporary queer people use to express themselves in all forms of art and literature. At Tate St Ives, enshrined in a glass cabinet is a burnished red teapot depicting two canoodling mermen entitled *The Mermen of Zennon*, by gay artist Simon Bayliss. This was created by Bayliss in an effort to 'relay contemporary queer experience in Cornwall'. The 2021 children's picture book written by Ian Eagleton and illustrated by James Mayhew, *Nen and the Lonely Fisherman*, tells the story of a fisherman and a merman falling in love and has been heralded as an example of inclusive children's storytelling. In Newfoundland, a group of men including trans men and nonbinary people formed the Merby's group. They celebrate queer body positivity and push

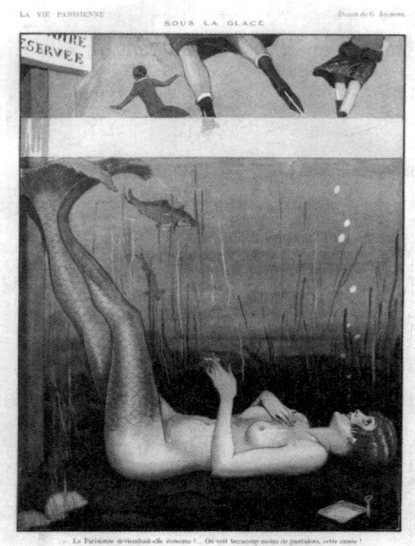

Smoking Lesbian Mermaid by George Leonnec, 1926 (The French text at the bottom of this illustration from *La Vie Parisienne* magazine describes the pictured mermaid's joy at a new fashion for Parisian women not wearing underwear, as they skate above her!)

back against toxic masculinity by dressing as mermen for a series of immensely popular calendars.

So why is this the case? Why are mermaids a symbol that is so instantly recognisable and remixable by queer people? The obvious answer is the mermaid is a glittery, camp and effeminate creature which is just appealing to gay and bisexual men. While there is a grain of truth in this it doesn't go nearly deep enough and leaves out the powerful connections with other queer identities such as trans women, lesbian women and nonbinary people. No, the story of why mermaids are a totem for queer people and the real reason why mermaids appear at Pride parades around the world is a far more ancient one.

WHAT IS A MERMAID?

The word 'mermaid' comes from the Middle English 'mere', meaning 'deep and marshy lake or ocean', and 'maiden', meaning a young virgin woman.[2] Mermaids have existed since the dawn of storytelling and they don't all look alike. Oral traditions and cave paintings depict ancient mermaids. They can be seen in indigenous Australian mythology, such as the tale of the Yawkyawks of Arnhem land, capricious creatures that live in freshwater pools and billabongs who are the daughters or wives of the great primordial World Serpent. This particular family of mermaids goes back at least 65,000 years, probably invented by the very first human arrivals to Australian shores. From the Inuit goddess Sedna, to the Western African Mami-Wata, human-fish beings have been created over and over again. Many of these are intended to be terrifying, dangerous or unsettling, such as the human-faced fish 'ningyo' of Japanese folklore, who are often genderless, horned and have multiple eyes.[3] Most barely resemble the mermaids that are popular in much of the world's media today, but are they mermaids all the same, even if not by name?

Indigenous performer and musician Rafael Montero, who also goes by the name Pampayruna, had this to offer when asked about the subject:

> I am an Aymara and Quichua indigenous, born in Jujuy, Argentina, but my parents' family are from a region in Bolivia with big lakes. I am a homosexual nonbinary person, natural chaman* and a classical singer. I respect the traditions and ceremonies of my ancestors, which we do still at home in Argentina and I now do in London. The ceremony to Pachamama, Mother Earth, and the consecration of instruments to Sirinx, the Godx† of the music who lives in the water.

Rafael explained how Sirino/Sirinx is often depicted today as a half-human and half-fish nonbinary being that blesses musicians' instruments, but their status as a 'mermaid' is complicated by colonial history.

> I think I would call them simply 'Sirinx', the indigenous populations, we don't know the Mermaid stylized in depictions of the occidental‡ Mermaids, but since we were colonised by the Europeans, we began

---

* 'Chaman' is the Spanish pronunciation of the word 'shaman', meaning someone who practices magic, divination or spiritual healing.

† In their words, the term 'Godx' and the use of an 'x' after the name of a deity is used to imply a nonbinary identity, neither a god or goddess, or a fusion of both.

‡ Occidental means anything that refers to Western (European and North American) culture. It is a counterpart to the term 'oriental': a mostly outdated word used to describe Asian people or traditions.

Portion of a tapestry, featuring Sirinx as described by Rafael. Peru, 1680–1720

to depict Sirinx as a European Mermaid. Maybe we call Sirinx now a Mermaid, since the Spanish word for Mermaid is Sirena and in some indigenous languages you don't have the vowel E . . . Sadly, the occidental civilisation has tried and still tries to convert us telling that they all know better than us and that they are progress. Non-binarism and queer-between indigenous people has been hidden since the beginning of the colonialism era, the binarism and homosexuality, depicted as an abomination for the Europeans, was normal in the times before the occupation by the Europeans. But we had to hide them because of the hatred of the occidental people.

Rafael is passionate about advocating for their Godx, telling museums about the story behind the symbols in their collections. Not 'just a mermaid', but a powerful gender-fluid being that only resembles a mermaid and blesses musicians. A god that predates *The Little Mermaid*, but has been unwritten and covered up through layers of colonialism and invasion.

To have a queer god for me is fantastic and I am so happy that my culture accepts it and that is accepted and not banned any more.

And specially because I am a singer and Sirinx is the Godx of the music. It fits perfectly!

Sadly, for many other stories, which either existed before written records or without contemporary living advocates and archaeological evidence, the exact narratives are now lost to us. Many of these creatures died with their storytellers, leaving only the vaguest echo of their unique forms and qualities. Those that have survived for many thousands of years do so only because of oral tradition, or because of living advocates like Rafael; told by spoken, not written word, and handed from generation to generation through active storytelling. Of these ancient 'mermaid' myths which were lucky enough to survive until the sixteenth century or beyond, most were themselves swallowed and subsumed by the European mermaid monomyth still popular today. Worldwide 'mermaids', which had many monstrous, wonderful, beautiful and terrifying forms, with as many diverse depictions and backgrounds as their creators, have become homogenised. Today's mermaids are collectively more white, more 'Disneyfied', through repeated erasure and appropriation.

The power of Sirinx, as described by Rafael, to represent nonbinary or third-gender people, suggests to me that there is perhaps something universally queer about these kinds of beings, even those that have been lost to history.

LADY OF THE SEA

When we think of the ancient classical world, our mind's eye is often distorted by the crumbling ruins we see on cramped tours and in fusty museums. We are so used to seeing ruins that we forget that for much of their history they weren't ruined at all. Also, particularly when it comes to the classical world, we often imagine a place of pristine white marble. We know now this isn't true – the unpigmented statues we see today were often originally painted in bright, gaudy colours. The bone-white, 'clean' and 'pure' depictions celebrated for hundreds of years by historians and aesthetes were often just an accident of ageing. To this day, when accurately coloured recreations of Greek and Roman art are revealed, they are met with shock and outrage. In 2008, a colourised statue of Emperor Augustus unveiled at the Vatican Museum was commented on by art historian Fabio Barry as looking 'like a cross-dresser trying to hail a taxi'.[4] One of the very oldest recognisable mermaids existed in this ancient setting, in the city of Ashkelon, 100 CE, fifty kilometres south of what is now Tel Aviv in Israel, close to modern-day Gaza.

This entire part of the world, stretching from the Eastern Mediterranean, Greece and further on to modern-day Syria and Iraq, was for thousands of years an enormous melting pot for many warring and trading civilisations, tribes and peoples. The bustling societies here were linked by the famous Silk Road trading route. This connected cities here with the Roman Empire and China, as well as further south to Egypt and the kingdoms of Sub-Saharan Africa. The city of Ashkelon (known then as Ascalon), built along a river of the same name, would be filled with myriad citizens speaking a mix of Aramaic, Hebrew, Greek and Persian. As with any thriving classical civilisation the city would also be home to a patchwork of religions, beliefs and overlapping faiths; the result was a fascinating milieu of cultures and identities.

Away from the markets and houses of the city centre were the carefully tended cool-water pools full of live fish. Pools such as these would have been a familiar sight throughout this part of the world, from Syria to Jordan, and in each case they served a similar purpose as sacred sites of worship. In Ashkelon, the water would seem to offer refreshing respite from the harsh summer sun but everyday folk would avoid dipping their feet in the sacred waters. This small oasis belonged to a goddess, Atargatis.

Her name changes depending on where she is recorded, and it is possible she is either one god with many names, or many gods with a shared lineage. Some have argued that she was the result of the fusion of three goddesses: Atirat, a god of the sea and fertility; Anat, a god of war; and Attart, a god of love.[5] Some called her Atargatis, or Atar'atheh or Tar'atheh in Aramaic. The Romans later named her simply Dea Syria, the Syrian goddess. For the sake of simplicity I will mostly be using the name Atargatis but I know that this is not always the case and is up for debate. Whatever her name, these guardian goddesses were depicted as beautiful women with long flowing hair and most of them were surrounded by fish. All acted as guardians to the cities they were built in.

Works probably by Lucian, the Syrian-Greek writer and satirist from the first century BCE, describe a temple to Atargatis. He connected her with the Greek god of love Aphrodite, as many authors would do, finding the closest familiar comparison within their own religion. He writes that within the temple, beyond the fish-filled pool, was a statue of the goddess sat beside her consort, the god Hadad. Both were made of solid gold and bedecked in precious stones, Atargatis's crown supposedly containing a huge red jewel, with rays of light radiating from behind her. She rode two lions, held a sceptre and wore a carved belt known as the cestus. This belt had the magical power to make her irresistible to anyone who looked upon her. Apparently the eyes of the golden goddess, or 'The Lady' as she was known, seemed to follow you around the room.[6]

Few of these effigies survive today, and those that do vary hugely from place to place in exactly how they depict her. Depictions of protector goddesses frequently show fish nearby, either in carvings around her head or caught in her hair. In the city of Ashkelon beyond the temple, the symbol of the fish and the woman might have fused around 2,000 years ago, and she would then appear with a fishtail. We see this on coins, tokens and later engravings. In this form she is unmistakably a kind of ancient mermaid. Today she is often colloquially and inaccurately referred to as 'the first mermaid' or 'the mermaid goddess'.

Tales of how a mortal woman became the revered fish-aligned deity are varied, but one account by the ancient Greek historian Diodorus Siculus from around 100 BCE, quoted by Lucian, talks of a noblewoman called Derceto who fell in love with a young man. The Greeks named her Derceto, 'ceto' likely being a reference to the Greek word for sea monster, or whale.[7] In the story she became pregnant out of wedlock and in her shame she threw herself into the river of Ashkelon. The story goes on to say that the gods took pity on her, and that she was transformed to have the body of a fish and the head of a woman. From here she became a benevolent goddess, one of love, beauty and protection. It is also said that in accordance with her origin story, followers and the people of the surrounding regions would abstain from eating fish and treat them instead as a sacred animal.[8]

At the many temples to Atargatis and similar sacred fish women one might also see a priestess as she pays homage or tends to the fish. From

the writings of Apuleius, a North African historian and philosopher of
the Roman Empire from 150 to 180 CE, these priestesses would be wearing
long, elaborate, saffron-dyed robes and would have painted toenails. The
prodigious amount of jewellery they wore would shine and glitter like fish
scales and they may have been seen carrying a wooden rattle or even a
flute for ceremonial events. These priestesses would patrol the sacred
pools ensuring nobody disturbed the blessed waters, or, worse, tried to
catch the fish.[9]

An important thing to mention about these priestesses is that in the
writings of Apuleius and Lucian they are described as having been assigned
male at birth. On aligning with the goddess Atargatis, young acolytes
would self-castrate as a sign of their faith. After going through this incredibly painful transformation and proving their devotion, these so-called
'eunuchs' would live their lives ostensibly as women, dressed in traditional
feminine attire and existing solely as priestesses to their beloved goddess.
From the depictions that survive and the writings that describe these
'mermaid priestesses', we can only guess how they may have identified
themselves. Today, they might use any number of terms to describe their
lived experience; nonbinary or trans women are just two examples. But for
these people, their identity was more about their role as spiritual envoys
for the goddess, and depending on the observer they might be respected
and admired, or seen as 'beggar-priests'. Whatever the case, from this early
start we see a fishtailed woman connected with gender nonconformity
and body transformation.

SIRENS AND GORGONS

While the priestesses of Atargatis danced and prayed, the ancient Greeks
were spinning their own myths about watery hybrids. This may have
been happening around the same time as the tale of the fishtail goddess
of Ashkelon, but would expand further towards the present than her
mythos. The stories of mermaids we tell today in European-influenced
societies are still deeply inspired by these Greek origins.

Within the Greek pantheon mermaids were divided into many forms,
but there were two main divisions: the naiad, mermaids that lived in

freshwater rivers and streams; and the oceanids, who dwelt in the sea. These humanoids might be depicted as naked women with two legs, or with fishtails, and were often the children or attendants of the sea god himself, Poseidon.

The trait of singing in the mermaid myth also has its origin with the Greeks. This happened when the story of the oceanids were mixed up with an entirely different creature, that of the siren. Originally sirens were depicted as half-human and half-bird, their claim to fame being their beautiful singing voices and a love of causing shipwrecks. The two creatures seem to blend, with sirens and mermaids becoming synonymous. Arguably this was down to either a mistranslation of Greek manuscripts or the thematic overlap between the two beings.[10] The half-fish form took precedent over the half-bird creatures of classical myth. Today, if you Google siren, you are far more likely to see a picture of a mermaid than a bird with a woman's head. This blending would connect mermaids with music and theatre, both perceived as feminine and lascivious pursuits, and would also give them a dark predatory backstory.

The victims of mermaids have even been suggested to have similar traits to the monster, making them even more susceptible as can be seen in bestiaries.* Consider this thirteenth-century entry on mermaids and how it seems particularly damning of a mermaid's victims, flamboyant men with loose morals and a love of theatrics:

> The sweetness of the sound enchants their ears and senses and lulls them to sleep. As soon as they are fast asleep, the sirens attack them and devour their flesh, and so the lure of their voices brings ignorant and imprudent men to their death. In the same way all those who delight in the pomp and vanity and delights of this world, and lose the vigour of their minds by listening to comedies, tragedies and various musical melodies.[11]

Today 'siren' still has its legacy in the word for mermaid in a number of Romance languages such as Italian and Spanish, which all call them

---

* These are mostly medieval zoological texts that list animals (both real and mythical) alongside their descriptions.

'sirena'. Strangely, in modern Greek the word for mermaid is not siren but 'gorgona' which comes from yet another creature, the gorgon.

Gorgons may not immediately seem at all mermaid-like, being most well known as a triad of monstrous sisters called Euryale, Stheno and the most famous of all, Medusa. Images of gorgons are traditionally women with wild staring eyes, snake hair, wings and the tusks of boars, resembling something like a fusion between a witch, vampire and demon. This strange quirk which links them with mermaids is probably down to another legend entirely, the Gorgona of Thessaloniki, a vengeful and powerful sea demon who was believed to be the sister of Alexander the Great. She was connected to gorgons with her petrifying* gaze and snakelike hair, but was also a kind of mermaid, being half-fish or sea monster. It is interesting that Alexander, the ancient king of Macedonia also known for his romantic relationships with men, would have an aquatic sister who would defend his name long after his death, a sister who birthed the modern Greek concept of the mermaid as something distinct from other parts of Europe.

Ancient Greece is often celebrated, rightly and wrongly, as an incredibly queer place, full of same-sex love and gender-bending. Of all the writers from the Hellenic world of the ancient Greek Empire, it is the poet Sappho of Lesbos who is probably best known for her queer connotations. Sappho had a life that is still shrouded in mystery. It is not fully known which parts of her life are fact and which are fiction, added to her story long after her death. We know that she was a profoundly skilled wordsmith, and that for much of her life she lived on the Greek island of Lesbos with a number of women as her students. Her poems are often fragmented, with whole sections missing; some original manuscripts were used in the bandages of Egyptian mummies. We do not have any accurate depictions of Sappho from when she lived, merely interpretations by artists who came much later. One symbol we see appearing among illustrations of Sappho on her island are depictions of oceanids and naiads, mermaids.

One reason for this is related to Sappho's death. There was a popular story described by the Greek playwright Menander, only surviving in

---

* Literally freezing victims or turning them to stone.

fragments today, that claims that Sappho threw herself off a cliff out of love for a male ferryman called Phaon, much like the ancient legend of Atargatis.[12] Some believe this story was intentionally created to obscure Sappho's sexuality, her attraction to other women. This account gave Sappho a romanticised tragic, heterosexual death, and might have been a way to 'clean her up'. This account was popular, particularly among a much later, God-fearing Victorian audience who were known to neuter and dilute anything in classical history that was deemed to be 'deviant'. Whatever the case, this drowning myth has led to water and mermaids being connected to Sappho in the popular public consciousness.

Still, her queerness survived even within the grips of this heteronormative revisionism. A print of Sappho's death by the French artist Adrien Nargeot in 1837 shows a host of mermaids clutching and caressing the fallen Sappho. This is positively subtle compared to Édouard-Henri Avril's painting in the early 1900s of Sappho, where she is attended to by a beloved female follower (by 'attended to' I mean receiving oral sex!). This image also includes an orgy of fishtailed sea nymphs in the background. These mermaid-like forms, representing Sappho's female students and fans, engage in mutual cunnilingus with each other in a highly charged erotic image. These scandalous sexy mermaids may have been produced to titillate a presumed heterosexual male audience, but the image is still one of queerness and subversion, in line with Sappho herself.

Sappho and her poems written on the island of Lesbos are what give us the word lesbian, and the term 'sapphic' to describe same-sex desire between women. We see the mermaid as a symbol used by artists to explore a woman's romantic relationships with other women, right at the origin of the naming of the lesbian identity. Indeed, when Compton Mackenzie wrote his book *Extraordinary Women* in 1928, a thinly veiled exploration of the gay women he encountered while travelling in Capri, he changed the location's name to the fictional island of 'Sirene', a play on the word siren and Sappho's legacy: 'Everybody's immoral in Sirene. It's the air. Can't help it, poor dears.'[13]

The Greco-Roman mermaid of Sappho's lifetime may also have influenced depictions of mermaids beyond Europe. Many Southeast Asian nations (such as Indonesia, the Philippines, Japan and Sri Lanka) are made up of islands and have strong maritime connections and rich folklores deriving from the sea. For example, sea spirits, creatures and monsters are littered throughout ancient Filipino cultures, perhaps even predating Greek and Roman civilisations. But through the influence and popularity of aquatic humanoids in Greco-Roman myths, legends and art, as well as much later European imperialism bringing an adoration for the neoclassical, some of these ideas have become mixed.

As a result of colonial influence on the Filipino language, the popular term for a mermaid is 'sirena', again echoing the Greek link between the aquatic oceanids and the deadly singing sirens. Filipino stories cast these sirenas as beautiful men and women with fishlike tails, gorgeous voices and mercurial temperaments. Some stories warn that mermaids drown sailors and fishermen in honour of a dark god, embodied in a magma-spewing underwater crevasse deep beneath the waves.

But the term 'sirena' is not only used in the Philippines to denote a mythical fish woman. 'Sirena' came to be a derogatory term often used to describe a gay man, or transgender woman, the suggestion of an insult for being not only girly, but also half-formed and not quite human. There is also another layer around the idea of transgender women being a 'trap', ensnaring heterosexual men with their beauty in spite of their 'secret'.

The Filipino rap star Gloc-9 is known for writing award-winning lyrics which cover topics such as social injustice and politics. In the fourth track of his album *Mga Kwento Ng Makata* (Stories of a Poet) released in 2012, there is a song entitled 'Sirena'. It is an account of the trials and tribulations of a young gay man growing up in the Philippines, who compares himself to a mermaid, as a source of joy and pride rather than shame. This song reclaims the slur as an empowering metaphor for the way the queer spirit survives against all odds.

SEX ON FINS

Greek and Roman retellings of the mermaid myth framed the depiction of mermaids in the West for centuries to come. By the Renaissance, European mermaids still had many classical traits, but also gained new ones. The mermaids of the 1500s became even more highly sexualised, with stories of sailors suffering from homesickness and cabin fever look-ing overboard and confusing a dolphin, seal or manatee for a beautiful maiden. No matter how true these accounts might be, the idea stuck. Mermaids were seen to represent a presumed heterosexual sailor's sexual frustration, and for this reason mermaids were a popular pin-up, and remain so today. The sexualised bare-chested woman would appear as a figurehead, adorning paintings, maps and tattoos across the maritime world. Mermaids were also a way to depict nude women using the excuse of highbrow classical art. From the eighteenth century the mermaids' association with repressed lust would also lend itself to pornographic and subversive illustrations that deviated from social norms, including expli-cit depictions of queer sexuality.

In the 1876 edition of the popular magazine *Beeton's Christmas Annual*, an intricate illustration of two mermaids kissing beneath mistletoe accompanied a whimsical poem about Christmas at sea. The image was designed largely for the eyes of the presumed 'gentleman reader'. It was definitely provocative, and a bold statement to include a same-sex kiss in a widely circulated nineteenth-century text.

The sexiness of mermaids has nearly always been contrasted with their monstrous natures. Even when beautiful, these beings are written about often with horror, and appear alongside chimaeras (monstrous animal-human hybrids) and sea monsters in medieval grimoires. When they are not beautiful, their strangeness and visible inhumanity is often at the forefront. At the heart of mermaid body horror is an inverted sexuality, or a monstrous presentation of gender nonconformity through 'abnormal' genitals and physicality that blurred sex binaries. In his book *Merpeople: A Human History*, Vaughn Scribner refers to accounts of mermaids with stumpy webbed hands and front-facing buttocks, or mermaids that 'did not exhibit the beautiful female form of myth. A horned, bald head replaced flowing hair, whilst the specimen's face was defined by masculine rather than feminine features.'[14] In another case from 1762 a mermaid that appeared like a 'full-chested woman' also had a beard of seashells and a body covered in 'tufts'. Mermaids are often creatures of duality; sexy and feminine and yet might also be perceived through conservative religious doctrine as monstrously androgynous.

POOR UNFORTUNATE SOULS

Hans Christian Andersen may be best known for his children's stories and fairy tales, but within his diaries and letters we get a much fuller picture of the man. As a boy, Andersen was reclusive and awkward, teased mercilessly by other children for being strange and sensitive.

> I very seldom played with other boys; even at school I took little interest in their games . . . My greatest delight was in making clothes for my dolls or stretching out one of my mother's aprons between the wall and two sticks before a currant-bush which I planted in the yard, and thus to gaze in between the sun-illuminated leaves.[15]

Andersen grew up to be a socially inept, emotionally tortured but exceptionally creative young man, pouring his heart into everything he wrote and into every person he met. Despite, and sometimes because of, the singular intensity of his feelings for others, very few of his romantic advances were reciprocated. He writes with surprising candour about his desire for sex and intimacy, even including symbols and codes which

Little Mermaid by Edmund Dulac

many believe related to masturbation.[16] Adding to his issues, Andersen was bisexual, falling head over heels in love with many men and women throughout his life.

One prominent example was his love for the handsome young Edvard Collin. The two communicated frequently through letters, and the surviving writings from Andersen leave no doubt about the depth of his affection. 'I long for you, yes, this moment I long for you as if you were a lovely girl from Calabria, with her dark eyes and stirring glance', and 'How often do I not think about you. How open does your soul not lie before me. I wonder if you understand me, understand my love as I have perceived you. At this moment I see you as I suppose blessed spirits see each other, I could press you to my heart!'[17] Edvard Collin did not reciprocate his feelings, writing in his own journal: 'I found myself unable to respond to this love, and this caused the author much suffering'. Andersen fell into a deep depression exacerbated by Edvard's forthcoming marriage to a woman, and it was then, when isolating himself on the island of Fyn, after reading *Undine* by Friedrich de la Motte Fouqué, that he wrote the first treatment of the story that would become *The Little Mermaid*.

The original account of 'The Little Mermaid' is quite far from the version created by Disney 150 years later. In Andersen's story, the nameless mermaid must have her tongue cut out with scissors by the sea witch. It's much more bloody and gruesome than what Disney's Ariel experiences and significantly less family friendly. When she comes onto land with her new legs, every step the mermaid takes with her feet is like walking on broken glass. To make matters worse, the mermaid does not get her prince in the end; instead she sacrifices herself for his happiness. And as a final downer, mermaids do not have souls in Andersen's story. When she dies, she is turned into sea foam, with only the dangling promise that one day she might earn a place in heaven.

The writing of this tragic tale is a clear response to Andersen's own grief and turmoil over Edvard and other men or women he longed for. While Hans would eventually end up being buried in a plot shared by his beloved Edvard and Edvard's wife, in life he never got his prince, so neither did the Little Mermaid.

Seeing the original 'Little Mermaid' as more than just a children's story – as an allegory for a queer man's unreciprocated love – casts the whole tale in a new light. It is powerful, and no coincidence, that Andersen chose the mermaid as a symbolic representation of his own painful and repressed emotions, writing, 'But a mermaid has no tears, and therefore she suffers so much more.'* There is a poignantly personal tone, one of someone who, like the half-fish protagonist, cannot freely express their heartbreak. Andersen put himself and the people he knew and loved directly into even the most fantastical tales he wrote, saying, 'Every character is taken from life; every one of them; not one of them is invented. I know and have known them all.'[18] Therefore 'The Little Mermaid' is not just a fairy tale, but also the most tragic love letter never sent.

> She was a strange child, quiet and thoughtful; and while her sisters would be delighted with the wonderful things which they obtained from the wrecks of vessels, she cared for nothing but her pretty red flowers, like the sun, excepting a beautiful marble statue. It was the representation of a handsome boy, carved out of pure white stone, which had fallen to the bottom of the sea from a wreck.[19]

MERMUSES

In 1886 painter Evelyn DeMorgan, inspired by Andersen's writings, created *The Sea Maidens*, which today hangs in the Queen's House in Greenwich. In her painting, five mermaids languish over each other at the water's surface. They are beautiful but alien-looking creatures, with identical half-bored facial expressions, intended to be the sisters of the Little Mermaid looking out at the human world. There is truly something strange about the painting: each of these mermaids has the same face – not just similar but identical. The face they share is that of Jane Hales.

It is said that Jane and Evelyn had an intimate relationship that was powerful, and went beyond that of a simple artist's model or house

---

* Interestingly an epitaph Disney decided to use at the very start of their most recent adaptation of the franchise despite no direct queer allusion in the film itself.

servant. Evelyn, her husband (William) and Jane are all buried in plots side by side in Brookwood Cemetery. DeMorgan appeared in Tate Britain's 2017 exhibition *Queer British Art 1861–1967*, which explored her adoration of the female form, particularly that of Jane.

Another painting, Myrtle Florence Broome's *Merman Reaching Up*, from sometime in the 1930s, is perhaps less well known. But it is still beautiful and speaks to an expression of 'sapphic' love and friendship, showing a merman underwater grasping for a human foot. Myrtle was an archaeologist and illustrator of Egyptology; she and her and fellow artist Amice Calverley travelled extensively throughout Egypt together, the two women staying in a mudbrick house to complete a set of illustrations of the temple of Menmaatre Seti I. I cannot suppose the exact nature of Myrtle's relationships with the women in her life, nor claim that she was a lesbian simply because she never married. That being said, when courted by a police officer and invited to visit his family, Myrtle said cryptically, 'It would never have worked.'[20]

Oscar Wilde was also intrigued by Andersen's story of the tragic mermaid and in 1891 wrote his own version called 'The Fisherman and His Soul'. An equally sad tale, depicting a fisherman and a mermaid as star-crossed lovers, they end up dying because of their relationship; the

Merman Reaching Up by Myrtle Broome

fisherman must cut out his own soul to make room for his forbidden love for the mermaid. Both are buried together in an unmarked grave where 'no sweet herbs grow' and yet afterwards strange white flowers bloomed there. The mermaid, popularised and re-energised by Hans Christian Andersen, became a powerful symbol for people who don't fit in. She, the mermaid, is a way to express painful love, or hopeless lust, or simply otherness.

In Germany, the Institut für Sexualwissenschaft (which translates as the Institute for Sexology but is now known as the Institute for Sexual Science) in Berlin was founded by Magnus Hirschfeld in 1919 as a place for the academic and social study of sex and gender. It became a safe space for queer people; those who today would define as gay, bisexual, transgender, nonbinary and intersex would meet here and form friendships and lifelong connections. One of the only surviving photographs depicts a vibrant and happy group of queer people after a masquerade, in fancy dress, including a Medusa-inspired headpiece. Tragically this came to an end with the rise of the National Socialist Party. The Nazis abhorred what they considered degenerate behaviour, demonising and persecuting homosexual men, women, queer people or anyone who did not fit the

Costume Ball at the Institute for Sexual Science in Berlin, before 1928

rigid gender binaries and sexual roles of their pure Arian future. All such individuals would fear criminal proceedings at best, at worst a painful and prolonged death. Lists of members kept by the Institute, so that the queer found-family might be able to connect with each other, were taken by the Nazis and used to locate many of the people we see smiling in this beautiful photograph. Some members fled the country; others less fortunate may have ended their lives in concentration camps.

The vast majority of books, letters and photographs kept by the Institute were burned by the Nazis. Among them was a collection of stories by Heinrich Heine, a radical thinker and part of the 'Young Germany' movement. One of his most famous story poems, 'Die Lorelei', tells of a beautiful but lonely mermaid who sings sailors to their doom. Among the burned remnants of records and personal effects from the Institute would have been the charred remains of the writings of Heine, including a story of a misunderstood mermaid.[21]

This story of Lorelei wasn't just loved by the queer rebels of Berlin. It was also reinterpreted by Noël Coward, playwright and infamous gay playboy (and my great-uncle, somewhat removed!). In his musical revue in 1928, *This Year of Grace*, Coward devoted a song to Lorelei. For this revue, Noël Coward worked with set designer Oliver Messel. Both Noël and Oliver had a mutual love of nautical themes and devised an intricate art nouveau underwater set piece for the song. Oliver commented that the ensemble was 'flawless' and the two gay men became firm lifelong friends.

In 1935, one hundred years after Hans Christian Andersen penned his story, Sir Charles Wheeler created a set of fountains based on mermaids and tritons which today sits in the centre of London's Trafalgar Square. The masculine triton sculpture with his rippling back and flexed arms shows a remarkable attention to the intricacies of the human anatomy. It was in fact based on drawings of a young model called Tony Asserati. According to Asserati's niece, Tony, a model and bodybuilder, was also probably bisexual. Tony modelled for many artists and sculptures, most notably for a number of erotic nudes painted by gay artist Duncan Grant.

Any one of these stories might be mere coincidence, but together they emphasise how the mermaid as a symbol has been connected with and claimed by queer people throughout history. To wildly misquote Oscar Wilde: 'To find one queer mermaid may be regarded as a coincidence; to find so many seems like a story!' This all brings us back to the mermaid we started with. Of all the mermaid stories so far, for many reading these words today this is the one we know best. (Or at least think we know best.)

PART OF YOUR WORLD

Walt Disney first started to produce animated films in the late 1920s and the studio continues to this day. *The Little Mermaid* was produced during a lull in the studio's output and with a desire to return to the 'golden age of Disney', when the studio created classic films such as *Pinocchio* and *Snow White*. Following their successful traditional pattern of adapting popular children's fairy tales, work began on a new adaptation of 'The Little Mermaid' in the mid-1980s. This was to be a revival for the company, and it would usher in a new era for animated productions.

On the team writing and producing this ambitious project was Howard Ashman. At thirty-seven he was already an experienced writer and lyricist for musical theatre and film. Howard brought his identity as a gay man into his work; he wrote the song 'Sheridan Square' in 1984, a song that references the gay district in New York and how during the HIV epidemic it was becoming quieter and quieter. The song itself becomes an ode to his friends, such as Johnny, Steve and Martin, that had passed away and shows the heartbreak Howard was experiencing; burying his friends, one by one, who were all being killed in their prime by a then mysterious sickness that preyed largely on gay and bisexual men.

With the AIDS epidemic raging in real time, Howard began work on this new Disney film, though his work on *The Little Mermaid* wasn't limited to the music. In addition to writing some of Disney's most beloved anthems from the film, Howard also influenced the characters and animation, in particular the design of Ursula the sea witch. As discussed at the start of the chapter, early designs showed her as the spindly hag of many previous Disney films, but Howard and his cowriter Alan Menken brought a different inspiration to the animator's table, that of one Harris Glen Milstead, aka Divine.

Divine was an infamous drag personality of the seventies. Famous for her self-styled trashy behaviour and intentionally crude, outlandish and provocative performances, Divine made a name for herself through multiple collaborations with queer film director John Waters. Films like *Pink Flamingos* and *Female Troubles* depicted Divine in full deviant comedic grandeur. The fact that this drag queen was the inspiration for the appearance of one of Disney's most beloved characters is one of the worst-kept secrets.

When you look at the two characters Divine and Ursula side by side, you can see how clearly one was influenced by the other: the same dramatic heavy lashes, large and curvy figure and the same arched, aggressively drawn-in eyebrows. The artists drawing Ursula had the image of the drag performer firmly in their minds as they created the demonic six-legged diva.

It was during production of *The Little Mermaid* that Howard was diagnosed with HIV. He kept this a secret for some time until the disease began to take its toll. In the 1980s, there was no clear path for those infected and receiving the news was akin to a death sentence. Slowly, just like those friends he had written about in 'Sheridan Square', Howard started to succumb to the so-called 'gay plague'.

Howard died on 12 March 1991. The last film he worked on, Disney's *Beauty and the Beast*, would release to audiences just over six months later. Disney included a small card at the end of the credits to the film. 'To our friend, Howard, who gave a mermaid her voice, and a beast his soul. We will be forever grateful. Howard Ashman: 1950–1991.'

VOICE FOR THE VOICELESS

The legacy of the mermaid myth and queer people resonates throughout history and for all kinds of people. Four years after Howard's death the largest transgender youth support network in the UK was founded – it was called Mermaids. I was lucky enough to work with this group for three years at the National Maritime Museum. Together a group of young people worked with the queer artist Eve Shepherd to produce a new bronze bust for display in the museum, to tell the stories of people often unrepresented by the rest of the collection. This group of transgender, gender-nonconforming and nonbinary teenagers explored the museum's collection and created a concept to celebrate their lives. They called the finished piece the *Person of the Sea*. This genderless person with their seagull wings and scaled spine is a combination of mythical creatures, such as the siren, and of course the mermaid. They stand in the museum today and if you press a button they speak with the voice of a young trans man. A voice who defends their right to exist in the museum.

A number of families and parents who are part of the Mermaids group shared the fact that for many of their children the mermaid is an incredibly popular symbol. For these children, the mermaid is inspiring as a creature who can change their form, transform their body and exist in multiple guises. Understandably, this has a strong appeal. Also, Ariel, as with all mermaids of any gender identity, has no visible genitalia. Her identity as a young woman is defined by her mind and her heart, not by what is, or isn't, between her legs.

For these reasons, Mermaids UK, something young trans, nonbinary and gender nonconforming youth connect with, just seemed like the perfect name. Also – and this is my own opinion – there is something about the mermaid being a monster that isn't monstrous that makes them so appealing to all queer people. This is particularly the case for those in the community who have been the most demonised and vilified.

From costumes at parades and parties to the tattoos that we adorn ourselves with, mermaids have earned themselves a place on the queer mantlepiece alongside the rainbow flag. Today many of us barely give them a second thought when we buy an ironic merman card for our friend's birthday, dye our hair blue and purple in time for Pride, or dress up as a gender-bent Ariel for Halloween, but the history is there all the same. Just beneath the surface of the cheap tat and silly merchandise are the voices of queer people that came before us. People that not only saw something of themselves in the mermaid myth, but also shaped it into what it is today. The story of mermaids might be make-believe, but it is also the very real story of thousands of years of queer people understanding themselves through a hybrid being of beauty and danger.

Horn of Plenty

Compared to other mythical creatures, the unicorn is quite a simple beast: a horse with a horn stuck in the middle of its forehead. It is also so well known and so well recognised that even young children will know it for what it is.

But why is it the unicorn that has become a contemporary LGBTQ+ totem – why not a dragon, or a peacock, a mantis shrimp or a manticore? The unicorn was not born this way; it has adopted the traits we associate with it over thousands of years, including a certain camp flourish and innate proximity to queer people. The original unicorn would be barely recognisable to its modern fans, and yet even there we find connections with people that today might define as LGBTQ+. The unicorn has queerness flowing through its rainbow mane; it was always primed to become the beast it is today.

In Amrou Al-Kadhi's memoir, *Life as a Unicorn* (2020), the British-Iraqi drag performer and writer outlines this felt connection perfectly:

> I feel a great affinity with unicorns. They are the ultimate outsiders, destined to gallop alone. They share a body of a horse, and are similar in form, but are of a different nature, almost able to belong in an equine herd, but utterly conspicuous and irrefutably other. For, no matter what, their fantastical horn cannot be concealed, signifying that they are of a different order entirely. In some mediaeval renderings of unicorns, the horns bring with them the sense of the pathetic; they are a deformity that invites the outside world to taunt the special being, almost like a dunce. As someone who has felt displaced for so long, I've harboured resentment for my

obtrusive horn, which has made it impossible for me to assimilate anywhere.

ANCIENT UNICORNS

The oldest named creature with an appearance that approximates to what we think of as a unicorn today is arguably the re'em, appearing in the Hebrew Bible dating back to around the first or second century BCE. This creature is often described as having a single horn sprouting from its head, and 're'em' has been translated to mean 'unicorn'. Some have argued that this is a mistranslation; the re'em might simply be a two-horned beast viewed from the side, giving it the appearance of a single horn. It is therefore also translated in some editions of the Bible as a 'wild ox', or as a species of extinct cattle known as an auroch, both of which have prominent horns.

Even earlier, the civilisation living in the Indus Valley, near modern-day Pakistan, around 4,000 years ago used soapstone seals to create shapes that seem to depict a one-horned animal which you could connect with the unicorn myth. Again, many have argued this is just a regular non-mythical, two-horned creature viewed from the side, or even a rhinoceros. Still the image seems popular and prominent, associated with a powerful merchant family, which might have paved the way for future incarnations of 'real' unicorns.

Around 79 CE we come across arguably the first known official and uncontroversial name for a one-horned equine creature that predates the word 'unicorn'. In Pliny the Elder's *Natural History*, which features all manner of real and fictional creatures, there is the 'monoceros', from the Greek for 'single horn'. This creature is described as 'the fiercest animal' which 'in the rest of the body resembles a horse, but in the head a stag, in the feet an elephant, and in the tail a boar, and has a deep bellow, and a single black horn three feet long projecting from the middle of the forehead. They say that it is impossible to capture this animal alive.'[1]

From here on unicorns are written about in many medieval bestiaries as dangerous and terrifying monsters. When they are depicted they are often far more goatlike and feral-looking than the well-groomed creatures we mass-consume today. Their associations are various, but they are nearly

A bestiary featuring a unicorn

always hard to capture, mysterious and fearsome. It is worth remembering that those reading and writing these lists of animals truly believed such creatures existed; to them the unicorn was not a myth but a dangerous, exotic creature living somewhere in uncharted regions of Eastern Europe, or what is now Turkey.

But single-horned beasts are not just a European creation: the 'qílín' (or 'kirin' in Japanese) is a legendary chimera, or hybrid creature, that appears throughout Chinese mythology. Some qilin have one horn and have been conflated with the Western unicorn myth, and are today colloquially known as 'Chinese unicorns'.

Translating qilin, '麒麟', as merely a subspecies of unicorn really does miss out the many other qualities that make it distinct. In Mandarin Chinese dújiǎoshòu, '独角兽', refers to the Western depiction of a unicorn, whereas a qilin is a divine spirit in Chinese mythology, associated with peace and harmony. While it has horse-like traits and often a single horn, it also has elements of dragons, ox, deer and flames incorporated into its design.

Before the introduction of Christianity, same-sex relationships appeared relatively frequently in Chinese folklore, and are particularly associated with mythical creatures. Many beings such as the nature spirits ('仙', xīan) and even dragons ('龙', lóng) are known to prefer relationships with those of the same gender, making homosexuality a kind of magical property.

The Yellow Emperor Huangdi is supposed to have bred the very first qilin in 2600 BCE and kept it in his garden. This emperor's success and even his death were foretold by the legendary creature and he is therefore associated with it. The emperor, as well as having many wives, is argued by queer historian Louis Crompton as having taken men into his bed-chamber, although this may have simply been gossip.[2] So among its many associations with luck and prosperity, the qilin arguably has some associations with a kind of male virility that would not be uniformly heterosexual. Today in Chinese medicine 'qilin pills' are used as a remedy to help with male infertility and erectile dysfunction.

HAVING THE HORN

Back in Europe, whether elephant- or goat-like, the key unchanging part of the 'traditional' unicorn, re'em or monoceros, was the horn. This becomes deeply important in informing the creature's character and how it would be used as a symbol. Horns and antlers are seen as symbols of virility and sexual potency all over the world. In Ghana, for example, a cow horn might be presented by a warrior to a chief as a symbol of his strength and masculinity. In the ancient Greek myth about the birth of the king of the gods, Zeus is suckled by a goat as a baby, and as he feeds he breaks away part of the horn, creating a symbol we refer to as 'the cornucopia'. A horn filled with fruit and flowers is still a symbol of virility, growth and health today: the horn of plenty.

In Celtic belief that Tarvos Trigaranus was occasionally something of a proto unicorn. This was most commonly a bull with three cranes perched on its back. But it could also be depicted with three horns, an additional central horn jutting from its forehead. According to Roman writers, who are not always known for their accuracy, this symbol was worshipped and associated with male virility and druidic divination. A regular bull was already a symbol associated with manhood by the Celts, but in certain examples of Tarvos Trigaranus this was seemingly elevated to an even more powerful sexual totem. Many Celtic and pagan rituals in the UK and Europe appear to have used horns to bring forth the rutting masculinity perceived in deer, elk and rams into their human bearers. Mainly because a horn, a stiff, jutting piece of bone associated with male animals, was normally a stand-in for the phallus, the human penis.

The chivalric romance told through the verse *Parzival* by the medieval knight and poet Wolfram von Eschenbach shows how the unicorn took some of these phallic traits into the thirteenth century, during the so-called High Middle Ages:

We caught the beast called Unicorn
That knows and loves a maiden best
And falls asleep upon her breast;
We took from underneath his horn
The splendid male carbuncle-stone
Sparkling against the white skull-bone.[3]

Also during the thirteenth century, Guido Cavalcanti writes:

The unicorn and I are one:
He also pauses in amaze
Before some maiden's magic gaze,
And, while he wonders, is undone.
On some dear breast he slumbers deep.[4]

The symbolism would not be lost on a medieval audience. The connotation is decidedly sexual, creating images of the penis, unbuttoning of breeches and, arguably, penetration and ejaculation.

Feral, goatish unicorns, with grizzled heads and sharp teeth are common throughout the early to mid-medieval period. Here they represented male sexuality, dangerous, potent and uncontrollable. For while few could tame a wild unicorn, a virgin woman was the one exception. Many images depict a young woman sitting with a unicorn, the beast laying its wild head on her lap and allowing itself to be caressed. The woman might be gazing down at it lovingly, and in many not so subtle allusions she is tightly gripping the creature's horn in both hands.

Today we use phrases like 'being horny' and 'having the horn', and while they have become unisex, the origins of all these phrases, as with the unicorn's single entendre, lie largely in male sex and lust.

PLEASURE AND PAIN

The public humiliation and punishment broadly known as 'rough music' or 'charivari' was rife throughout Europe from at least around the thirteenth century. In some cases people accused of anything from thievery and adultery to sodomy might be beaten in a kind of pantomime performance designed to humiliate, and even execute, its victims.

Many of these activities took place around the UK, involved pagan imagery and included the use of horns, such as a ritual known as 'riding the stang'. Here a person would be beaten with bull's horns, or tied to a phallic pole and hit with sticks called 'stangs'. We know men engaging in same-sex sexual relations experienced such punishments. In 1716 in Westonbirt, Gloucestershire, two men, George Tennant and Walter Lingsey, were put through a 'mock groaning', a kind of fake marriage ceremony, then beaten, for having been caught having sex.[5] Therefore for those engaging in sodomy the connotations of a unicorn horn, a symbol of male sexuality, might have added meaning as a punishment for sexual transgression.

For a queer woman, or trans person, the symbol of a horn might also represent a way of augmenting your own body. Many of the oldest dildos and sex aids are made from animal bone, antlers and horn, such as a collection found in Germany dating back to 30,000 years ago, and their appearance in Japanese erotic shunga prints. The horn could be a tool for sexual pleasure outside heterosexual sex. (This is not to discount the symbol of a carved or man-made phallus used by some trans men as part of their gender expression.) It is interesting that when Samuel Butler wrote his poem 'Dildoides' about a collection of sex toys, he notes, 'Some were compos'd of Shining Horns, More precious than ten Unicorns'[6] and he uses a unicorn as a comparison for their worth as sexual objects. A unicorn with its clear phallic connotations but still separate from an actual man might also be liberating for people exploring sex and gender beyond the rigid norms of the time, without the need for men.

During the fifteenth century the unicorn would find a new place as a symbol for wealthy families and even royalty. It would also become a popular symbol in heraldry, the images used as statements of power and legacy by those who could afford it. The power and virility of the creature would be amplified and its seedier pagan nature would be masked. The unicorn is hereon mostly horse-like, although sometimes winged or with a lion's tail, and is nearly always pure white. This airbrushed unicorn would be intended to communicate masculine strength, but combined with Christian purity and respectability.

Through this, unicorns became symbols of nationalism and pride, a way to show off a family's or an individual's wealth, and thus become more ornate, more decorated and more valuable.

DEMONIC HORSE

A unicorn was not necessarily always a symbol of virtue hereafter; some of its earlier forbidden pagan eroticism might occasionally leak through. In 1516 the artist Albrecht Dürer created one of his most enigmatic pieces, an etching he called *The Abduction of Proserpine on a Unicorn*. In this piece a woman is dragged screaming by a man on the back of a horse with a single horn. But the picture doesn't fit the classical myth of Proserpine (known as Persephone, the goddess of Spring in ancient Greece) being abducted and taken to the underworld, as the title might suggest. The closest match to any known story would be the fate of the Berkley Sorceress. This folktale, according to a collection of stories recorded in the historical encyclopaedia *The Nuremberg Chronicle* published in 1393, tells of a witch from Gloucester who sold her soul to the devil and was carried

The Abduction of Proserpine on a Unicorn by Albrecht Dürer, 1516

to hell by a 'demonic horse'. Dürer helped illustrate the *Chronicle*, and was perhaps inspired to create his own version of the tale.

Dürer himself was probably attracted to men and women, writing to his close friend Willibald Pirckheimer about his lust for both 'handsome' soldiers and beautiful girls. He even created a portrait of Willibald, with the knowing comment 'With the cock in your asshole!' underneath.

As the art critic Brian Sewell commented, Dürer's work is often 'a puritanical response to the human body, very rarely beautiful in face or figure, erotic interest so tightly reined as to be virtually undiscoverable – and then only in men as creatures of prominent codpiece and long muscular leg'.[7] As an added twist the man pictured in this painting is perhaps a kind of self-insert: many have commented on the likeness of the bearded unicorn rider to Dürer's own appearance.

Dürer's relationship with his wife Agnes was not a good one; he called her an 'old cow' and in letters to each other he and Pirckheimer joked about sharing her as a sexual object. After Dürer died of malarial infection, Pirckheimer blamed poor Agnes, writing, 'For God's sake, I can blame no one other than his wife, who made his heart heavy and tormented him, to the extent that he took leave of this life all the more quickly.'[8]

Dürer's unicorn piece will probably remain somewhat unknowable, but it is interesting that a unicorn would be the vehicle for him to project an erotically charged power fantasy, perhaps tinged with a cocktail of homoeroticism, vanity and misogyny. But Dürer was not the only one using unicorns to enhance his own sense of virility.

SELLING UNICORNS

By the sixteenth century the purported horn of a unicorn was a much-prized and sought-after substance. Alicorn, as it was known, was believed to be able to detect poison, cure illnesses and confer great mystic powers. Unsurprisingly the horn was also associated with sexual potency and fertility; the powdered horn was a kind of aphrodisiac. The horn would in fact be a carved walrus tusk or the tooth of a narwhal, an animal whose skeletal remains were easily mistaken for those of unicorns. Once labelled as alicorn, these mystic objects were held in great reverence and were enormously expensive. Some were gifted to lords, kings and queens, such as Catherine de' Medici, who received a 'unicorn horn' from her uncle. These might be turned into sceptres, or displayed within cabinets of curiosity.

The horn also had darker magical properties, associated with the occult. Ivan IV, aka Ivan the Terrible, a man who supposedly entertained performances of cross-dressing men in his courts, was said to use a unicorn horn in an attempt to predict his own death. He would carve a circle into a tree with an alicorn and place spiders within it; if the spiders died, so would he.

So the unicorn becomes a symbol of extravagance, magic and nobility. We see it decorating palaces and shields, now dripping in gold and wearing crowns, each iteration outcompeting the others to be the most decadent and regal. But as with everything that is grand and overdone, it is liable to fall out of favour. The gilded unicorn of aristocracy was a little obvious and gauche for those wishing to be fashionable, and through losing some of its masculine energy to sparkle and glitz it started to be seen as somewhat mass-produced and tacky.

In the Victorian era, the unicorn myth was further rewritten. In its portrayals it was so pure a creature, so whitewashed, that it was largely used to entertain children. The unicorn had transitioned from a creature of presumed masculinity and danger to something dainty and innocently feminine in appearance. The Victorians, as will be seen in the chapter on fairies, had a habit of taking creatures of complex ancient origin and sanitising them. The unicorn mostly lost its edge, becoming a fairy-tale beast synonymous solely with magic and purity.

Despite this move towards gilded simplicity, the unicorn was always a creature of duality, the large phallic symbol jutting from its head encouraging artists and writers to lean into their own sexuality and express latent desire. The unicorn was a fantastic way to mask erotic and provocative messages while still communicating them to their intended audience.

UNIPORN

Even in Victorian England, the unicorn had its lewd moments in private circulation. Aubrey Beardsley, a young nineteenth-century writer and illustrator, wrote about the sexual adventures of a kinky knight called

Tannhäuser. In this there is a decidedly X-rated scene involving Venus, the goddess of love, and her pet unicorn, Adolphe:

> Adolphe sniffed as never a man did around the skirts of Venus. After the first charming interchange of affectionate delicacies was over, the unicorn lay down upon his side, and, closing his eyes, beat his stomach wildly with the mark of manhood! Venus caught that stunning member in her hands and lay her cheek along it; but few touches were wanted to consummate the creature's pleasure. The Queen bared her left arm to the elbow, and with the soft underneath of it made amazing movements horizontally upon the tight-strung instrument. When the melody began to flow, the unicorn offered up an astonishing vocal accompaniment. Tannhäuser was amused to learn that the etiquette of the Venusberg compelled everybody to await the outburst of these venereal sounds before they could sit down to déjeuner. Adolphe had been quite profuse that morning. Venus knelt where it had fallen, and lapped her little apéritif!'[9]

Beardsley wrote this as part of an unfinished 'romantic novel' called *Under the Hill* in the 1890s. The piece was only published in 1907, after his death, with an anonymous note printed at the beginning which read: 'It has been deemed advisable, owing to the freedom of several passages, to issue only a limited number of copies for the use of those literary students who are also admirers of Beardsley's wayward genius.'[10]

Beardsley's career had taken a nosedive after the trial of his close friend (and sometimes frenemy) Oscar Wilde, who was convicted of sodomy in 1895. Whereas before Beardsley had been a celebrated art nouveau illustrator and respected avant-garde author, he was now shunned by polite society as a pervert for his association with Wilde and other 'aesthetes'. Now he could only find a paid outlet for his 'wayward genius' creating pornographic materials for small limited-edition presses.

Before his death from tuberculosis at the age of twenty-five he asked that all his 'obscene drawings' be destroyed. The piece about Venus and Adolphe quoted above shows that Beardsley, a young queer man with dangerous friends, knew exactly how a unicorn could be subverted back to a sexual being to both shock and titillate his Edwardian readership.

HERE BE BISEXUALS

By the twentieth century another element of the mythical beast comes more into play. The unicorn is something fantastical, and no longer believed to truly exist at the edge of man-made maps as it once was. Therefore it is now also symbolic of anything that is frivolous and imaginary, something make-believe. This brings it into connection with the bisexual community. Here the term 'unicorn' has been used to describe a bisexual woman who is willing to engage in a threesome with an ostensibly heterosexual couple, it being used largely from the man's perspective.

The 'unicorn' is considered to be someone who, much like the mythical beast, is a wonderful impossibility; for a man using this term, having another woman to spice up their love life, without threatening the status of their masculinity or heterosexuality, is seen as some sort of wonderful daydream, too perfect to really exist. In an article from *Vogue India*, sexuality educator Apurupa Vatsalya explains:

> Unicorn hunting is when a heterosexual couple seeks a bisexual woman to join their equation temporarily or permanently. The premise is that the primary relationship is between the hetero couple; the bi woman is a racy add-on. While any type of consenting relationship between adults is valid, the way unicorn hunting is being currently navigated is dehumanising and seems to be rooted in unrealistic expectations.[11]

Any person deemed a 'unicorn' in this scenario is expected to be sexually available but not to form any romantic or emotional connections that threaten the heterosexual relationship. Those looking for this kind of woman (although it can also be a man) may refer to 'going unicorn hunting'. This is a dark throwback to the mythic origins of the beast, bringing to mind the image of brave knights tempting unicorns into the open through the enticement of a virginal woman.

The term 'unicorn' is considered demeaning and dehumanising, making the bisexual woman an object rather than an active agent in sex, and erasing the meaning of a bisexual identity to simply being a straight man's plaything. More so, it plays on the trope that, like the unicorn, bisexual people aren't real, that they just haven't made up their minds. And yet, as with other slurs and insults we shall explore, the word can be reclaimed. Some bisexual people love the unicorn as an icon that can be played with. Today unicorn T-shirts, pins and accessories with the bi flag incorporated into their mane are commonplace. On the website Bi.org, the 'unicorn scale' is used to rate the quality of bi inclusion in film; the more unicorns the better the representation of bisexuality.

BEYOND THE SPARKLE

The unicorn emblem is somewhat divisive across the LGBTQ+ spectrum, with some claiming it as a kind of modern heraldry, whereas for others it is simply mass-produced commercial branding. During the war in Ukraine, Oleksandr Zhuhan and Antonina Romanova volunteered to fight against the Russian invasion. Both of them, a queer couple, became known as the 'unicorn' soldiers for their use of the unicorn insignia on their arms. They say of the symbol 'they (the lesbian, gay, bisexual, transgender and queer community) chose the unicorn because it is like a fantastic "non-existent" creature'.[12] This story calls back to the history of the unicorn as a standard or banner for warring sides, except now it is not a kingdom but an identity that is being championed and fought for.

On the flipside you have Instagram photos of gay men lounging on inflatable unicorns in Gran Canaria, or of bisexual couples buying each other unicorn Valentine's Day cards or funny T-shirts. These may not be intentionally calling back to the complex history of these puritanical yet pagan, perfect and perverse hybrids. Instead they are simply cute and fun; an ingroup membership symbol for contemporary gay and queer people. Therefore this fascination with a particularly elusive horny equine, which has been playing out for queer people across centuries, has resulted in both shallow and deep cultural significance.

Today the unicorn is also one of the purest icons of 'camp', 'childishness' and 'femme-ness'. Unicorns are also incredibly popular with children, particularly and stereotypically young girls. While the meaning derived from these fantasy creatures for kids and queer adults might come from very different places, there are similarities with why both groups connect with these beings so readily. The unicorn's loud femininity is unapologetic and proud, a brash and vibrant femme-ness that refuses to be diluted: a feeling that a seven-year-old girl from New York, a nineteen-year-old bisexual woman from Madrid and a forty-seven-year-old gay man from Tokyo might all want to celebrate.

Unicorns as highly commodified, safe and ofttimes neutered symbols can also become emblematic of some of the contemporary issues and backlash around the commercialisation of Pride itself. The shops that sell unicorn-bedecked Pride merchandise will not necessarily stand up for queer rights if it threatens their profit margins. When Lady Gaga appears dressed as a unicorn, or is pictured riding one, she is making a statement that being queer is not frightening or monstrous, but it also helps sell her brand to an audience of billions of consumers.

Today the unicorn is at the very heart of debates around queer acceptance and assimilation, both being subversive and commercial in their broad appeal. These horny horses have become a kind of accidental ambassador for queer people, as they are beloved and socially acceptable among many heterosexual, cisgender folk. Maybe we are hoping that if people can love a unicorn, in its overdone splendour and tacky weirdness, they can learn to love us, too.

3

Radical Faeries

As with the unicorn and the mermaid, the fairy's origins are as far away from their glossy or Disneyfied counterparts as you might imagine. The first fairies (or faeries)* in European folklore are not just mischievous, they are often downright malevolent; wicked nature spirits, which delight in playing cruel tricks on unsuspecting people. Blamed for people going missing in the woods, for dead crops, malformed or unborn children and even responsible for murder. Indeed, sometime between 1656 and 1663 a list of deaths from Cumbria included the ominous entry 'Frightened to death by fairies'.[1]

The fairy of today is rather different, a sparkly playful creature, normally a diminutive human with dainty butterfly wings. These fairies are often (though not always) feminine in presentation, and may help or hinder a person, but only ever with an aura of childlike innocence. Yet for LGBTQ+ people 'fairy' might also represent a vintage slur, as well as a source of significant power.

THE 'F' WORD

Since the early days of the 1900s, the term 'fairy' has been a common insult used to describe effeminate queer men and the transgender people

---

* Both 'fairy' and 'faerie' are correct spellings but refer to subtly different things. Fairy is the most commonly used and refers most prominently to contemporary depictions of these beings. Faerie is a spelling that intentionally throws back to Celtic language and folklore, and is used to describe the older and more malevolent aspects of these creatures.

who have been confused for them. This term is, at the time of writing, rather outdated, but in the interwar period of the 1920s all the way up until the 1990s, fairy was a common insult. Alongside 'pansy', 'dandy', 'poof' and even the now common descriptor 'gay',* these are all terms which loosely mock a perceived homosexual man's femininity, frivolity and lack of strength. A fairy is perceived as something weak, girly, silly, and looked down upon by a society that prizes masculinity in its men.

Today the insult 'fairy' is largely a relic of an older generation's lexicon, and yet it persists in the minds of living LGBTQ+ people. The term has been adopted, and become for some a kind of countercultural identity. Fairy wings and a sprinkling of glitter are common accessories for many gay men at fancy dress parties. But as with every other creature in this book, there is much more to the fairy and its link to queerness than perhaps meets the eye.

The evolution of fairies from their dark pagan beginnings also tracks with the equally dark perception and treatment of the queer people they may have been associated with, even hundreds of years ago. It can be argued that it was LGBTQ+ people in theatre, dance and underground communities that forged the connection between fairies and themselves. We weren't necessarily just the passive receivers of an insult about being girly; there is evidence that we actively sought to become a tribe of fairies long before this.

The earliest reference to 'fairy' meaning gay or queer is in the writings of a pseudonymous author who refers to themselves, alternately, as Jennie June, Ralph Werther and Earl Lind. The author perceives themselves as an 'androgyne' or 'an invert' in that their gender expression and attraction to others is not what would have been determined by the sex they were assigned at birth. In their 1918 book *Autobiography of an Androgyne*, Lind writes the following: 'On one of my earliest visits to Paresis Hall† – about January, 1895 – I seated myself alone at one of the tables. I had only

---

* There is evidence that before becoming a socially accepted term for homosexuality, 'gay' was a coded term referring to prostitution and sex-work amongst women and thus calling a man 'gay' inferred a quality of both femininity and indecent promiscuity.

† A well-known gay bar in New York named after the condition of 'general paresis' which described the mental instability and hallucinations brought on by long-term syphilis.

recently learned that it was the androgyne headquarters or "fairie" as it was called at the time. Since Nature had consigned me to that class, I was anxious to meet as many examples as possible.'[2] Therefore if the author's words are factual and representative of the time, as long ago as 1895, people who today might describe themselves as queer and gender-nonconforming were also talking about themselves as being part of 'fairie'. But why choose this name for themselves?

DANCE OF THE SUGARPLUM FAIRY

An elderly Irishman called Roderick MacNeil was recorded in 1871 talking about the origin of fairies as handed down through Gaelic oral tradition. He stated that after Lucifer rebelled against God,

> The Father ordered that the gates of heaven and the gates of hell should be closed. This was instantly done. And those who were in were in, and those who were out were out; while the hosts who had left heaven and had not yet reached hell flew into the holes of the earth, like the stormy petrels. They are the Fairy Folk – ever since doomed to live under the ground, and only allowed to emerge where and when the King permits.[3]

This understanding places fairies closer to demons and angels than other beings, but the Victorians drew and painted their fairies in an almost entirely angelic guise, without the darker rebellious and cursed backstory. Their fairies are beautiful men and women, although most frequently the latter, who cavort and dance in nature. They are playful, not cruel; fair of face, not frightening. So it is of little surprise, then, that fairies became a popular theme for the performing arts during this period, which revelled in beauty and escapism. While the writings of Shakespeare's *A Midsummer Night's Dream* explored the fairy world long before this, it was the Victorians who cleaned them up and made them dance in tutus.

La Sylphide was a ballet produced and choreographed in 1832 by Felipe Taglione. The story of the piece follows a Scottish man who is forced to marry his cousin, until a beautiful and mysterious 'sylph', played by

Felipe's daughter Marie, comes down and takes him away to be wed. A sylph is a term originating in the sixteenth century for a kind of air sprite, so in the style of the time Marie was dressed all in white with tiny butterfly wings. The play was a sensation. From here on ballet and fairies were for many synonymous, bringing to mind those appearing in the likes of *The Nutcracker* and *The Sleeping Beauty*.

Nineteenth-century ballet was a world of escapism and magic for those who enjoyed it, but it was also a rich subculture that both rewarded masculine and feminine heterosexual archetypes, while also making room for cross-dressing, flamboyance and a certain amount of behind-the-scenes subversion. In ballet, fairies abounded, and not just the ones on stage. The relationships between LGBTQ+ costume designers, dancers, wealthy benefactors and stagehands were notoriously complex and interwoven. Lynn Garafola, dance history professor at Barnard College, New York City, states that in particular the Russian ballet gave gay and bisexual men 'a cultural center that could not be articulated openly', and that 'it was a safe haven for gay men during a period of intense persecution'.[4]

Queerness and fairies were closely linked within this art form in a complex web across theatrical roles, jobs and celebrities. For example,

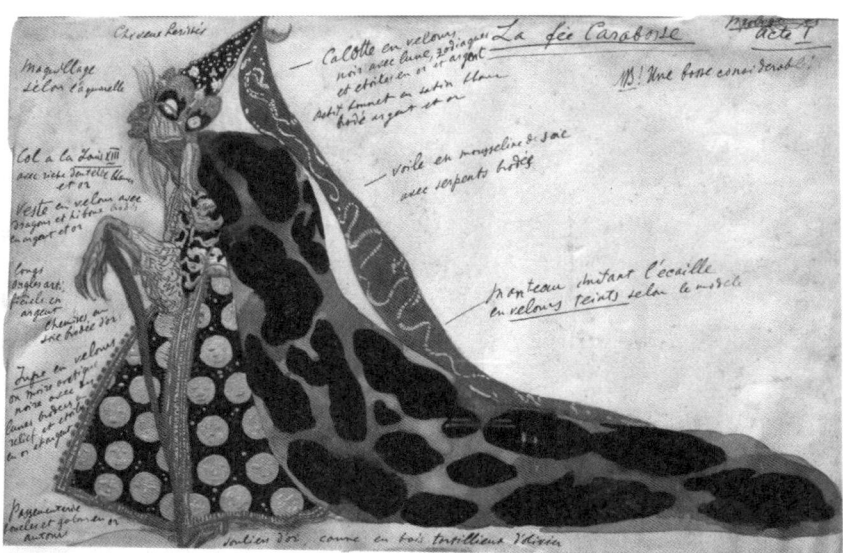

Costume design by Leon Bakst (1866–1924) for Carabosse,
the wicked fairy godmother in *The Sleeping Beauty*

Carabosse, the dark fairy from *The Sleeping Beauty*, was brought to life by Maestro Enrico Cecchetti, a male ballet dancer cross-dressing as the wicked sprite. He was bedecked in a costume envisioned by the legendary Léon Bakst, a Russian artist who was part of a queer cohort of illustrators and designers beloved by the art critic Sergei Diaghilev. Diagilev was deeply in love with the bisexual dancer Vaslav Nijinsky, who was himself known for performing as a fairy, a sprite and a faun. So here we have layers of queer men in and around this industry who knew of each other, had relationships with each other and created their own secret networks and social groups.

It is unsurprising then that the fairy became a known and beloved symbol for queer people at this time, even those in the audience; conjuring images of the freedom and liberation glimpsed through the world of ballet and theatre, connected with the attractive and flamboyant performers.

PRINCIPAL BOYS

For queer women and many of those assigned female at birth, the fairy also brought certain freedoms of expression. In 1904 the very first theatrical production of *Peter Pan* was staged at the Duke of York Theatre in London. Based on the children's story by J. M. Barrie, Peter is a boy who can fly with the use of fairy dust, alongside his faithful fairy friend Tinkerbell. His clothing and character are directly inspired by images of nature sprites and fairy folk, and his name partly derives from panpipes, and therefore the Greek Pan, god of the wilds. This first theatrical performance cast the actress Nina Boucicault in the role of the puckish Peter. The decision to cast a female actor as Peter was probably neither a subversive nor an artistic one, however, and related more to the laws around child labour; it was also believed to be a challenge finding children who would have the acting chops to carry an entire play. Yet, this decision has led to more than 120 years of Peter being played by actresses on stage.

Many women who specialised in these cross-dressing roles were known historically as 'principal boys' or regarded as playing a 'breeches role'. The sight of a woman in said breeches, acting as a man, had a powerful effect

Maude Adams as Peter Pan, 1905

on audience members of all genders and inclinations. The fanbase of principal-boy actresses included a well-known retinue of adoring women. Vesta Tilley, a famous 'male impersonator', received a letter from one frequent admirer called Elsa which begins, 'No doubt you will be confused to hear from me again' and continues, 'I was so upset to hear that you were retiring I dare not think about it'.

In America, Maude Adams played the very first Peter Pan in 1905 on Broadway, and her short hair and the so-called 'Peter Pan collar' designed for her costume would inspire a trend among women all over the world. As Maude was a lesbian, known for her partners Louise Boynton and Lillie Florence, this 'boyish' fashion statement might also be a clear but coded message between gay women in the early 1900s.

THE PEOPLE OF DANU

Beings that are similar to fairies exist in stories around the world, from the Hawaiian dwarf-adjacent being called a 'menehune', to the Japanese 'yosei'. 'Fairy' is only a loose Westernised catch-all term for a number of disparate mythical beings that have a multitude of origins. Still, the majority of fairy stories and tropes we think of today in Europe and North America originate in Scandinavian and Celtic legends. In older Irish folklore, fairies and their ilk are believed to descend from an entire race of magical people, the Tuatha Dé Danann. These magical folk are closer to the supernatural entities outlined in the introduction; frightening beings fond of using witchcraft and 'glamour' to enact their chaotic desires on unsuspecting human victims.

The Tuatha Dé Danann are a mythical Irish people, who by being connected to forbidden pagan gods have lost their humanity. Descended from these people are another group of beings called the Aos Sí, the original name for Irish fairy folk. They are shadows cast by the stories told long before Christianity. Ireland's ancient history of Celtic gods of forests and spirits, of rivers and streams, were recast, through Christian propaganda, as monstrous tricksters and wicked fiends. Fairies mark a place where some of the darker folklore of the 'before times' continued to keep a hold over the beliefs and traditions of an otherwise deeply Christian people.

As is often the case when a culture and people go through a religious change, the old ways and the old gods are perceived with a sense of shame or suspicion. How could these wicked pagan beliefs have held sway over the Irish people's ancestors for so long? What dreadful practices went on across the so-called Emerald Isle before the arrival of the one 'true' god and his doctrine? Therefore many practices forbidden by Christianity but practised by earlier people were attributed to the supernatural and pagan Tuatha Dé Danann. Because of this transference, alongside blasphemous magic and nature worship, we might also find same-sex desire and fluid gender expression becoming a part of the fairy folk's character.

The Celts had many beliefs that the medieval Irish church found abhorrent. The worship of a pantheon of gods who, like the Greek and the Roman deities, were flawed individuals who fought, screwed and squabbled with each other, and who also deified natural phenomena, and the land; a particular tree, river or cave might contain a spirit or godly being. While all religions have their own rules of conduct, the Celtic rules and systems would be a stark contrast to those of Christianity. To draw in broad strokes and based entirely on second-hand sources, Celtic paganism would have a much looser and occasionally more celebratory approach to sex, fertility and reproduction in its entirety. We see these themes more openly and viscerally represented through erotic imagery and artwork showing the explicit act of sex and portrayal of sex organs. Carvings such as the Sheela Na Gig, which depicts a crudely carved woman exposing her exaggerated vulva, are thought to date back to beliefs from this time, connected to one of the three forms of the warrior goddess known as the Morrígan. We can see that sexual behaviours that would be frowned upon, and maybe even punishable under Christian doctrine, might be acceptable in a pagan Gaelic Ireland.

Diodorus Siculus, a Greek writer born in ancient Rome, commented that among the Celtic tribes of the British Isles, same-sex relationships and pederasty between men and boys were a rite of passage. There are also Irish Celtic parallels with the homoerotic Greek and Roman mythical heroes, parallels which bleed into later folklore; for example, the twelfth-century Ulster Cycle involving the warrior Cú Chulainn (the Hound of Culann) and his beloved Ferdiad. These men have a relationship strikingly similar to the one between the Greek hero Achilles and his lover Patroclus.

When forced to fight each other Cú Chulainn announces, 'With all my heart – I wish it could be anyone other than he. Not because I fear him, but because I have such affection for him.'[5] It is also noted that in a previous battle Ferdiad slew a hundred warriors just to retrieve his companion's sword. Even more powerful are passages of the original text, for example:

> Ropdhar cocle cridi,
> ropdhar caemthe caille,
> ropdhar fír chomdeirgide,
> contulmis tromchotlud
> ar trommníthaib.[6]

Which can be translated as:

> We were heart-companions once;
> We were comrades in the woods;
> We were men that shared a bed,

When we slept the heavy sleep,
After hard and weary fights.

At the end of this myth, after killing his beloved Ferdiad in armed combat, Chulainn is devastated, making 'loud and lengthy lamentations over his fallen companion' and cries out that:

Play was each, pleasure each,
Till Ferdiad faced the beach;
Loved Ferdiad, dear to me:
I shall dree his death for aye
Yesterday a Mountain he, –
But a Shade to-day.

Part of this story includes a character called Queen Medb, who encourages the fight between the two beloved men. She is thought to have inspired Shakespeare's depiction of Queen Mab of the fairies.

There is indeed a history of same-sex desire and friendship between men being connected to the Celtic realm of fairies within writings even in Christian Ireland. In a poem by Eochaidh Ó hÉoghusa, the bardic poet for the Maguire family from the sixteenth century writes: 'Another man beguiled me, Maguire of the fairy-like weapons; he beguiled me, and I him.'

And in what is believed to be Eochaidh's final poem:

If I do not love Myles it is not through lack of desire. I am afraid that my heart will show him the secret of my mind. Venus, the goddess of love, may wound my mind with mad love for him. Seeking to seduce me, she had shown me the bright expanse of countenance, the modest joyous face with lovable fairy-like disposition.[7]

These intriguing writings come much later than the pre-Christian Celtic peoples who may have inspired the original idea of the Tuatha Dé Danann and later Irish fairy folklore. In truth, it is difficult to say exactly to what degree same-sex desire and gender fluidity would be understood by the Celts and their progenitors up to 3,000 years ago, as there is simply a dearth of first-hand sources for their beliefs and realities of daily life. Most of our understanding of the peoples of England, Wales, Scotland and Ireland before the Roman occupation of Britain beginning in 43 CE and the later introduction of Christianity around 400 CE comes entirely from outside observers. There are no known written texts from Ireland prior to the late sixth century, and the writings afterwards are mostly translated and edited through the judgemental lens of Christianity. So it is difficult to know exactly how the Irish Celts might perceive people that today would identify as something akin to LGBTQ+.

Still, the fairy folk of Irish myth were not intended as accurate portrayals of the Celts; I would argue they were a parody of their strange beliefs and sinful lives. The fae folk known as the Aos Si were described as a dark, mysterious, frightening, lawless and overtly sexual people. In early tales they do not obey the laws or customs of polite society. For example, a person possessed by or replaced by a fairy would behave out of character, being violent, sexual or just 'strange'. Sex outside marriage, gender non-conforming behaviour or any deviation from societal expectations of what a man and woman should be could be attributed to fairy intervention, with terrible consequences.

Some families became convinced that their loved one, be it a child or a wife, was under the spell of a fairy, or was a changeling in disguise, in some cases occasionally going so far as to result in a victim's own family putting them to death. Such incidents have been recorded all the way up to the nineteenth century, with the most famous case being that of Bridget Cleary, who was burned alive by her family in 1895. After his arrest her husband claimed she had been replaced by a fairy impersonator and felt no regret about what he had done.

Some historians have argued that many who were accused of being charmed by fairies, or replaced with one, were possibly just neurodivergent or suffering from a physical or mental illness.[8] A gay or genderfluid family member might arguably be seen as being under a similar spell. Even today some unaccepting families will talk of their gay or transgender child as having been replaced or changed, an explanation that is still used to justify conversion therapy. For those living among stories and beliefs of the Aos Si, back in the eighteenth and nineteenth centuries, people we might describe today as LGBTQ+ could easily be described as 'fairy touched' or 'fairy struck'.

Interestingly, as it was believed that fairies of all genders had a prefer-ence for little boys, there is an account from Connemara in Ireland of parents dressing children of both sexes in red flannel petticoats to avoid them being taken.[9]

AWAY WITH THE FAERIES

'Radical Faeries' Harry Hay and Don Kilhefner started a movement in the late seventies which combined the neopagan and spiritualist ideas of the 1960s with the budding gay rights movement of 1970s America.

The very first formal event for the Radical Faeries kicked off with the Spiritual Conference for Radical Faeries, a meeting held for gay men at an ashram in Arizona in the summer of 1979. The movement used the fairy as a symbol to unite gay men together and used pagan rituals and ceremonies to empower them. The Radical Faeries are still very much alive today, when they are now made up of people of all genders and sexualities, although the majority of members describe themselves as men who love men. The organisation even has its own specific spin-off chapters, such as the 'Black Leather Wings' for queer people who are part

A group of Radical Faeries gather for an Equinox ritual in London, 2017

of the leather community, and 'the Sisters of Perpetual Indulgence', who dress as nuns, using drag and camp sensibilities to mock homophobic religious institutions while raising money for charities and campaigning for LGBTQ+ rights and healthcare.

Talking to Lavender, a current member of the Radical Faeries movement, they said, 'I wonder if faeries, like other mythical, magical creatures – merpeople, vampires, werewolves, and the like – appeal to LGBTQ+ people because like us they are beings that live/have lived on the fringes and in between worlds. And also I suppose I just feel like queer people are inherently magical.' Lavender joined the movement while looking for a retreat that was safe and welcoming for queer people. When asked to define what made a Radical Faerie, they said, 'I still think it's hard to pinpoint exactly what makes a faerie. But I think faeries are generally people – mostly gay men still, though that is ever-expanding and-changing, we are becoming more and more diverse – who wanna go deep in connecting with each other, care for nature and each other.'

The reclamation of the term fairy as an identity, a political movement, a community, an aesthetic or simply playful self-expression has been happening for a long time in queer spaces. It is clear that from its earliest pagan origins through to its contemporary mass-consumed Disneyfied version, the fairy is a symbol that connects with many LGBTQ+ people far beyond being a dated insult.

PART 2
Bad Blood

(Cursed beings and shapeshifters)

'Listen to them – the children of the night. What music they make!'

From *Dracula* by Bram Stoker

4

Big Bad Wolves

In the twelfth century, Marie de France, a poet and storyteller, wrote of a tale that she wished not to forget. It was a story that had been handed down but seldom recorded.

The tale was that of 'Bisclavret' or 'the garwolf' and tells of a noble knight married to a 'worthy woman'. Mysteriously, every week the man was absent for three full days and nobody knew where he went. Fearing that he had taken a lover, the knight's wife asked him about his odd behaviour. Under duress the knight confessed that he transformed into a wolf and went hunting in the deep woods. Frightened, the wife betrayed her husband by asking an old flame of hers to steal his clothes, thus trapping him in animal form. Eventually she married this new man, and for a whole year the knight was stuck as a wolf with everyone wondering where he had gone.

A while later the king was out hunting and came across a strange-looking beast that resembled both a wolf and a man. But before he could kill the creature, it knelt in front of the king and begged for mercy, fawning before him. Marie writes:

> He seizes the King's stirrup-ring,
> and kisses his foot and leg.

The king was moved by this affection and offered his protection. So the wolf-knight became a constant companion, at night even sharing the king's chamber.

> Every man thinks it a precious thing,
> For it's so gentle, well-bred, polite,

It never would do what isn't right.
Wherever the King might go
It didn't want to be separated, so
It went along with him constantly.
That it loved him was easy to see.

At a party thrown by the king, the normally gentle garwolf went wild. He attacked a man and woman, tearing the woman's nose off her face, to the horror of the guests! The truth finally comes out: the mutilated woman is the wolf-man's former wife, who was at the party with her new spouse. Both the man and woman are banished from the kingdom and all the lady's female heirs are born without a nose, cursed to be disfigured like her.

The knight is given his old clothes by the king, and left alone to transform. Afterwards an intimate scene takes place between the two men:

On the king's royal bed, they see
Lying fast asleep, the knight.
The king ran to hug him tight;
He kissed him a hundred times that day.
When he catches his breath, he hands
Him back all his fiefs and lands,
And more presents than I will say.[1]

Werewolves, and people that transform willingly or unwillingly into beasts, are a popular queer trope today. Even in their ancient origins, pre-dating Bisclavret, werewolves have created room for sexual liberation and expression that aligns with what we might deem queer today.

KEEP IT IN THE FAMILY

Throughout history there are accounts of people turning, or being turned, into wolves. But the most cited 'original werewolf story' is the ancient Greek tale of King Lycaon* of Arcadia. There are many versions of this

---

* His name is also occasionally spelled Lykaion.

myth, but the most popular is narrated by the geographer Pausanias around the second century CE. Lycaon was a king who attempted to test the omnipotence of the king of gods himself, Zeus, by feeding him human flesh. The flesh he used was that of Lycaon's own son, Nyctimus. The thunder god king was not amused at the mortal's hubris and infanticide, so transformed him into a wolf as punishment. In wolf form, Lycaon kills and eats all his own children. In some accounts, his children are turned into wolves as well. Either way, the name 'Lycaon', mirrored in the Greek word 'lykos', meaning wolf, is where we get 'lycanthropy', the word used to describe the condition of being a werewolf.

In a slightly different telling of the Lycaon myth, the tale begins earlier with the nymph Callisto, a daughter of King Lycaon and a follower of Artemis, the goddess of the hunt. The nymph was interested in nobody other than Artemis herself, so when Zeus tried to court her he was unsuccessful. As with many of the women who were targets of Zeus's affection, Callisto's own preference meant nothing to the lustful god, and she was tricked by him. Specifically he used the guise of Artemis, the one person Callisto was attracted to, as a ploy to seduce her. The person Callisto perceived as Artemis was in fact Zeus all along, but it has been the source of a number of queer interpretations and tellings. The painting *Jupiter in the Guise of Diana Seducing Callisto* (the title here is using the Roman names

Jupiter in the Guise of Diana Seducing Callisto by Jacob Adriaensz Backer

for Zeus and Artemis) by Jacob Adriaensz Backer* painted sometime before 1651 shows an intimate moment between the two women. Despite the title revealing one of them to be a male god in disguise, the image is ostensibly of two women embracing.

The child born of Zeus's assault was a boy called Arcas. Sadly, Callisto – as with Medusa and many other women like her, who were assaulted by male gods – suffered one final indignity. The goddess Hera, jealous of her husband Zeus's infidelity, turned Callisto into a bear, and wanted to do the same to her son Arcas, who had to be hidden away from the vengeful goddess.

In this version of the Lycaon werewolf myth, it is Arcas, Lycaon's grandson, who is sacrificed and fed to Zeus; not Lycaon's own son, Nyctimus. The death of Arcas as a son of Zeus, even if he was born through sexual assault, is the instigating event which invokes the wrath of the king of the gods, who again transforms Lycaon into a wolf.

Later Arcas is magically resurrected, but discovers his mother in bear form. In some versions of the legend he tragically kills her, not recognising who she is, and in others he is also turned into a bear, both of them eventually becoming the constellations known as Ursa Major and Minor, the big and little bear. Mother and son reunited in the heavens.

Here we see an entire mythos of transforming humans and demigods, bears and wolves being mixed into the ancestral blood of living human descendants. Also with the legend of Callisto, and Zeus in drag as Artemis mixed in, we have a strong contender for an asexual, or an arguably lesbian origin to all future lupine supernatural abilities.

BLOOD AND MILK

While the ancient Greek werewolf was not quite the same beast we would later see in pulp horror films, there is a sense of the sins of the father being visited upon his children which ties the two storylines together. In both cases the transformation, whether it is a gift or a curse, is something that

---

* Until recently this painting was miscredited to Gerrit van Honthorst.

is handed down from person to person orally, either through eating flesh, or being bitten by an infected person. To many ancient Greek writers it was believed to be a bizarre and barbaric thing, but also a very real practice, kept alive by a particular group of people, the Arcadians.

The Arcadians were a Greek tribe of the central Peloponnese and were seen as one of the oldest Greek peoples, the height of their civilisation existing around 400 BCE. The origins of these people are often tied to the legend of Arcas himself: the son of Callisto and Zeus through trickery, and the grandson of King Lycaon. He was one of the first kings of ancient Arcadia, teaching people how to weave and bake bread.

In ancient Arcadia, in devotion to the story of Lycaon, King Arcas and a version of Zeus born from this myth, a religious festival was held, a set of secret rituals and a rite of passage for young men. On it the poet and philosopher Lycophron (whose name, incidentally, means 'wolf mind'), writing around 300 BCE, said of Arcadian men:

> One of the sons of the oak (Arcadians), the wolf-shaped devourers of the flesh of Nyktimos, a people that were before the moon, and who in the height of winter heated in the ashes of the fire their staple of oaken bread.[2]

He implies here that people from Arcadia, related to King Lycaon, were bound to the legacy of their 'wolf-shaped' ancestors. Almost 500 years later Greek writers such as Pausanias also extended the ability of transformation to living Arcadians during the festival of Lykaia.

> It is said, for instance, that ever since the time of Lykaon a man has changed into a wolf at the sacrifice to Zeus Lykaios, but that the change is not for life; if, when he is a wolf, he abstains from human flesh, after nine years he becomes a man again, but if he tastes human flesh he remains a beast forever.[3]

The suggestion was that during this time, young men would travel up to Mount Lykaion, named after the king in the original story, where human sacrifices were made to Wolf-Zeus. Any young men who ate the flesh and entrails of the victim would transform into wolves for a period of nine years.

If they failed to abstain from eating another person during this time they would be stuck in wolf form for eternity. Remains dating back over 3,000 years imply that human sacrifice did take place on this mountain on a large stone altar, which gives credence to at least the sacrificial origins of this story.

Elements of this ritual were borrowed by a similarly wolf-themed festival in ancient Rome. Known as Lupercalia, reflecting the Latin 'lupus' for wolf, this was a large-scale fertility festival. As the Roman mythological origin story relates to the twins Romulus and Remus being suckled by a she-wolf named Lupa, this too was woven into their version. What resulted was a wild, erotic and frenetic celebration. Caesar himself was supposed to have witnessed the festival where 'many of the noble youths and of the magistrates run up and down through the city naked, for sport and laughter striking those they meet with shaggy thongs'.[4]

During this raucous event Mark Antony, a longtime supporter of Caesar and celebrated general, was chosen to be a 'luperci'. A luperci was one of the young men who sacrificed a goat or dog, covered themselves in blood and milk, and ran naked through the streets, laughing, touching and slapping members of the public. The very embodiment of what we might call 'wolfish' behaviour.

In Antony's youth there was much gossip about his sexuality, his interest in men as well as women. While some of this was mere political scheming, such as the assertion that he had had sex with Gaius Scribonius Curio, it is known that alongside his famous love for Cleopatra, Antony also fell for a young Jewish man known as Aristobolus. In the first-century writings of the historian Flavius Josephus it is said that Antony 'stood in admiration at the tallness and handsomeness'[5] of Aristobulus. It is later described that the attractiveness of Aristobulus and his sister was such that it was believed to be some kind of a trap 'to entice Antony into lewd pleasures with them'. Later King Herod says:

> He did not think it safe for him to send one so handsome as was Aristobulus, in the prime of his life; for he was sixteen years of age: and of so noble a family: and particularly not to Antony; the principal man among the Romans; and one that would abuse him in his amours; and besides, one that openly indulged himself in such pleasures, as his power allow'd him, without control.[6]

The fact that Antony was chosen as a Luperci, a wolf priest, for the festivities even at the ripe age of thirty-nine, is therefore perhaps unsurprising as the unburdened sexuality associated with wild canines might also be associated with bisexual desire in humans. This is a reductive description of bisexuality and even links with contemporary stereotypes around bisexual people being promiscuous and predatory.

Wolf festivals, revolving around the transformation between human and bestial forms, were very much devoted to all forms of male sexuality. While they were known to improve fertility for women, and believed to be good luck for those who were pregnant, it was not just women who would have been the recipients of the wanted, or unwanted, attention of the Luperci. For those men who enjoyed the vision of naked men running through the streets, the event was as equally erotic as it would be for female observers. From a Greek and Roman perspective, to become a wolf for a night was to be given free rein to indulge in all manner of predatory sexual urges. The wolf did not differentiate.

GOING BERSERK

Another major influence on the European werewolf legend comes from Norse mythology and beliefs. The seafaring groups of people from the first to the eleventh centuries that are today loosely described as Vikings shared a number of gods, spiritual beliefs and theological conventions. These included the idea of a caste of warriors that were known to go into a trancelike state when fighting. These 'berserkers' were men who embodied the spirits of aggressive mammals, mostly bears, wolves and wild boar. By wearing the skins of these animals and possibly taking hallucinogenic drugs, or purposefully inflicting pain on themselves (for example by biting down on their own shields),[7] they could go into a rage where they would fight fearlessly and tirelessly. The word 'berserker' comes from the Norse words for 'bear' and 'shirt', referring to these men's wearing of animal skins in battle. It is also where we get the word 'berserk', meaning to go crazy or lose control.

Berserkers were also often mixed with ideas around animal magic and transformation. Whether or not these warriors simply fought with the ferocity of the animals they embodied, or literally became them, depends on the text. Bödvar Bjarki, for example, is a hero of Norse legends who was cursed to shapeshift into bear form, and there are suggestions of other warriors becoming wolves, similar to the contemporary werewolf myth.

Berserker warriors were often described as ugly and strange outsiders. For example, *Egil's Saga*, an epic story of an Icelandic family of heroes and their adventures and shifting allegiances, talks of a group of warriors that may be berserkers as follows: 'There be men here outside newly come, twelve together, if men one may call them, for they are liker to giants in stature and semblance than to mortal men.' Although often villains or solitary weirdos in Norse stories, due to their violence and strange behaviour, they could also be written about more kindly. *Egil's Saga* actually opens with two shapeshifting protagonists. Ulf, nicknamed 'Kveldulf', meaning 'evening wolf', is a central character, named both for his temper and his shapeshifting abilities. And we also meet his dear companion, a warrior named Kari, who was also a berserker. They are introduced as follows: 'Ulf was a man so tall and strong that none could match him, and in his youth he roved the seas as a freebooter. In fellowship with him was one Kari of Berdla, a man of renown for strength and daring; he was a Berserk. Ulf and he had one common purse, and were the dearest friends.'[8]

Within Viking society fierce bonds of friendship between warriors would be seen as manly and proper. These two characters sharing a purse implies a similar bond to what we see with many classical heroes and warriors in ancient Rome and Greece. This does not necessarily mean there is a romantic or sexual element, but nor does it preclude this. Today the Vikings are largely held up as a hypermasculine hyperheterosexual and purely warlike group of people. The truth is more complex and nuanced. Primarily, these different groups and tribes of people had a rich and layered culture. We can see within the Norse language words that might be used to describe same-sex attraction, intimacy and even gender nonconformity.

'Ergi', for example, was an insult, used to describe a man perceived as weak or feminine. The god Odin himself was accused of 'ergi' by the god Loki, for using a branch of magic largely practised by women called 'seiðr'. A translation of the *Poetic Edda* reads, 'They say that with spells, in Samsey once like witches with, charms didst thou work; And in witch's guise among men didst thou go; Unmanly thy soul must seem.' The historian Eirnin Jeffor Franks translates the term 'ergi' as not just 'womanish', but something closer to the word queer, wherein cross-dressing and gender nonconformity would be associated in Norse belief with magic and transformation: 'In the past, the terms "argr" and "ergi" were applied to these spiritual functionaries. It is fairly certain that the ergi priest-magicians wore a mix of feminine and sacerdotal attire'.[9]

Loki is also not just a character who calls out other people's 'ergi' but is perhaps the most famously genderbending character in Norse mythology. As a shape-shifting trickster god, Loki is known to have taken the form of a milkmaid for a while and raised children, and in one bizarre incident to have transformed into a female horse to copulate with a stallion, and give birth to eight-legged offspring! Within the Norse understanding, transformation and magic could push a person's identity beyond the limits of man and woman, and could allow for all manner of unlikely pairings.

Today's werewolf, a creature of monstrous transformation, borrows heavily from these Norse beliefs, where strangeness, otherness and even a kind of magic femininity might allow for shapeshifting into a new body. It is also interesting that today's werewolves are partly inspired by legendary roaming warriors, driven by the animus of a wolf or a bear, who might travel together, sharing their lives and all their earnings in same-sex partnerships.

BEAR MAIDENS AND FOX WEDDINGS

Among the many belief systems and myths that have been compared with contemporary ideas of werewolves, one culutural tradition that is frequently cited, and often clumsily connected, comprises Native American stories of animal transformation. This has led to an understandable hostility among many people of indigenous descent, having their beliefs and heritage conflated with movie monster tropes and teenage paranormal romantic fiction.

This supposed werewolf connection is often attributed to the belief in so-called 'skinwalkers' and 'mai-coh' (meaning wolf) among First Nations peoples of North America. In Navajo 'yee naaldlooshii' is described as a person who uses magic to cause harm, and may transform into an animal such as a coyote or control the bodies of others. The coyote is a totemic animal, a trickster spirit and powerful deity, and a symbol for queer indigenous people today:

> In our Native Tradition we have creatures called tricksters: Raven, Coyote, Rabbit, Monkey – these are all tricksters. Tricksters are the ones who, when everything is going well – life is wonderful and POW – they come along and whack you in the head. The really nice thing about tricksters is they can change gender – they can cross back and forth.[10]

The Ojibwa have the story of a bear maiden. In this tale there are three sisters, but the very youngest is born as a little bear. The little bear, after repeatedly being bullied by her sisters, manages to find each of them a man to marry. At last she finds herself a human husband, but he refuses to be with her in her current form, so she asks to be sacrificed in a fire. Instead of dying she transforms into a beautiful human maiden and decides she doesn't want to be with a man after all.[11]

The association between tricksters, transformations and gender fluidity is also a staple beyond the Ojibwa:

> Among the native American Oglala Sioux, two-spirit or third gender shamans-to-be dreamed of the female divinity Anukite, or Double Woman . . . Double Woman had many faces: she could appear as twins, as a beautiful maiden, a woman warrior, an hermaphroditic buffalo calf, a vampiric deer. The young person who dreamed of her would become a two-spirit shaman and a member of 'They [who] dream of face-on-both-sides'.[12]

The Tewa may have a similar understanding, blending ideas of gender transformation with animal metamorphosis, saying: 'if you are a man, and if you are a woman, then you can be a bear.'[13]

***

The Fox's Wedding, 1800

In Japanese culture a number of natural phenomena – including the appearance of atmospheric ghost-lights, known as will-o'-the wisps, or a rainbow, or when it rains while the sun is shining – can be referred to as 'kitsune no yomeiri'. This term means 'the fox's wedding'. In Japan the fox is not always just an animal; rather, kitsune are also mischievous spirits often taking the form of beautiful women. In some tales these beings lead elaborate wedding processions, where certain mortals may be invited or caught up in the festivities.

The kitsune is a spirit of nature that can shapeshift and transform, also classed as a type of 'yokai' among other supernatural beings. These creatures could be cruel, playful or kind, depending on the story. Some kitsune might prey on humans, draining them of their life force in a sexually vampiric manner. Sometimes these kitsune will have homosexual inclinations, being male foxes in disguise and targeting young men who wander alone and away from their hometowns.[14]

Kitsune, like witches, fairies and demons, can also possess a human host, changing its behaviour. People under the control of a fox are in a state known as 'kitsune-tsuki' and historically have been described in similar ways to demonic possession: laughing uncontrollably, cursing and barking like a fox. Within this behaviour there are examples of men and women becoming controlled by a fox spirit that is the opposite of their own gender. For example, a young woman possessed by a male fox might talk about wanting to bring rice cakes back to her fox-wife.

> I am no evil spirit, only a fox who happened to come wandering by. I have a young family in my den who were hungry . . . Will you please let me have some paper, so that I can wrap this up and take it home for the old lady and my children to eat.[15]

Many of those affected by kitsune-tsuki may also exclaim adoration and devotion to the 'kami' (deity) known as Inari. In one case, an otherwise illiterate man wrote a dedication to the 'great god' Inari, complete with a drawing of a messenger fox. Inari is a being that appears in many guises, and seemingly has no fixed gender. Sometimes Inari is a beautiful maiden, sometimes an old man carrying rice, and sometimes they appear in a form that is androgynous, combining masculine and feminine features.[16] Inari is associated with the kitsune, who are sometimes their servants, or followers. It is perhaps unsurprising that the gender-bending-yokai foxes would have an equally transformative master.

Kitsune are not the only transforming creatures in Japanese folklore; the 'tanuki' is another overlapping myth. The tanuki myth, as with kitsune, is based on a real animal, the raccoon dog, which is a canid closely related to foxes. These beings, like kitsune, are playful creatures of transformation, who love drinking and playing tricks on people. One notable trait is that they are believed to have enormous, stretchy testicles, encapsulated in a popular playground song which translates as 'tan-tan-tanuki's bollocks, even without wind, they swing-swing!'[17] Therefore tanuki are nearly always male, although they don't always stay masculine in appearance when appearing to humans. In one myth a tanuki takes the form of a man's deceased wife shortly after her death. As he goes to embrace her, the man realises this cannot be possible, and breaks the illusion, transforming his wife back into the form of a male raccoon dog:

> 'Is it possible for a dead person to come back?' He grabbed her, pulled her towards him, and he stabbed her three times with his

sword: she disappeared into thin air. His retainers rushed in, lit torches, and searched everywhere, but there was nothing. When morning broke, they discovered a trace of blood on the hold of the door latch. Thinking this was very strange indeed, they searched and found a hole in a grove located at the northwest corner of the property. They dug this up and found an aged tanuki, stabbed three times and lying dead.[18]

In many cases these shapeshifting yokai use gender-bending and human desire for the sheer mischievous fun of it.

Historically Japanese attitudes to sexuality and gender during the formation of these myths has, as in every other human society, been an ever-changing and nuanced one. In the times of the origins of many of these yokai legends and tropes, there were living humans who moved between gender identities and had sex outside heterosexual pairings. For example, in Japanese monastic tradition same-sex partnerships among men, one of whom was often underage, were a known milestone. The archaic term 'shudo', from 'wakashudo', meaning 'the way of adolescent boys', was also a synonym for same-sex desire. Over time some of these behaviours and roles fell in and out of fashion, and are seen as more or less acceptable. But we can still see the fossils of the lives and experiences of real people in the fantastical, perhaps most clearly in transformative fox and raccoon dog folklore.

WHAT BIG TEETH YOU HAVE

'Little Red Riding Hood', like so many fairy tales and children's stories, has a long and complex history, and there isn't necessarily just one origin. The story as most people know it today was solidified in the seventeenth century as 'Le Petit Chaperon Rouge' by French writer Charles Perrault. It has since been retold many, many times, the most well-known adaptation being by the Brothers Grimm. It is worth stating that in some versions of this story, the wolf is described as a 'bzou', such as in 'The Story of Grandmother', a retelling by Louis and François Briffault in 1885. A bzou is another word for werewolf.

One origin is within Norse mythology and revolves around the tale of
the previously mentioned Loki, the trickster god, Thor, the god of thunder, and Freyja, goddess of love and war. In the 'Þrymskviða' ('Þrym's
Poem'), part of the Viking *Edda*, Thor and Loki are on a quest to find
Thor's hammer, Mjöllnir. It turns out that the hammer has been taken by
Þrym, the king of the 'jötnar', troll-like beings. Þrym asks for Freyja's
hand in marriage in return for the hammer, and so Loki and Thor hatch
a plan whereby Thor poses as Freyja in a wedding dress, despite his protests, and Loki becomes his very willing handmaiden:

> Then bound they on Thor the bridal veil,
> And next the mighty Brisings' necklace.
>
> Keys around him, let they rattle,
> And down to his knees hung woman's dress;
> With gems full broad upon his breast,
> And a pretty cap, to crown his head.
>
> Then Loki spake, the son of Laufey:
> 'As thy maid-servant thither I go with thee;
> We two shall haste to the giants' home.'[19]

While at the wedding feast, Thor's table manners and enormous appe-
tite are noted by the guests:

> Then loud spake Thrym, the giants' leader:
> 'Who ever saw bride more keenly bite?
> I ne'er saw bride with a broader bite,
> Nor a maiden who drank more mead than this!'

Next Thor's eyes are commented on:

> Thrym looked 'neath the veil, for he longed to kiss,
> But back he leaped the length of the hall:
> 'Why are so fearful the eyes of Freyja?
> Fire, methinks, from her eyes burns forth.'

It is this comedic sequence of questioning Thor's appearance while in drag that seems to have inspired the most famous part of 'Little Red Riding Hood'. Red Riding Hood famously says to the wolf, who is disguised as her grandmother, what big teeth she has, and what big eyes she has.

The wolf in the story of Little Riding Hood primarily symbolises dangerous, predatory men, and is a warning to young women and children, particularly during or after puberty. Charles Perrault explains the moral of his tale, saying:

> From this story one learns that children, especially young lasses, pretty, courteous and well-bred, do very wrong to listen to strangers. And it is not an unheard thing if the Wolf is thereby provided with his dinner. I say Wolf, for all wolves are not of the same sort; there is one kind with an amenable disposition – neither noisy, nor hateful, nor angry, but tame, obliging and gentle, following the young maids in the streets, even into their homes. Alas! Who does not know that these gentle wolves are of all such creatures the most dangerous![20]

The wolf is a predatory animal, and so is a powerful synonym for a male sexual predator. Indeed, in many tellings Red Riding Hood ends up in bed with the wolf before being eaten. But there is also a clear gender-bending reading of this: the wolf dresses as an elderly woman, and this is at least partly inspired by the tale of a male thunder god dressed as a bride. This feeds into a long-running trope that, sadly, still exists today: that of the transgender trickster.

By dressing as a woman, the belief is that a man might gain access to women to commit harm and abuse, similar to the earlier myth of Zeus and Callisto. Also, such a trick might be played on a man, fooling him into believing he has met a 'real' woman, just like the tanuki myth. Either way, this harmful stereotype is still used in political discourse. In the *Daily Telegraph* of 26 January 2023, cartoonist Matt Pritchett created an image of a wolf dressed as a grandmother, looking at Little Red Riding Hood, who says: 'So, you ate grandma and now you want to be sent to a women's prison?' This uses the metaphor of a wolf in disguise directly as a substitute for transgender women, the assertion being that trans women are using their identity as a way of preying on cisgender women.

Yet, as with every cruel stereotype, there is sometimes an opportunity for reclamation by queer people. The term 'werewoman' commonly describes a female werewolf, but etymologically speaking 'were' means man, so it would translate literally as 'man who becomes woman'. For this reason there has been some reclamation of this term by transgender women. A page described as 'New Werewoman Handbook: A Manual for the newly transgendered' was created on 1 December 2011 and uses werewolves as a tongue-in-cheek way of talking about the journey of gender transition: 'What separates a regular man or woman from a werewoman? For starters, your garden variety person spends their entire life in one gender. Boy becomes man OR girl becomes woman; either-or. Not so for a werewoman. We change genders frequently; although some more frequently than others.'[21]

BITE THEM YOUNG

Werewolf stories can be used to reflect a number of difficult elements of the queer experience: the journey from shame to self-acceptance, and the awkwardness and danger of being LGBTQ+ during puberty. Even stories that do not have explicitly queer characters, or are even subtly homophobic, are often aware of this connection.

In the 1985 hit film *Teen Wolf*, Scott, the protagonist and teenage lycanthrope, literally stumbles out of a wardrobe while transforming. His best friend Stiles comments, 'What's it like coming out of the closet?' Later, when Scott approaches Stiles again, wanting to share his embarrassing werewolf secret, his friend says, 'Are you going to tell me you're a fag? I mean if you're going to tell me you're a fag I don't think I can handle it!'

Later in the film, Scott's father, who is also a werewolf, tries to console his son, saying, 'Don't believe all that stuff you see in the movies. With certain obvious exceptions, werewolves are people just like anyone else.' And: 'The werewolf is a part of you, but that doesn't change what you have inside.' The allusions to coming out as queer, to both friends and parents, are clear, even if the characters are otherwise entirely heterosexual, and these moments are played for strictly 'no-homo' laughs, but show a knowingness of how well the werewolf and being a queer teenager go together.

In J. K. Rowling's Harry Potter series there are a few werewolf characters. The main one is Remus Lupin, a teacher and heroic father figure. Although not explicitly referenced in the books, J. K. Rowling later stated that 'Lupin's condition of lycanthropy was a metaphor for those illnesses that carry a stigma, like HIV and AIDS'. The character of Lupin is beloved, and so this can be seen as an attempt to fight stigma. But there are other perhaps unforeseen implications to this reading of the werewolf condition as synonymous with HIV, which many have found offensive.

Within the Harry Potter books it is stated that Lupin was turned into a werewolf by another evil werewolf called Fenrir Greyback. Fenrir's character is described as follows:

> He regards it as his mission in life to bite and to contaminate as many people as possible; he wants to create enough werewolves to overcome the wizards. Voldemort has promised him prey in return for his services. Greyback specialises in children . . . Bite them young, he says, and raise them away from their parents, raise them to hate normal wizards.[22]

Lycanthropy can be both an empowering symbol for queer people or an incredibly negative one, depending on how it is used and what connections it is used to make. In this case, it is rather clumsy, and, through the insinuation of the existence of evil child-predator werewolves, could lead to further stigmatisation for queer people with HIV.

SEXY BEASTS

It can be a funny thing trying to explain the gay community and its codes to anyone outside it; some of the terminology can sound a bit like a trip to the zoo. A bear is a large hairy man; a cub is a smaller, younger hairy man; an otter is a thin or athletic hairy man; and a wolf is similar to an otter, but usually older and more promiscuous, while still younger and more muscular than a bear, etc., etc.

The use of animal-based terminology in contemporary queer parlance goes beyond even this: there are chickens and oxes; there are pups, gym bunnies and rats, foxes – even dolphins and pigs. These particular descriptors are largely used among gay and bisexual men; lesbians and bisexual women, and nonbinary people, also have their own terminology and inside jokes that overlap, but aren't quite as animal-focused. But the sheer preponderance of animal slang among men who love men has always struck me as both funny and illuminating when considering the history of animal transformation and queer identity.

The significance of these terms, and the subcultures they encompass, varies wildly between individuals. For some of the people who reached out to me over social media, the terms bear or otter are largely just physical descriptions that allow them to find people they are attracted to, and people who might be attracted to them. For example, Ricky said, 'I drifted towards the bear scene rapidly, principally because of my interest in Hirsute Pursuits. Even then there was disagreement as to what constituted a bear, with some going for hairiness, some going for size/stature, some insisting it was a look and some insisting it was an attitude. For me, facial and body hair was central.'

For others there is a deeper meaning, a sense of found family and community at odds with societal beauty standards that often celebrate only a very specific body ideal for queer men. Luke Marlowe says, 'The media constantly go out of their way to describe gay men as "less than human" – so why not embrace that? There's a masculinity and an animality that can come out in gay spaces – and the "packs" that gay people can often be found in – for company and for safety.'

These categories came into the lexicon in the 1980s among a group of men who frequented the Bear Hug gay bar in San Francisco. 'Bear' as a queer tribe was established among the wider queer community through the release of *Bear* magazine in 1987 by Richard Bulger and Chris Nelson. As with many queer publications, this began with xeroxed pages stuck together into forty-five editions and advertised through other small LGBTQ+ magazines. These archetypes are now well understood, even outside the LGBTQ+ community, and are even starting to be accepted in everyday parlance. But there are areas where this 'animism' and non-human identification becomes more pronounced – not just a word and a flag, but a truly lived character and identity. In these spaces there has been more of a cultural backlash and level of derision, even if it is all arguably cut from the same cloth.

Within the myriad different kinks* there are a number of communities which resonate with the idea of animal identity and transformation: for example, the kink side of the 'furry' fandom, the 'pup' community and 'omegaverse' erotic fiction. All these groups involve an appreciation of anthropomorphised animals and related content, often focused on wolves and other canines.

Within the furry community, only 20 per cent of people surveyed self-defined as heterosexual, meaning the majority fall somewhere within the LGBTQIA+ spectrum, although solid data on trans identities is lacking.[23] Animal role play, for example pup play, where the roles are based around dogs and their masters, is particularly practised by queer men, originally as a subgroup of the 1980s gay leather scene.

All the communities described here are often derided, perceived by many as products of bizarre imaginations or a 'gross' fetish. The mix of sex, identity and animal traits is often mocked as perverse, embarrassing, cringe-inducing and synonymous with bestiality. Yet the reason why there is such mockery aimed at these communities is largely down to their prevalence. It is increasingly difficult not to come across these communities, their art, their conventions and their tropes. From my perspective, I simply see human beings doing something humans have done for an incredibly long time: finding familiarity, joy and, yes, sexiness in the other. I can see a direct throughline from the erotic classical depiction of hybrid creatures like satyrs, mermaids and centaurs going back thousands of years, to someone creating their own 'fursona'.

While to some the kinks surrounding animal roleplay and fursonas may seem extreme, from a queer perspective they are merely an extension

---

* A kink is any kind of sexual preference, interest or fantasy that is deemed unconventional or outside 'ordinary' sex. This can come in myriad types but includes role play, bondage, voyeurism and exhibitionism.

of sexual identification with nonhuman characters. I believe they follow the line from werewolf folklore, where certain animals, particularly wolves and canines, have been folded into a folkloric understanding of forbidden human sexuality.

GOING THROUGH CHANGES

As a whole, werewolves and animal shapeshifters are clearly strong vessels for expressions of queer lives and desires. The fact that they mix body transformation with the inherent sexuality and danger that is associated with wolves and predatory animals leads them to reflect back a lot of the lived experience of LGBTQ+ people throughout time. The animal side of the werewolf can make for uncomfortable parallels with which some people may not want to connect. For others, the sheer body horror and edgy sexiness of werewolf folklore is what makes them so compelling. Also, compared to the other folkloric strands so far, there is something primal and connected to the natural world about the werewolf that I think is grounding for many queer people. Seeing themselves as unnatural through the lens of society, it can be deeply validating to find oneself in a creature that, while supernatural, is also simple in its bestial and carnal nature.

The werewolf in its constant changing forms, between man and monster, encapsulates the way queer people are used to existing between, or underneath, regular 'normal' society. So a being that bends and breaks the rules of what it is to be human, at least once a month, under a full moon, can offer marvellous escapism.

5

Children of the Night

Paros is a Greek island located in a circle of islands called the Cyclades in the Aegean Sea. In classical history it was famous for its white marble, which was used to create famous sculptures such as the Venus de Milo and the Nike of Samothrace.

My family has been visiting Paros since before I was born, and so our connection with the island is a strong one. During these trips I developed a fascination with Greek myths and monsters, constantly drawing them and scaring myself with imagined stories based on the minotaur and gorgons. It is because of this that my childhood memories of dark cicada-filled nights and the smell of Greek night flowers are also forever associated with the thrill and fear of the supernatural.

Paros is a good place to commune with the darkly fantastical, even if my younger self didn't fully understand why. An amphora vase made on Paros depicts warriors in battle. It was found in a polyandrion, a war grave filled with the ashes and remains of young men, from 750 BCE. Ancient Greeks had many superstitions around the undead and evil demons. Large millstones are often found covering buried bodies; this was to stop the deceased from rising from their graves.

The island of Paros also has a smaller sibling. Antiparos takes about twenty minutes by boat to reach and is known mainly for its picturesque fishing port, pebbled beaches and one enormous cave, nestled in the hill of Agios Ioannis on the south of the island. It is a gaping, dripping maw, full of stalactites and stalagmites and lit by naked bulbs that run along the ceiling. A deadly drop into darkness was, back in the nineties, only narrowly avoided by a few precarious-looking rusty handrails which guarded the edge of the slippery steps. Today it has been made somewhat safer. The air in the cave is always moist, salty and deep-cold despite the seething Mediterranean heat outside. Other than the coachloads of tourists who visit daily in the summer months, the dark enclaves of the cavern are home to an assortment of 'nychterides' (night creatures), including pipistrelle and horseshoe bats.

Other than the bats, those who visit the caves today largely come to see the graffitied stalactites which contain signatures of notable people who have visited over the past 300 years. For example, the marquis de Nouadel, a French ambassador to Constantinople, entered the cave in 1673. Finding a rock formation that looked like an altar, he celebrated a mass down in the darkness. His message reads: 'Here Christ himself celebrated Midnight Mass on Christmas 1673'. Some have even argued that the cave was home of the giant one-eyed cyclops Polyphemus, as described in Homer's *Odyssey*. All this means that the cave has this incredibly gothic feel, at odds with the bougainvillea and the brochure-worthy, blue-roofed churches outside. As a child I thought maybe this was where a vampire would sleep, resting in the moist darkness and then transforming into one of the small bats at dusk, to prowl the villages of Paroikia and Naoussa. In some ways I wasn't entirely wrong.

MAD, BAD AND DANGEROUS

Around 1810, the twenty-three-year-old Lord Byron travelled the islands of Greece as part of his Grand Tour. These tours were a kind of rite of passage undertaken by wealthy, educated European men to enable them to see classical antiquities. They would visit the museums, galleries and the ancient temples of Italy and Greece, while also sampling whatever earthly delights might take their privileged fancy. The tour, while not exclusively undertaken by queer men, was an opportunity for many whom we might label as gay or bisexual to explore that side of themselves. The likes of Byron would view the homoerotic frescos, the depictions of Dionysian orgies and the impossibly muscular ancient heroes and gods with an added level of interest.

Many queer men came to Greece, Italy and the Near East believing they might find a freedom of expression in the ancient past that they did not find in the realities of contemporary Georgian and Victorian society. In fact, some fifty years after Byron's trip, influential gay writer John Addington Symonds would try to find words to describe his own same-sex desires. He would name it Greek in origin from his study of 'man love' in ancient Greek texts. The affinity of queer people with Greece is longstanding and still has its echoes in the crowded circuit parties of Mykonos today, and the popularity of same-sex weddings on the island of Lesbos.

On Byron's trip to Antiparos he and a few friends made their way up the mountain to the cave and it is then that Byron supposedly left his name on a stalactite. I say 'supposedly' because I have never found it.* So while it is by far the most famous autograph in the cave, it might not even be there! If it is, it has had to suffer hundreds of years of erosion by thousands of suncream-covered hands. Still, we know that Byron visited the island, and no doubt the cave, too.

Because of his love of Greece and its people, and his later support of the Greek struggle for independence, Byron became a kind of folk hero of his own. He is beloved by many Greeks even today, known as Λόρδος Βύρωνας, 'Lordos Vironas', and is seen as a saviour or hero of almost mythic proportions. Back home things were more complicated.

In England and Europe, Lord Byron would become the leading figure of the Romantic movement, and a political and social fascination for the press. He was a beloved and derided outcast; a man who was infamously 'mad, bad and dangerous to know'. He is frequently described as handsome and charismatic, but also as having a violent temper, being deeply vain, and showing very little regard for anyone else in his life. Although for a long time respectable historians have been markedly tight-lipped and awkward when describing Byron's sex life, we now know Byron was romantically involved with multiple men as well as women. One puzzled biographer comments: 'It is not so simple to define Byron as homosexual

---

* Or at least I have never found the 'real' one. I have found multiple examples of Byron's names and initials, but I am unable to verify them so these may well be forgeries. The cave is literally covered with writing on every surface, and while many of the signatures and scrawled epitaphs are hundreds of years old, they sit alongside modern graffiti and counterfeits.

or heterosexual: he seems rather to have been both, and either.'[1] Luckily we do have a word for that today: Byron was in all likelihood (at least by modern standards) bisexual, and, for the conservative nature of the times, flagrantly so.

But it would not be wise to call Byron a queer icon: his behaviour was divisive, abusive and occasionally downright cruel, even to those he claimed to love. Still, it is important to remember that Byron's life has been so overly dramatised and embellished that it is difficult to tease apart the facts from the fiction. Whether or not he was truly the bad-boy whirling dervish of burning sexuality he is made out to be, or a pitiable incestuous and self-absorbed narcissist, depends on your perspective and which accounts you read. Either way, Byron was a celebrity, and very much a sex symbol of the time. He left in his wake a sea of broken hearts and adoring fans, of all genders, but just as many critics. Because of one of these one-sided relationships, Byron is arguably the father of the modern vampire.

POOR POLLY DOLLY

John William Polidori. The story goes that the young Anglo-Italian doctor met Byron originally as a personal physician on his travels around Europe. Polidori confided to Byron that while he had trained in medicine he was desperate to reinvent himself as a writer. Polidori's travels with Byron would no doubt have brought him into contact with all manner of people and places that would have fed a desire for a more literary and bohemian existence. One night in 1816, Polidori, who was only twenty-one, found himself in the company of Lord Byron and the celebrated literary couple Mary and Percy Shelley. This illustrious group decided to write ghost stories as a competition. It is here that Mary Shelley wrote the introduction to what would one day become *Frankenstein* (a story explored in Chapter 11).

After this night, Polidori, clearly desperate to impress his new friends, took the short piece Byron had been working on (before the drunken lord became bored of the game and wandered off) and at the request of a mysterious and possibly fictitious 'lady' fleshed it out into a novella about a beautiful and extravagant man who was secretly a vampire. The story was called 'The Vampyre' and the antagonist, or antihero, the vampiric Lord Ruthven, is clearly a caricature of Lord Byron.

The relationship between Polidori and Byron was at this stage already fraught; while Polidori was in awe of Byron and some have argued hopelessly infatuated, this soon turned to resentment. Byron repeatedly pushed Polidori away, finding him boring and needy.

He mocked his efforts to become a writer, nicknaming him 'Polly Dolly', much to Polidori's chagrin.

It is said that around this time, once when boating together, Polidori accidentally hit Byron in the head with a paddle, but rather than apologise Polidori commented, 'I am glad to see you can suffer pain.' So the character of Lord Ruthven in 'The Vampyre', an attractive, cold and ultimately wicked creature who hurts and destroys all those around him through literally draining their life essence, can be read as a clear jab at Byron.

> He gazed upon the mirth around him, as if he could not participate therein. Apparently, the light laughter of the fair only attracted his attention, that he might by a look quell it, and throw fear into those breasts where thoughtlessness reigned. Those who felt this sensation of awe, could not explain whence it arose: some attributed it to the dead grey eye, which, fixing upon the object's face, did not seem to penetrate, and at one glance to pierce through to the inward workings of the heart; but fell upon the cheek with a leaden ray that weighed upon the skin it could not pass. His peculiarities caused him to be invited to every house; all wished to see him, and those who had been accustomed to violent excitement, and now felt the weight of ennui, were pleased at having something in their presence capable of engaging their attention.[2]

'The Vampyre' mysteriously left Polidori's side and was handed from person to person without his knowledge. It was published in a magazine without his consent, and as a final affront it was mistakenly attributed, described in the tabloids as 'A Tale Told By Lord Byron'. The story took off, and people loved what they believed to be a dark but self-referential horror by the infamous socialite, when in fact it was intended as a scathing critique by a jilted acolyte. Neither Byron nor Polidoro were happy with this outcome, but the misattribution to Byron stuck for some time, partly because it was so much more exciting.

After Polidori claimed authorship the fee was reduced from £300 to a paltry £30.[3] A few months later, aged only twenty-five, humiliated, depressed and in debt, Polidori is believed by many to have killed himself by taking prussic acid.

After Polidori's death, the myth of the vampire suddenly became synonymous with the dark and mysterious bisexual young Lord Byron. Later writings such as Bram Stoker's *Dracula* borrowed heavily from this archetype, casting the vampire as a wealthy, darkly handsome and cultured man of taste and class. It is likely that Stoker was intrigued by this image partly because of struggles with his own identity and sexuality.

Bram Stoker is believed by many historians and biographers to have been a repressed gay man. He had close affiliations with many notable queer writers, including Oscar Wilde, yet in 1912 Stoker went on record calling for the imprisonment of all homosexual authors in Britain. I have wondered whether this was an attempt to mask his own sexuality from prying eyes.

The most well-known example of Stoker's conflicted self is expressed through his close relationship with the gay poet Walt Whitman, and in particular his introductory letter:

> If you are the man I take you to be, you will like to get this letter. If you are not I don't care whether you like it or not and only ask that you put it into the fire without reading any further. But I believe you will like it. I don't think there is a man living, even you who are above the prejudices of the class of small-minded men, who wouldn't like to get a letter from a younger man, a stranger across the world – a man living in an atmosphere prejudiced to the truths you sing and your manner of singing them.

Towards the end of his letter Stoker writes: 'How sweet a thing it is for a strong healthy man with a woman's eyes and a child's wishes to feel that he can speak to a man who can be if he wishes father, and brother and wife to his soul.'[4]

The coding of a vampire, being a man living alone with his fortunes in an ancient family castle, engaging in salacious and forbidden acts, is clearly drawn from the scandalous accounts of Byron's real life. The bisexual 'bad boy' Lord Byron, through Polidori, and later Bram Stoker's lens of writing, in many ways gave birth to the first truly modern vampire.

But while contemporary vampires may have had a queer father in Byron, they also had a mother in Lilith.

DARK MOTHER

The vampire has existed as a concept for thousands of years, across different cultures; it has shifted form multiple times. The word vampire has Slavic roots originating either from the word 'upyr', meaning a kind of witch, or from the word 'vperit', meaning to violently thrust into. Either way there is a tone of dark magic and perhaps dangerous sexuality baked into the very word.

From a biblical perspective the first vampire might have started out in the Garden of Eden. In Judaic mythology, Adam had another wife before Eve, a woman called Lilith. Lilith refused to sleep with Adam, and in doing so refused to honour the words of God. In the *Alphabet of Ben Sira*, written in 700 CE, Lilith says, 'I will not lie below', and Adam responds, 'I will not lie below, but above, since you are fit for being below and I for being above.' Here Lilith argues, 'The two of us are equal, since we are both from the earth.'[5] For this breach of gendered sex roles, and for fighting for equality alongside Adam, she was cast out of the Garden.

Here Lilith becomes the mother of all demons and is transformed into a succubus. A succubus is an evil being, often of feminine appearance, who feeds off the life force of men and children; the associated Hebrew word 'lilit', meaning either 'of the night' or 'flying demon', and categorises beings such as hags and witches. In some stories Lilith is the progenitor of a very particular kind of demon, the vampire.

The story of Lilith was most likely written as a warning to women: to know their place in a strict patriarchal set-up, or else have their womanhood twisted into something evil and depraved. But the depiction of

Lilith has for many taken on a different meaning: she has become a symbol for women not doing or looking as they are expected.

Many have taken Lilith to be symbolic of a queer woman, or anyone who rebels against patriarchal and heteronormative assumptions. In this form she has been used both to disempower and empower queer people throughout history. For example, popular 1950s spiritualist Samael Aun Weor wrote that same-sex attraction was a kind of 'infrasexuality', or perversion. He describes this as being within 'the sphere of Lilith'. He believed that gay and bisexual men and women, like the myth of Lilith, were perverted on a spiritual level which made them rebel against what he believed to be the normal sexual order.

Lilith has also been reclaimed, as conveyed in an article by Rebecca Lesses in the Jewish Women's Archives. She writes that Lilith 'represents a woman whom society cannot control – a woman who determines her own sexual partners, who is wild and unkempt'.[6]

The female vampire enshrined in the myth of Lilith, with dark sexual appetites, has also existed separately in folklore around the world. From the Filipino 'manananggal', whose upper torso sprouts bats wings and tears away from her legs at night, to the Zulu monster called a 'tokoloshe' and Ghanaian vampiric demon known as the 'adze', all are shapeshifting beings with rapacious, twisted sexual appetites and a desire for human life force.

In Europe, alongside the Byronesque vampires of Dracula and Nosferatu, we have a whole host of vampires who are feminine in their presentation and wickedness, as well as being decidedly queer. The archetypical version is 1872 *Carmilla* by Sheridan Le Fanu, the story of a mysterious vampiric countess in disguise who turns her sights on a young heroine, Laura, whom she hypnotises and slowly drains of life. Here Carmilla talks to Laura, showing deep affection, while drawing her innocent female prey closer into her thrall:

> She used to place her pretty arms about my neck, draw me to her, and laying her cheek to mine, murmur with her lips near my ear, 'Dearest, your little heart is wounded; think me not cruel because I obey the irresistible law of my strength and weakness; if your dear heart is wounded, my wild heart bleeds with yours. In the

An engraving from the gothic novel *Carmilla* by Sheridan Le Fanu, 1872

rapture of my enormous humiliation I live in your warm life, and you shall die – die, sweetly die – into mine. I cannot help it; as I draw near to you, you, in your turn, will draw near to others, and learn the rapture of that cruelty, which yet is love; so, for a while, seek to know no more of me and mine, but trust me with all your loving spirit.'

And when she had spoken such a rhapsody, she would press me more closely in her trembling embrace, and her lips in soft kisses gently glow upon my cheek.[7]

The poet Samuel Taylor Coleridge wrote an eerily similar character in an unfinished poem started all the way back in 1797. In the poem, Christabel (the protagonist) forms a strange relationship with the mysterious, other-worldly and beautiful Geraldine who she discovers near an old oak tree. Gerladine fears the light, hates the touch of iron and is incapable of praying, just like a classic vampire. More interestingly she has a profound effect on Christabel, putting her under a spell, and encouraging her to undress alongside her:

Quoth Christabel, So let it be!
And as the lady bade, did she.
Her gentle limbs did she undress,
And lay down in her loveliness.

But through her brain of weal and woe
So many thoughts moved to and fro,
That vain it were her lids to close;
So half-way from the bed she rose,
And on her elbow did recline
To look at the lady Geraldine.[8]

These are perhaps the first of what becomes a popular trope, the lesbian or Sapphic vampire. It is important to note that both these depictions of female vampires predate Dracula, Nosferatu and even Polidori's 'Vampyre' by a number of years, the vampire in European fiction having long been a largely feminine creature deriving from female original sin and the fall of Lilith.

FANGBASHERS

In 1934, the Hays Code, also known as the Motion Picture Production Code, was introduced in America. This was a set of rules and requirements which aimed to keep cinema clean and respectable for family audiences, based around staunchly Catholic values. The fourth item on the list of things that should be censored or removed from cinema was 'Any inference of sex perversion', meaning that any depiction of non-heterosexual, or even non-heteronormative relationships, was to be seen as immoral and thus not fit for film. To try to show such a relationship in a film would almost certainly result in it being banned from public viewing.

Many filmmakers were able to get around this ruling, through showing gay, bisexual or transgender characters in their films only as villains or monsters. The only way to depict queerness and still have a successful film in Hollywood was to show it in a negative light. The vampire, which already has such a rich heritage of queer identity to draw from, was

A promotional poster for *Dracula's Daughter*, 1936

therefore a perfect vessel to use in this way. We see clear coding, with vampiric men being camp, effeminate, dramatic and well-dressed, and vampiric women being dominant, striking, butch, predatory or visually transgressive.

One of the best examples of this is in the 1936 film *Dracula's Daughter*, wherein the character of Countess Marya Zaleska, played by Gloria Holden, spends seventy-two minutes stalking and seducing the helpless Lili (her name itself almost certainly a reference to Lilith: the fallen first wife of Adam).[9] The film's screenplay contained such explicit lesbian allusions that before they could begin filming the studio asked the director to make a number of changes to certain scenes. For example: 'It will be definitely established that she has been attacked by a vampire. The whole sequence will be treated in such a way as to avoid any suggestion of perverse sexual desire on the part of Marya or of an attempted sexual attack by her upon Lili.'[10]

While the film was watered down to bypass censors, it still reeks of same-sex desire, and Marya is still a dark lesbian caricature. We see this throughout cinema of this time, where the vampire, whatever their gender, is a stand-in for any number of sexual deviants. This is a product of the history of the literary vampire, but also a result of directors and actors being unable to explore alternative representations of gender or sexuality in any of the 'good' characters.

Another powerful element to the vampire myth is the way they prey on the innocent, and through an embrace, an intimate bite to the neck, they spread their disease, the understanding being that those seduced by a vampire will themselves become vampires. The significance of this is not lost on the queer community. Indeed, for most of the twentieth century and arguably the twenty-first, gay, bisexual and trans people have been described in the press with eerily similar language. This all came to a head with the HIV epidemic, where queer people were not only being described as predatory perverts, but as dangerous people who could infect you and your loved ones.

The so-called 'gay plague' of HIV cemented the link between LGBTQ+ people living in the eighties and nineties and the classical image of the vampire. No longer were vampires mythical creatures asleep in coffins, catacombs and caves; you could find them in a crowded nightclub or bathhouse. Also, much like that of a B-movie monster, their blood was poisonous.

In spite of the taboo around queer people, or maybe because of it, in this period we see another resurgence in writings with queer vampires: for example, *Interview with a Vampire* by Anne Rice and 'The Southern Vampire Mysteries' series by Charlaine Harris. Both are authors who from the late 1970s through to the early 2000s would make a name for themselves in writing fiction focusing on vampires, many of whom were queer. Sometimes they even make direct connections to LGBTQ+ politics and issues, such as referring to 'Fangbashers', a mirror to the nickname for real life homophobes 'Fagbashers'. This appears in Harris's TV adaptation *True Blood*.

Slowly, vampires became cool, partly due to this association with edgy queer cultures. The aesthetics of the well-dressed wealthy aristocrat were modernised with black leather jackets, tight T-shirts, piercings, tattoos and bleach-blond hair. From *The Lost Boys*, released in 1987, directed by a gay man, to *Buffy the Vampire Slayer* of 1992, the queerly gothic vampire ruled supreme.

Even when the vampires of the nineties and 2000s were not overtly queer in their relationships – even if they were depicted as overtly cisgender and heterosexual – the visual cues are still there. Everything about the modern vampire aesthetic hints at underground gay BDSM nights and lesbian goth bars. Queer, as a visual affectation or code, is, for a presumed heterosexual audience, synonymous with danger and sex. Danger and sex sells, as long as it doesn't overstep. Therefore, on the screen the 'vampire boyfriend', a popular teenage trope who is coded as gay, must still perform a shallow approximation of heterosexuality. Meanwhile, vampiric women may wear black leather and severe eyeshadow, but they are created to be fetishised by heterosexual men. Despite all this, queer people love vampires.

Whether it be the homoeroticism in sparkly teenage vampires or the grandeur of baroque counts and countesses of nineteenth-century fiction, we see ourselves reflected in the vampire's dark mirror. The LGBTQ+ community don't just enjoy vampires, we also understand that at some level we are the true children of the night.

PART 3
Black Magick

(The occult and supernatural)

What lips my lips have kissed, and where, and why,
I have forgotten, and what arms have lain
Under my head till morning; but the rain
Is full of ghosts tonight, that tap and sigh . . .

From 'The Well of Loneliness' by Radclyffe Hall

Witch-hunts

In September 1649 the village of Kilbarchan, in the central Scottish lowlands, was rocked by a bizarre scandal involving Maud Galt and her servant Agnes Mitchel. Maud and her husband John Dickie had lived in the village for many years; it was God-fearing, famous largely for its accomplished weavers and named after the chapel devoted to its very own patron saint, Barchen. Other than census records, they pass unrecorded until an official meeting of the Church of Scotland in Kilbarchan. Agnes Mitchel broke the solemn silence to make a shocking accusation of her mistress. She announced that Maud was 'abusing ane of hir servants with ane peis of clay formed lyk the secreit member of ane man'.[1] Simply put, Agnes said her mistress was using a clay dildo on one of her own servants, another woman. It was then revealed that the servant in question was in fact Agnes herself; she had simply been worried about admitting her identity as the victim, for fear of recrimination.

Agnes next revealed, to the no-doubt startled crowd, the actual clay penis that she said Maud had used on her, which she had brought with her to the church. This claim was even backed up by other witnesses, who said that they had seen Maud arguing with Agnes. They posited that this might have been about her desire to share her story publicly.

In much of Scotland at this time there was a terrible suspicion around deviant and heretical behaviour, actively whipped up by the church. Neighbours were encouraged to spy on each other, and entire communities would quickly turn on whoever was deemed an outsider, as soon as the wind of accusation seemed to be blowing their way. It is perhaps unsurprising, then, that further rumours appeared, whether or not those sharing them actually believed what they said or simply wanted to join in with the pile-on. Aspersions were cast on Maud's character in general: she was believed to have a fiery temper and was seemingly not well liked by some in the community. Some suggested that strange misfortunes had occurred to them after angering Maud, and blamed her for these incidents; it was implied that they were not just strange, but uncanny, supernatural, even. The story of Maud using a dildo to penetrate another woman was swiftly combined with this revelation, the narrative now being that this was all part of her use of vengeful dark magic against her enemies – the dildo was clearly evidence of something otherworldly. The story of the clay penis would therefore fan the flames of what would become an accusation, not of lesbianism, or even assault, but of witchcraft!

Luckily for Maud she did not end up being executed, unlike at least 1,500 people between 1590 and 1662 (75 per cent of whom were women) who did have their lives taken due to accusations of witchcraft.[2]

***

In 2021, between February and April alone, some twenty-four people were arrested and beaten in Cameroon by security forces.[3] These were startlingly brutal attacks: people were dragged from their homes, cafés and bars, largely under cover of darkness, without warning or explanation. Those attacked were targeted because they were believed to be gay or were gender nonconforming in presentation. In Cameroon, 'homosexual' can cover any perceived deviation from strict heteronormativity, and is used to lump men and women together irrespective of their actual sexual or gender identity. For example, among those arrested were two young transgender women called Shakiro and Patricia, who were taken from a restaurant and handed a five-year sentence for 'attempted homosexuality'. They were deemed to have committed this 'crime' simply by wearing women's clothing in public.

This assault is part of a persistent and ongoing attack on the LGBTQ+ people of Cameroon that has been happening for decades. It has been repeatedly labelled a 'witch-hunt' by the Human Rights Watch and many others in the foreign press. The term here is not merely a journalistic flourish; just as in a classic witch-hunt, people have been incited to inform on their friends and neighbours and 'out' whoever they believe to be gay or 'abnormal' out of a religious or moral duty. This attack, and the law that supports it, is based on colonial laws left behind by European occupation; laws that criminalised 'sodomy' and instilled a moral and religious outrage against those not perceived to be heterosexual.

More so, historically the idea of homosexuality in Cameroon has been closely linked to fears of witchcraft and devil worship. Shelagh Roxburgh writes that 'rumours that suggest homosexuality, witches, and cults are working collectively and covertly to destroy Cameroonian society' are common.[4] Indeed, in 2006 Archbishop Victor Tonye Bakot of the Archdiocese of Yaoundé in Cameroon accused people of using homosexuality as a form of witchcraft to advance their careers and acquire money. The archbishop's rant was published in the papers and used to fuel a similar push among the public and officials to find and punish so-called 'gay witches'. It has even been weaponised against political rivals, where competing parties will accuse opponents of the combined crime of sodomy and witchcraft.

I have opened this chapter with two stories separated by both space and time. One is a story of a woman more than 370 years ago in Scotland, the other of human rights violations in an African country that is ongoing even today. Yet the connective tissue between them is clear, and one with a deep, dark and complex story. It is not simply a historical quirk that witchcraft and queerness go hand in hand: the witch and the queer person are married in belief and folklore the world over. This remains so even in popular culture and contemporary queer identity.*

---

* Note this chapter deals with the queer folkloric symbolism of the witch, which is made up of both the real history of men and women accused of witchcraft as well as the fictitious stories later associated with witchcraft in the public consciousness. It will not give you a thorough account of the true history of witchcraft overall. There are numerous misconceptions about 'real' witches and 'real' witch-hunts today, for example the idea of there being a secret underground pagan religion during the medieval period practised by peasant women. There is no historical foundation for this, yet some of the tropes around the contemporary idea of a witch lean into these ahistorical accounts, stories, fairy tales and artworks; these are explored in this chapter as well. In reality, witch-hunts are best understood as a complex political tool and as a kind of extreme religious or moral paranoia observed all over the world. For a deep and thorough exploration of the history of real witches, witch-hunts and witchcraft in general, please see the writings of Julian Goodare and Ronald Hutton (cited in this chapter).

RAT WITHOUT A TAIL

How does one spot a witch? Well, the reasons for individual accusations of being a witch vary hugely, from personal grudges to perceptions of unruly or aberrant behaviour, to a woman being seen as having too much power or control. Today the discussion of witches has become a potently feminist issue, and many authors, such as Annie Harrower-Gray, have explored how women who could not, or refused to, conform to patriarchal notions of womanhood might find themselves thrown onto the pyre, tragically often by their own families, loved ones or community.

Yet while accusations of witchcraft during witch-hunts are often meaningless and flimsy in and of themselves, in European and American history certain traits come up repeatedly. Those deemed ugly were particularly vulnerable to accusation: the Rev. John Gaule, a self-appointed 'witch-hunter', suggested that any woman with 'a wrinkled face, a furr'd brow, a hairy lip, a gobber tooth, a squint eye, a squeaking voice, or a scolding tongue is not only suspected but pronounced for a witch'.[5] A witch might also have had a body that did not conform to the feminine archetype of the time, with marks, growths, scars or enlarged genitals. How a woman dressed and presented herself might also get her in trouble. Bridget Bishop, the very first woman put to death in the Salem witch trials, was accused of wearing an odd costume, namely a black cap and red bodice.[6]

Another feature indicative of being a witch was sexual deviance or promiscuity. This might be as simple as a woman having sex out of wedlock, or a woman who was sexually active but did not have children. We also see, as with the opening case of Maud Galt, any woman having sex with another woman or using a sexual aid was particularly suspect. Laura E. Hedrick writes in her paper 'Male and Female He created them', 'There are many examples from both France and Spain that show women flogged for tribadism (see lesbianism) and burnt or otherwise executed for possession or use of a dildo.' Similarly, Elsbeth Hertner von Rehen from Switzerland 'met spirits of the dead who advised her to have sex with a demonic woman', as described in Julian Goodare's comprehensive book *The European Witch-Hunt*. Despite this, Goodare believes that 'homosexuality was uncommon in witchcraft cases',[7] to which I would suggest that direct assertions of female sexuality of any kind were uncommon, often being hidden behind euphemism or suggestion. Looking beyond this I personally think there is a definite overrepresentation of same-sex desire among those accused of witchcraft. Maybe by the end of this chapter you will agree that these traits from 300 to 400 years ago have influenced the way we perceive witches today, and in particular how we see a witch's sexuality and expression of womanhood.

While internationally witches can be fair or foul in appearance, the archetypal female witch in European folklore and storytelling is often embodied in a somewhat ugly and unwomanly creature as perfectly depicted in the Rev. John Gaule's treatise. While nearly always being a woman, she has her natural womanhood and gender stripped away. A witch's actions and appearance subvert what a good woman should be. At the beginning of his 1606 play *Macbeth*, Shakespeare writes of three 'wyrd sisters' with the gift of prophecy. Their appearance is such that Macbeth's friend Banquo asks, 'What are these, so wither'd and so wild in their attire?', using the neutral pronouns 'these' and 'their' since he is so confused by the way they look. He continues, 'You should be women, and yet your beards forbid me to interpret that you are so.'[8] We are therefore invited to believe that these witches are a hybrid of feminine and masculine traits, hideous and somehow unsexed. The witches themselves play on this, when one produces a finger she has severed, 'a pilot's thumb', which in many performances would be waggled suggestively around the waist. Another sister comments lasciviously on how she will drain a sailor through sexual dreams, but says, 'like a rat without a tail, I'll do, I'll do, and I'll do'. This is outlined by Selima Lejri, a historian of theatre and literature:

> The fantastic image of the castrated rat is completed by the sudden display, by that same witch, of a 'pilot's thumb', which she most probably takes from underneath her clothes and exhibits, in a bawdy gesture, as a phallic fetishistic object that would invest her with magical power and double her whimsical projection into a hermaphrodite creature.[9]

Therefore this entire introduction to *Macbeth*'s witches, arguably one of the most archetypal portrayals in European literature, could even be read as one witch suggesting that she once had a penis but – like a rat without a tail – was castrated, becoming a woman. The otherworldly weirdness of these sisters is marked by the way they mix genders and are both sexless and hyper-sexual at the same time.

Wearing 'strange', unladylike clothes, looking masculine or being feminine 'ineptly', using sex toys, having relationships outside the boundaries of a heterosexual union and not passing, are therefore commonly associated with witches. All of these traits, while not exclusively queer, are definitely part of the LGBTQ+ experience and are traits many queer women and nonbinary people, of all identities, are still judged for today. All are linked with the witch, and all might explain why queer women and nonbinary people would have an affinity for such a reviled creature. From a butch lesbian to a trans woman, to a bisexual woman; to be visibly different aligns with the witch archetype created hundreds of years ago. People with those equivalent identities and expressions would no doubt be suspected during a witch-hunt, of which we find direct evidence.

In his 2017 article 'A Woman Like Any Other', historian of homosexuality Jonas Roelens outlines a tragic and fascinating case that perfectly illustrates how gender and sexual subversion might go hand in hand with accusations of witchcraft. In Bruges in 1618, two women, Mayken and Magdaleene, were accused of having had a year-long sexual relationship with each other. The accusation, made by the husband of Mayken, who was on trial for execution, implied that Magdaleene was a 'hermaphrodite' who had seduced his wife and run away with her. Magdaleene, who was framed as the predatory instigator, not only had her sex called into question, but was also accused of being a 'poisoning witch'.

Around this time women who were found to have sexual relationships with other women would often be referred to as 'tribades', from the ancient Greek 'τρίβω', (tríbō) meaning to rub together. As outlined in the fantastically old-fashioned *Pictorial History of Morals* by E. Wedeck, tribadism is described (in a chapter entitled 'Deviations and Aberrations', no less) as 'an etymologically variant designation for lesbianism. It is the female counterpart of homosexuality. This type of association was anciently linked with the island of Lesbos.' The book goes on to describe tribadism and lesbianism as a 'divergence' and a 'physiological and emotional condition' and as being 'equated with a harlot'.[10] The images that accompany the text in this part of the book are not explained, and witches are not mentioned in the description of tribadism, and yet the segment includes prints of 'A young and old witch on their way to a sabbat by means of levitation' and 'A witch is sacrificing a human being to the goat-formed archfiend', both by Goya.

The term is not just a classical synonym for lesbian; 'tribadism' gained a stranger meaning, in that these individuals were believed to have enlarged clitorises that they used to stimulate their partners, marking them out as biologically different to 'normal' women. Female anatomy, sexual pleasure and sexuality were so poorly understood that accusers could not imagine how else two women might have intercourse – and certain physical differences of anatomy were also believed to be the hall-mark of a witch.

There is little evidence that Magdaleene was intersex; this was prob-ably an accusation hurled at her simply for being a woman who did not conform and slept with other women. It is clear that Mayken, her part-ner, believed that Magdaleene was not physically different from any other woman, despite multiple intrusive medical 'inspections'. Here,

A woodcut of Hermaphroditus: the male-female principle of alchemic transmutation straddling the winged globe of chaos, 1625

'hermaphroditism'* is less a biological assessment and more an ignorant explanation for 'deviant' behaviour between women that the courts could not comprehend.

Compared with Maud in the opening of this chapter, Magdaleene was far less lucky when it came to punishment. She was tortured with thumbscrews and put on a rack, which would have agonisingly stretched her limbs to breaking point. This was done to extract a confession of witchcraft, which included supposedly having poisoned oranges and prophesised the death of a group of people. Despite this extreme physical torture, Magdaleene would not confess to being a witch. While Mayken was freed and simply asked to pray for her sins, Magdaleene, as the instigating party, was kept imprisoned for two years for the crimes of 'seducing several women' and 'several implications of witchcraft'.

In the nineteenth century, despite an upsurge in beliefs in other supernatural forces, we see less public obsession with witches as real supernatural entities among European people. The white people of England and America would be more likely to view witchcraft through a colonial lens, and depictions of witches might focus instead on non-European people. These people, particularly those of indigenous races, would be seen as inherently different, and therefore it was believed that if there was still a spark of dark magic left in the world, it would reside in these people alone.

Around the turn of the nineteenth century we see a number of writers, many purporting to be anthropologists or explorers, who discussed witchcraft through their observations of indigenous people. Within these stories are frequent portrayals of gender and sexual identities that might have startled a Victorian and Edwardian audience, and these are often subsumed into the inherent 'weirdness' of the indigenous witch.

---

* 'Hermaphrodite' is an outdated term for a person whose biological sex cannot be determined, or blends male and female characteristics. 'Hermaphroditism' is still a term used in biology to describe the presence of both male and female characteristics. For humans, this is known as being intersex and intersexuality occurs in up to 1.7 per cent of the population.

THE 'PUEBLO GIRL'

In the British Museum there is a collectible postcard from 1879 showing a colour drawing of what appears to be a Native American woman in traditional dress, weaving fabric. The postcard is entitled 'A Pueblo Girl Weaving a Sash'. The image and its title is an entire fabrication and hides a secret. It is based on a real black-and-white photograph of a Native American weaver, but, despite having an almost identical appearance to the figure in the postcard, this was not a woman. This individual was called We'wha and was one of the Zuni people of New Mexico. The creator of the postcard changed We'wha's face, redrew it and feminised it; they slimmed down her form, made her seem smaller, more like a western Victorian's ideal of a 'Pueblo girl'.

As with many Native Americans, within the Zuni there is a rich history of people whose gender is neither male nor female, or which moves fluidly between the two. These people are often grouped together under the contemporary translation 'two spirit', but each nation has its own terms and understandings around such individuals. Among the Zuni, such a person might be known as 'lhamana'. Lhamana are traditionally assigned male at birth although they may be intersex, but take on an identity that allows them to partake in feminine traditions. This includes practising a mix of roles and ceremonies designated for men and women, as well as wearing a mix of male- and female-coded clothing. Beyond simply occupying a functioning role, many lhamana are particularly celebrated for their artistry, their strength, cultural leadership and spiritual balance. This is true for many two-spirit peoples; for example, Thomas Highway, an indigenous Canadian playwright, writes that 'They had, that is to say, not only a sacred but an essential role in the community.'[11] And in the book *Queer Myth, Symbolism and Spirit* it is stated that the winkte third-gender identity of 'nadleeh' 'were thought to be able to heal mental and physical illness and to aid in childbirth through the employment of magical songs'.[12]

Born in 1849, We'wha grew up at a time when the Zuni had only just started interacting with European Americans – and the results were devastating for her community. Because of the introduction of diseases from white foreigners to which the Zuni had no natural immunity, both of

We'wha's parents died early in her childhood from smallpox. Having been adopted by her aunt, it wasn't until We'wha's early teens that she was recognised as lhamana and began to learn the work and rituals of Zuni women and to dress in traditionally feminine attire.

We'wha lived an incredible life. We know much of her life and character, though only through the lens of the writings of her close friend Matilda Coxe Stevenson, an American ethnologist and activist. Stevenson described We'wha as 'the most intelligent person in the Pueblo. Strong character made his word law among both men and women with whom he noticed.' Note that Stevenson uses 'he' here, but would also call We'wha 'she', depending on the context. Later in her diary, Stevenson acknowledges that after years of friendship, 'As the writer could never think of her faithful and devoted friend in any other light, she will continue to use the feminine gender when referring to We'wha.'

I have chosen to use 'she/her' in describing We'wha, while other authors such as Will Roscoe, who has written extensively on the subject, have opted for 'he/him'. Some contemporary Native American commentators have stated that the use of gender neutral 'they/them' for We'wha would not be an accurate or respectful representation of the lhamana identity.

We'wha spent time travelling with her friend, going to Washington DC, where some of her pottery was displayed in the National Museum (now known as the Smithsonian), and she was referred to on 14 May 1882 in the Washington DC *Critic and Record* newspaper as 'the Zuni princess'. Sadly, by the time she returned to her community, relations between the Zuni and the US government had further deteriorated, and We'wha found herself at the centre of a strange and ultimately fatal dispute around witches.

In 1892 a young man from Pueblo called Nick Dumaka got hold of whisky brought in by the town's governor, Dick Tsanahe. Dumaka, considered an argumentative show-off who disrespected Zuni tradition, became drunk and violent. After getting into a fight with numerous people, he was left beaten and unconscious. Dumaka eventually came round and in a drunken stupor claimed to have supernatural powers. He announced that he was able to practise witchcraft: 'So you think I am going to die? So that's what you think? I won't die, for I don't have my heart where my heart is . . . I have my heart in my toenails'.[13]

Assertions such as this were traditionally taken extremely seriously by the Zuni, who strongly believed that witches of all genders could both hurt and kill people through black magic. Therefore, Dumaka was seized to be put on trial; the punishment was either execution or, if he confessed, to be sent into exile.

The news spread beyond Pueblo, and newspapers, thirsty for dramatic portrayals of Indian backwardness and barbarity, began to print exaggerated and false headlines, such as 'Two Zuni Indians Charged With Witchcraft Meet Horrible Death In The Hands Of The Tribe'. This was scandalous, as the Zuni were believed by many white Americans to be more peaceful and well-mannered than other tribes. Eventually officers from the US army were called to intervene, but rather than simply keep the peace, twenty-five soldiers arrived on horseback and stormed the town in an attempt to arrest governor Dick Tsanahe for having acquired the whisky in the first place.

According to the white Americans, We'wha was present when they arrived. They described her as 'a woman – or what at the time was supposed to be a woman',[14] who refused to allow them access to Dick Tsanahe's house, blocking the doorway and pushing one officer over. It seems that after spending time travelling and befriending white Americans, her opinion on their impact on her people had shifted more towards the negative. Seeing the friction within her community upon returning – the mistreatment, imprisonment, even the murder of Indigenous Americans – had made We'wha even more mistrustful of the motivations behind white colonial power.

For obstructing their passage, We'wha was arrested. As punishment she was imprisoned for over a month, and after being freed We'wha had to trek forty miles home on foot in the middle of winter. Shortly after, and probably as a result of her ordeal, We'wha died of a heart attack. Her friend Matilda Coxe Stevenson wrote that the Zuni community ascribed We'wha's sickness to witchcraft, believing a piece of bewitched mutton to have been fired magically like a bullet into her heart by a local woman she had angered.

Matilda Coxe Stevenson wrote extensively about the Zuni, including her friend We'wha. She did this as a white ethnologist, observing the religious practices and beliefs of the Zuni as an outsider. The works are expansive, and often deeply felt, but they are also patronising and othering when looked at today. Still, they formed part of the foundation of many white academics' understanding of indigenous culture for Western writers and historians. Therefore, ideas around witchcraft and 'Wizards', as Matilda referred to any indigenous men who practised magic, were very much informed by her accounts.

At the point of writing this, the Wikipedia entry for We'wha implies that she was prosecuted as a witch, something that never happened. Incorrect and dramatised ideas of indigenous magic and 'exotic' sexuality and gender representation are a common feature in fiction, even in today's popular culture. From the Disney depiction of Pocahontas to the indigenous-flavoured aliens in *Avatar*, the association between strange magical powers, mysterious or heightened sexualities and indigenous people has become a trope all its own.

THE ROTTING GODDESS

The parallels between women being accused of witchcraft and modern queer identity feel particularly poignant today. Even in those countries where there is more protection for queer people than in many parts of the world, safety is not a given. The idea of a witch as a historic symbol of those that came before, those fighting similar battles, can create an empowering kind of sisterhood. For nonbinary people and intersex people, whose gender identity and bodies are seen as falling 'in between' or straying beyond gendered boundaries, the witch can also be a liberating symbol.

There is no single origin of witchcraft, as equivalent roles and practices of magic have existed in societies the world over and since time immemorial. But in terms of the folklore surrounding witches in Europe, there have been many spirits, beings and gods that have embodied the particular aspects that define a witch, namely the practising of secret magic, connecting with the dead and the summoning of dark feminine energies. Of all of them, the most contemporarily cited is probably the ancient Greek goddess Hecate.

Hecate was the goddess of many things. She is associated with fertility, protecting children, crossroads, the dead, torches, keys and the practice of magic. Her most famous depiction is that of a triplicate goddess: three women, or a woman with three heads, but united as a single entity. In modern depictions each of the women became a different facet of the goddess, often labelled today as 'maiden', 'mother' and 'crone', relating to the three stereotypical phases of womanhood, although this is mostly a modern attribution, blended or confused with the Greek concept of the Moirai or Fates, who were also depicted as three women. Classical depictions of Hecate show all three of her bodies as young and maternal. In most versions the three women that make up Hecate hold hands, or stand back-to-back against a column, although in others they do embrace each other. In a mosaic from Boeotia one facet of Hecate kisses and holds another in a romantic manner. At this stage Hecate is still a beautiful goddess and so there are arguably positive allusions of same-sex desire. Sappho described Hecate as 'shining of gold' and being 'a handmaid to Aphrodite'.[15] Some have even suggested that she was surrounded by a eunuch, or gender-fluid, priesthood known as the Semnotatoi.[16]

Over time the goddess, who always had some associations with the underworld, started to take on a darker character. In the Roman

A marble statuette of Hecate

Pantheon, where she was known as Trivia, she gained a different set of traits. When the Roman writer Lucan composed his epic poem *Pharsalia*, he described her as a 'rotting goddess' with a 'pallid decaying body'. From here the association with death, decay, witches and witchcraft became more firmly cemented. There is something dark, forbidden, yet sexual about these later depictions. By the time of Shakespeare, the scarier, ugly form of Hecate had almost entirely supplanted her classical, more nuanced forms. In *Macbeth*, Shakespeare writes, 'Witchcraft celebrates pale Hecate's offerings', firmly aligning the goddess with his previously discussed 'wyrd' sisters. It is from here that the goddess who was once a powerful warrior, protector and guardian becomes something foetid, old and evil. A hag.

The hag is closely associated with the witch mythos, but is something more specific; a being that is old, uses dark magic and is not necessarily entirely human. The word 'hag' originates from the Germanic 'Hexe' and the Old English for witch, 'hægtesse'. The word hex today, being a dark spell or curse placed on someone is, of course, no coincidence. All these words might draw a connected or shared origin to the name of the goddess Hecate herself. But the hag is more than a monster; she is a

Witches Going to Their Sabbath by Luis Ricardo Falero, 1878

misogynistic warning for all women, of what you can become if you allow yourself to age, or don't conform to society's expectations of womanhood. You may become an unloved and unlovable old woman. A woman who is hideous, predatory and covetous, and not just of young men, but of other women, too.

In the painting *Witches Going to Their Sabbath* by Luis Falero of 1878 we see a number of naked women flying through the air, many of whom are young and beautiful, while others are old, crudely rendered and barely human skeletal creatures. In the foreground a withered hag of a witch clamps her hand on the buttocks of a young woman, in clear delight. Meanwhile in the background younger women seem to be in a kind of orgiastic bliss, with one woman mounting another.

Another, earlier artist, Henry Fuseli, painted *The Night-Hag Visiting Lapland Witches*, wherein the hag, based on Hecate herself, is at the centre of the piece but has sadly faded with time, although still clearly visible in the foreground is a young, muscular Lapland witch, who pauses while feasting on a child. She is looking up, enchanted by the hag's

The Night-Hag Visiting Lapland Witches by Henry Fuseli, 1796

appearance. The story within these archetypes is similar to the one we explored in Chapter 5, 'Children of the Night', with the idea that an older predatory woman, this time a hag, will prey upon a younger impressionable woman and introduce her to the dark arts.

The narrative, while not always sexual, often implies romantic seduction to make the initiation into the occult seem more frightening and twisted. It is a warning to young women not to be seduced by older women who will eventually turn them into what they have become: something satanic, something inhuman, a childless, unmarried 'thing'. While lesbianism is rarely explicitly referenced in European texts from the early medieval period onwards, there is a sapphic shadow cast by the witch, who does not have children of her own and so must tempt younger acolytes by whatever means necessary.

This mirrors many contemporary narratives about LGBTQ+ people as a whole: that we are 'groomers' who cannot reproduce normally so must recruit from the young and vulnerable. Within lesbian relationships, it reflects the stereotype of an attractive feminine partner and the older butch, 'mannish' woman who has led her astray. Think even of the wizened hag from *The Wizard of Oz* shrieking, 'I'll get you, my pretty!'

ALL PLEASURE

A witches' sabbath, the term used to describe a meeting of witches, often seems to be little more than an orgy, or a large ritualistic gathering involving men and women naked after dark, associated with the practice of the dark arts. This continues all over the world, where the simple discovery of a suspected neighbour being found naked at night is enough to incite a conviction of witchcraft. In his book on witches, Ronald Hutton includes a description from Valais in Switzerland, from the Middle Ages, a text known as 'Errores Gazariorum', that talks of nocturnal meetings between witches. It says that as well as eating babies, the revellers engaged in 'dancing, and a sexual orgy without regard to the gender or kinship ties of partners'.

The rites and rituals around witchcraft vary alongside their source communities and associated laws and codes; whatever norms a society has, witches are thought to break them. Therefore same-sex desire, non-procreative sexual intercourse and gendered sexual role-reversal are far from uncommon in historic writings on the witches' sabbath. For both male and female witches there is a commonly cited reference to a ritual known as 'kissing the devil's arse'. Rictor Norton describes this as the 'osculum infame', or the shameful kiss. For example, in a confession from 1609, translated from French, sixteen-year-old Jeanette d'Abadie claimed that 'the Devil made him kiss his face, then the navel, then the virile member, then his behind'.[17] After kissing the devil, often represented through the leader of the coven, on the anus or their genitals, a witch, irrespective of gender, could be initiated into the fold.

European folklore concerning gatherings of witches also includes a tradition that has, sadly, faded in contemporary significance. Across Germany, France and Spain from the year 900 to the late 1300s, pauper women would talk of going on supernatural journeys with an entire retinue of ghostly and demonic entities. They would leave their sleeping bodies at night to join a parade of beautiful women. This party was often led by the spirit of a graceful and noble woman, a mistress whom all others would serve. The feminine entity might be called Frau Holle (meaning gracious lady), Holda, Bensozia, Abundia, Habonde, Satia, Oriente, Sibilla, Richella or Perchte, depending on the story.[18] The accounts vary wildly, but the pagan group would dance and put on great feasts, and travel supernaturally from house to house.

In some accounts those leading the group were 'former rich and powerful women who were punished for their sins by being compelled to wander by demons'.[19] It is interesting that the sins of these beautiful women don't seem to be laid out, and that despite these sins those mortals who joined her retinue did so with love and adoration. Also it can be noted that in a poem called 'De imagine Tetrici' by Walafrihd Strabo, the spectral hostess was compared to the goddess Diana and even the poet Sappho,[20] both figures associated with liberated female sexuality and lesbianism. Many of these accounts seem to have been a joyous form of escapism for the lower-class women who experienced them, but sadly the stories were often only collected in order to accuse a woman of witchcraft or devil worship.

The fact that these were stories told by women, about spending time with other women, not in the company of men, is powerful. There is an intimacy, and a romantic adoration for the spirit hostess and her night parties that seems to come through in these descriptions. As Hutton writes, 'all were commoners, often poor, and often old, who experienced pleasures and honours in these dreams, visions or fantasies that they could never have enjoyed in daily life'.[21]

What we would today consider queer sexuality in terms of how LGBTQ+ people might want to enjoy, use or share their bodies would all fit neatly within historic constructs of witchcraft and ritual. Whether it was men engaging in anilingus, collective or group sex with mixed-gendered partners, or simply women wishing for romantic adventures with other beautiful women, all these experiences which did not fit with regressive Christian heterosexuality could be seen as the acts of a witch.

Interestingly, in contemporary witchcraft, within the pagan religion of Wicca, these acts are often subsumed into a concept of religious worship, and are made sacred. One of the charges of the goddess as outlined by Doreen Valiente, who wrote much of the religious liturgy for Wicca, said, 'Let my worship be within the heart that rejoiceth, for behold: all acts of love and pleasure are my rituals. And therefore let there be beauty and strength, power and compassion, honour and humility, mirth and reverence within you.'[22] This has become a profound statement for the many LGBTQ+ Wiccans who practise today and find in modern witchcraft a space for their queerness which, ironically, has been historically punished in those accused of witchcraft.

A GOOD WITCH, OR A BAD WITCH?

Within the faith of Wicca, often described as a modern pagan or neopagan religion, LGBTQ+ people are massively overrepresented. A 2015 survey showed that nearly 11 per cent of LGB people followed neopagan religions, twice the percentage of heterosexual people surveyed. Other surveys have found anything from 28.3 to almost 50 per cent of people who self-identified as pagan were also not heterosexual.[23] Data for transgender, nonbinary and intersex people within paganism is harder to find, but the trend is likely to be the same.

To understand the modern significance of the witch to LGBTQ+ people I put out a simple callout on Twitter to see whether those who identify as witches today and are also part of the LGBTQ+ community would be willing to share their thoughts with me. The response was astounding.

No other mythologised being, or creature, that I have discussed publicly online has resulted in such a strong and swift call to action. I was inundated with hundreds of people willing to share their experiences as queer practitioners of witchcraft.

While not all respondents felt a strong connection between their identity as a witch and their identity as part of the LGBTQ+ community – for example, Ben Joel wrote, 'I'm gay and I'm a witch, but I'm not a witch because I'm gay' – most did, and on a deep and fundamental level. Also, whether or not personally felt, all seemed to understand why the two communities overlap so much, and were able to go into incredible detail on why this might be.

One prominent theme that came up again and again was that many contemporary queer witches were raised in restrictive religious environments, particularly growing up in dogmatic Christian households and attending faith schools. These experiences are uniformly recalled negatively, particularly while coming to terms with their own sexuality and gender identity. For many, like Tom Pearson, becoming a witch was part of a challenging journey to find a spirituality that would recognise their identity and not demonise it: 'I was born and raised in a very conservative Christian family, in a God-fearing part of the East Midlands. The more I learned about my true sexual feeling the less connected with God I felt and the bigger the void in my soul that needed fulfilment grew. I learned to ignore this and filled the void with "cocktails and sodomy". However, about 6 years ago I began to have a spiritual awakening, but I knew that Christianity or any other formally institutionalised religion wouldn't be for me.'

Moss Matthey had a similarly traumatic experience: 'I was raised in a fundamentalist Christian cult who didn't tolerate any LGBTQ+ individuals, so had a lot of shame and internalised homophobia. When I left

I was shunned and left without any community. I eventually became a pagan and witch, the freedom and being able to express myself while maintaining a spiritual connection are really important to me. Rather than being ashamed of my sexuality it's an important part of my practice.' For many queer witches of all identities and backgrounds, modern-day paganism and witchcraft fulfilled a spiritual need that other organised religions could not. Becoming a witch was aligned with their journey of becoming a happy and spiritually fulfilled LGBTQ+ person.

Another recurring theme was freedom of expression in relation to gender, particularly among queer women, both trans and cis. Yennefer writes, 'While magic and its practices are open to all, my spirit is feminine and my being is as a woman and my magic allows me to authentically be that, even when presenting as a man for many years longer than I should have.' Meg Elison talks further about the way in which witchcraft flips societally ingrained norms around masculine and feminine presentation: 'I think "witch" is inherently queer, synonymous with sexual liberation and acts deemed obscene or forbidden in other places and groups. I think the fixation on witches in popular culture stems largely from the fear of any power at all in feminine people (sexually receptive people, bottoms, women, femmes, etc.) because power is meant to reside in the penetrator and any other arrangement is taboo.'

Popular culture seems to be part of many LGBTQ+ people's journey to becoming a witch. Daniel was particularly reflective of this: 'If you look at different forms of media, witches tend to be used as portrayals of the LGBTQIA+ spectrum in other media too – I'm a huge comics nerd, so as examples you have characters who are magically based that have a huge gay fan base (Scarlet Witch, Wonder Woman, Zatanna, Raven, Pixie), are interpreted as ace (Illyana Rasputin), or are openly queer (Nico Minoru, Wiccan). I think there's definitely a link between seeing someone struggling to control a power within them that's inherently part of their nature, and the real-life reckoning of someone's sexuality being something other than hetero, or gender being something other than cis.' Indeed, many witches who got back to me said that as queer young people they first learned of witchcraft through media portrayals, referencing *The Craft* and *Buffy the Vampire Slayer* as eye-opening examples.

Once finding witchcraft, while many commentators reminded me that Wicca and other neopagan belief systems are not without issues of prejudice such as homophobia and transphobia, they were able to find a profound sense of community and family, whether this was within a traditional 'coven' of fellow witches, or a more informal online community of like-minded people. Daniel also writes, 'There's quite a strong link in terms of "chosen family". Most of the people I know and talk about witchcraft with are not related to me by blood, but they're just as much a chosen family as my LGBTQIA+ chosen family.'

Finally, there was the unifying experience of being victimised and vilified that many respondents connected with as the root of their witchcraft. C. G. Aubrey wrote: 'I think that many people relate to being hunted, to being ostracised, to being condemned for nothing more than the crime of being themselves. But those same people create art and literature and healing, and humanity cannot thrive without them. The Witch is a precious commodity, but also a scapegoat waiting.'

Taking one's shared pain, but finding a community of others who understand and accept this trauma, and then being allowed to find spirituality without sacrificing your own selfhood, seem to be woven into the witch identity for a huge number of those who contacted me. And while only a few of the respondents referenced 'Hecate', or particular archetypes of the classical or medieval witch and hag, they understood full well what a witch 'meant' and how many of the negatives traditionally associated with her (or him) might be flipped into a source of power for a queer person.

DEFYING GRAVITY

Today, in popular culture, the witch can be reframed as a misunderstood hero, or as a victim of her society's religious paranoia and patriarchal expectations. Witches have gathered legions of queer fans, who read books, craft cosplay and attend musicals that recast witches and witchcraft as free and accepting. The hit West End musical *Wicked*, based on the books by Gregory Maguire, is enormously popular with LGBTQ+ adults, who see themselves in Elphaba, the Wicked Witch from *The*

Wizard of Oz, whose journey leads from yearning for social acceptance to leading a rebellion. The swelling lyrics of 'Defying Gravity' are a queer anthem, as likely to be heard coming from TikTok theatre kids as they are to be bellowed by a forty-five-year-old gay man in a Soho karaoke booth.

As described by nonbinary playwright and lyricist Hayley St. James:

> Elphaba is a queer icon not just because of her amazing vocal pyro-technics and her killer looks and witty comebacks. Elphaba's activism for the Animal community is very strongly reminiscent of the fight for LGBTQ+ rights in the United States, and her journey towards self-acceptance and control of her powers feels very much like a metaphor for coming out.[24]

Many reading this, who, like me, grew up in the nineties and early 2000s, will have first explored their own queerness through 'slash fiction' in fantasy worlds. 'Slash' is a term for fictional same-sex romantic pairings written largely online, which became enormously popular in the early 2000s but retain their impact today. The authors, often LGBTQ+ teen-agers, created queer narratives in what were otherwise heterosexual and cisgender fictional worlds, rewriting their favourite films, books and anime to include queer love between characters. But of all the franchises explored this way by its fans, perhaps the most infamously queered was the Harry Potter universe.

Irrespective of the author's beliefs and motivations, a world of sorcery and witchcraft was at the time of publication a natural escape for us LGBTQ+ teens who were still working out who we were. Today we are now queer adults, many of whom have outgrown the source material they once used as a launching pad and are able to critique it.

It is the symbol of the witch that really stays eternal, the significance of that particular folklore and history that lingers with many of us. Whatever your belief in their magic, the witch was a person (often but not always a woman); she/they/he were weirdos, oddballs, the elderly crone, the sacrilegious daughter, the ugly, genderless thing and the rebellious misfit.

The witch is a symbol that can be shared, must be shared, across the community. The witch has become a divisive icon, one that represents only the stories and plight of 'real women', one that can exclude trans and nonbinary people from seeing themselves in this history, and pits trauma against trauma, whereas I think the witch being read as a symbol for oppressed women alongside other marginalised people does not dilute any one reading or interpretation. In the words of Emma Watson, who played the gifted, muggle-born witch Hermione Granger: 'I'm here for ALL the witches.'

7

Demon Twinks

On 31 July 2021, queer DJ and event promoter Ty Sunderland wrote the now infamous tweet: 'There was a DEMON twink on Britney boat last night. Threw a drink at the dj equipment, wouldn't get off the stage unless I stopped the music then the party ended and he's somehow in VIP getting his ass ate like out in the open. We had to literally tell him to stop and go home!!'[1]

It's worth explaining here that 'twink' is slang for a young, slim, gay man, normally white and stereotypically blond, traditionally good-looking and effeminate. Online, 'twink' is normally a derisive term; just like the mass-produced, American confectionery Twinkies from where the slang originates, twinks are seen as 'disposable', and as spectacularly described in Paul Baker's book on gay slang, of 'little nutritional value, sweet to the taste, and creme-filled'.[2] Ultimately a twink is used as a symbol of a kind of shallow, youth-obsessed homosexuality, and someone described this way is often perceived as weak, irritating and self-obsessed. The term 'twink' has links with mainstream heterosexual terms like 'bimbo' or 'fuckboy' in the way it describes an otherwise physically attractive person as shallow, stupid, vapid or narcissistic. Gay 'circuit' terminology normally has this cruel edge to it; a category or term might start out simply describing a body type or age demographic of a gay man, but it normally ends up becoming something more barbed.

During the height of the coronavirus pandemic, Gay Twitter had a field day with this tweet. The image of a single 'twink', a much maligned but otherwise weak person taking an entire party boat ransom through sheer aggressive 'twinkness', was for many hysterical. Also, we had all been locked in our own homes for a year, so there was almost certainly a touch of schadenfreude about the entire situation. Of course the tweet went viral!

For ages afterwards, the term 'Demon Twink' took Twitter and other queer online spaces by storm. People speculated as to who this 'Demon Twink' might have been, and it has become a term within the lexicon of my own gay friendship group to describe an unpleasant, toxic, white gay man with a sense of entitlement and a taste for chaos.

I am not for a second claiming that this is a profound statement on the demonic nature of homosexuality. I am also not saying that the fact that these two ideas went together so easily and naturally in the public consciousness means something. But as an opening for exploring the way in which queer people have been labelled, and label themselves, as something hellish, satanic, devilish, otherworldly and profane, it is at least an entertaining one.

Also, when one thinks of demons one also thinks of possession, of young, traditionally femme bodies, instilled with sudden primal rage and animalistic lust by a dangerous outside entity. The same way a single, drunk, gay man could turn a party boat into pandemonium, so a demon might turn your loved one, your child, or yourself into something unrecognisable. Whoever the Demon Twink was, he won't be the last queer person believed to be gifted with sexual and chaotic energy above his station. He definitely wasn't the first.

FROM AMDUSIAS TO ZAHBUK

Of all beings I've attempted to define, a 'demon' is perhaps the most abstract and the hardest to pin down. Today 'demon' might summon images of a red-skinned devil, with black goatee, horns and pitchfork, but in Abrahamic religions a demon is any inhuman being or entity of malintent that is aligned with Satan, the devil, or evil itself. Demons therefore vary enormously in their appearance, from monstrous multi-limbed nightmares to seductive humanoids. They also can possess, inhabit, or take the form of the body of an everyday person.

In this way other mythical beings such as fairies, vampires, witches and genies have all, in certain circles, been described as demonic, and even subsumed under the category of demon. Real folklore doesn't stick to the neat categories that humans create for it. For example, in south-east European stories the 'kallikantzaros' is a mischievous, dirty, hairy, donkey-legged entity that combines many traits from the above creatures. Like fairies, the creatures are often known as 'the other folk' and can be tricked into doing helpful household chores; they share characteristics with Islamic 'djinn' such as the propensity to offer gifts and wishes to human mortals, while also being associated with the demonic realm of hell and the concept of sin. The author Polis Loizou uses the kallikantzaros in his novel *A Good Year* as a monstrous depiction of the guilt and self-loathing of a bisexual man living in 1920s Cyprus. He explained to me why he used this particular demonic folk entity:

> Not only to express my queer protagonist's personal demons, but also the state of his mental health. I began to see them as an allegory for depression, which comes and goes. But a more general interpretation could be that they simply represent bad times, whether for you, your family or even your country. As a queer man, the fear of infection by these creatures rang bells, too.

Demonic entities, in their many different guises, have therefore become a catch-all particularly for religious folk talking of pagan or 'heretical' beliefs, but also personal allegories for repressed desire.

Some demons appear literally as other mythical creatures. In the 'Lesser Key of Solomon',[3] a grimoire of demonology originally compiled in the seventeenth century which acts as an encyclopaedia of demons, the demon lord 'Vepar', despite being a male Duke of Hell, 'appeareth like a mermaid'. A few pages later, the demon Amdusias is known for 'appearing at first like a unicorn'. Therefore, through the lens of Christianity, Islam and Judaism, any being that seems heathen, monstrous or uncanny could be a kind of demon.

But demons are not an Abrahamic concept; they originate from the ancient Greek 'δαίμων' (daimon), meaning a lesser spirit or god, without any baked-in negative connotations. There are also similar cognates in Hinduism such as 'asuras', a kind of 'anti god' or 'titan';[4] the 'yokai' of Japan, which encompass all manner of supernatural beings and spirits;[5]

and the windigo, which is an Ojibwe word for a kind of 'monstrous abomination who exhibit grotesque physical and behavioural abnormalities and possess great spiritual and physical power' that stalk the North American plains.[6] These creatures are not called 'demons' by their believers, but have been translated as similar kinds of creatures to contemporary understandings of what a demon can be. The word 'demon' is therefore an incredibly broad category: beings that defy natural laws, and in general, although not always, intend to cause harm to people.

Many times in human history there have been pushes to meticulously catalogue and understand demons, in much the same way as one would creatures in the natural world. One reason for this is that the demon has a strong connection in European cultures with the occult and the practice of dark magic; the idea that a demon can be conjured or summoned if the correct rites and practices are observed resulted in detailed lists and manuals. This practice seems to have originated in ancient Mesopotamia, where there were hundreds of named demonic entities, each with their own physical description and motivations. Some of these may be bargained with, or even called upon as servants.[7]

'The Goetia', which is part of *The Lesser Key of Solomon*, is an anonymously written text from sometime after 1570, which lists seventy-two demons in total, as well as the seals which can be used to summon and bind them. To use a very nerdy twenty-first-century analogy, it is a demonic Pokédex! The beings in this list, which vary in their bizarre shapes and traits, also show interestingly gender-bent forms, surprising magical powers and varied sexual proclivities.

The twelfth Spirit Sitri, 'with a leopard's head and the wings of a gryphon', also has a human form that is 'very beautiful' which he uses to 'enflameth men with women's love, and women with men's love' as well as the power to render people naked. Gremory, or Gamori, is a 'Duke strong and powerful' but chooses instead to appear as 'A beautiful woman with a duchess's crown about her waist, and riding on a great camel'. In this form he, or she, can 'procure the love of women both young and old'. Andrealphus has the body of a muscular man, an animalistic head and glorious peacock's tail, whereas Aim appears in the form of 'a very handsome man in body' who will offer to 'giveth true answer unto private matters'.

Asmoday, also known as Admosdeus, is another demon that appears in the *Goetia*; he is described as a three-headed hybrid of man, bull and ram with a serpent's tail. He is also a trickster, who will attempt to deceive any would-be exorcist that does not know his true name and seal. It is in another text, 'The Testament of Solomon',[8] written sometime in the medieval period, where this same demon speaks his own intentions, saying: 'I transport men into fits of madness and desire when they have wives of their own, so that they leave them and go off by night and day to others that belong to other men; with the result that they commit sin and fall into murderous deeds.' It is from here the demon Asmoday becomes associated with the sin of lust, as he is recorded in 1689 in a list by bishop and theologian Peter Binsfield.[9] Because of this the demon starts to be known for enticing men to sodomy. His description in the *Malleus Maleficarum*, published in 1486,[10] implies just this: 'But the very devil of Fornication, and the chief of that abomination, is called Asmodeus, which means the Creature of Judgement: for because of this kind of sin a terrible judgement was executed upon Sodom.'* From this there are some accounts where Asmodeus becomes a protector of homosexuals. The physical description of Asmoday/Asmodeus could also be significant, with Plato suggesting that chimeric hybrids of man and beast might represent the many sides of the human psyche, in particular aberrant carnal desires: 'It doesn't shrink from trying to have sex with a mother, as it supposes, or with anyone else at all, whether man, god, or beast.'[11]

Another demon appearing in 'The Testament of Solomon' with similar 'queer' adjacent traits is 'Beelzeboul' (also known as Beelzebub, which is often used as a synonym for Satan himself). Beelzeboul says, 'The chosen servants of God, priests and faithful men, I excite unto desires for wicked sins, and evil heresies, and lawless deeds; and they obey me, and I bear them on to destruction. And I inspire men with envy, and [desire for] murder, and for wars and sodomy, and other evil things.' As with Asmoday, one of the ways Beelzeboul may both acquire power over another man, or show itself within a victim, is through sodomy. This being nonprocreative sex, particularly penetrative sex between two men, the fear is

---

* Sodom was a biblical city known for sinful behaviour; it would later become more specifically associated with non-procreative sex and homosexuality through the term 'sodomy'.

that the sanctity of heterosexual pairings is threatened by demonic sexual creatures. Similarly, the demonic fallen angels Zahbuk, Zsniel and Zshmael in the apocryphal 1896 translation of a thirteenth-century Jewish manuscript entitled 'The Sword of Moses'[12] are known for separating men and women from each other, to 'make them depart from one another, and that they should not comfort one another' through mysterious means.

The writings in these lists may be designed to shock and titillate, to intentionally go against religious norms, proving the horror of these beings. But the flipside is that they also show the kinds of gifts a demon might offer a budding queer demonologist, if they were to gain their favour; gifts which include body transformation, gender swapping, sexual magnetism for any sex and the acquisition of a magical 'familiar' or partner, most often in the form of a beautiful man. In 1905 the index of demons was republished as *The Goetia: The Lesser Key of Solomon the King* with a new introduction, describing the demons as manifestations of human psychology and the esoteric rituals as a kind of self-exploration. The publisher also provided his own illustrations. In the descriptions of the demons Samigina and Foras we see two crudely drawn priapic figures, meaning they both have enormous erect penises. In the description of Vepar, there is now a mermaid-like woman with flowing hair and large, distended breasts. The artist and author clearly found a conduit for his own sexuality in these 'ancient' writings, this person being none other than Aleister Crowley.

Marginalia drawing by Aleister Crowley from his personal copy of *The Goetia: The Lesser Key of Solomon the King* (Foyers, UK: Society for the Propagation of Religious Truth, 1904), Warburg Institute, University of London

'DO WHAT THOU WILT'

Aleister Crowley is perhaps the most famous person associated with demonology and the occult. Raised by conservative Christian parents and coming
of age at the turn of the nineteenth century, he became infamous for his
association with 'magick' (his own spelling),[13] witchcraft, paganism and so-
called 'esoteric' religions. He spent his life studying the supernatural,
travelling the world learning about various non-Western faiths, and ended
up founding his own religion, Thelema. 'Thelema' comes from the ancient
Greek word 'θέλημα' (thelema), defined as 'divine will', but is also used to
describe sexual desire.

Part-eccentric philosopher, part-charismatic cult leader, Crowley led
many adoring followers into a bizarre and complex world of ritual and
ceremony based around a pantheon of gods drawn from ancient Egypt,
but blended with practices drawn from belief systems as disparate as
yoga, Western mysticism and Qabalah. The early 1900s were in many
ways a restrictive and highly conservative time, borrowing much from
Victorian stoicism; public polite society was about blending in and
upholding British imperial virtues and values. Therefore a 'new' religion
that elevated sex to religious worship, that welcomed homosexual acts as
part of this, that encouraged elaborate costumes, orgies and cross-
dressing, actively and flagrantly going against Christian doctrine, was
deemed deeply perverse and abhorrent.

The English media perceived Crowley as a twisted and dangerous force,
possibly aligned with the devil himself. This perception wasn't entirely
unfounded. Crowley had cast himself as a prophet within his religion,
and was known for getting acolytes and followers to engage in satanic and
even life-threatening rituals, such as drinking the blood of a sacrificed cat,
talking with demons, or relinquishing their ego and selfhood through a
ritual known as 'crossing the abyss'. After a follower of Crowley's cult died
from drinking polluted water, the victim's wife told her story of the bizarre
rituals and ordeals she endured to the press. This was explosive, and in
1923 Crowley was labelled 'the wickedest man in the world'[14] and 'a man
we'd like to hang'.[15]

With Crowley considered incredibly eccentric by late Edwardian society, his sexuality was definitely speculated over but was probably seen to

be merely an outrageous extension of his heretical devilish persona – something Crowley actively courted. He was bisexual, having a multitude of sexual and romantic relationships with both men and women, generally ending badly for his partners irrespective of gender. In fact, written into his religion of Thelema was an intentional reframing of sexuality, in all its forms, as not shameful or sacrilegious, but powerful and full of 'magick'. The opening words of Crowley's sacred book of revelations known as 'The Book of the Law' distil its beliefs into a single phrase known as the Law of Thelema: 'Do what thou wilt'. We see Crowley's exploration of his once hidden bisexuality clearly revealed in his poetry and other writings.

> He who seduced me first I could not forget.
> I hardly loved him but desired to taste
> A new strong sin. My sorrow does not fret.[16]

Today, for some, Crowley's legacy and reputation are up for debate. While there are very fair readings of him as a pure narcissist who led the way for future dangerous cults, as an anti-Semite, misogynistic abuser and instigator of conspiracy theories and pseudoscience, there are others that wish to celebrate him as a free-thinker and a sexual liberationist. In *Aries*, the 'Journal of Western Esotericism', Manon Hedenborg White argues that Crowley deserves a 'rethinking', particularly regarding his attitude to sexuality, stating, 'Openly bisexual at a time when consensual sexual acts between men were still criminalised, Crowley can be situated among sexual visionaries such as Edward Carpenter, Havelock Ellis, and D. H. Lawrence, who viewed erotic liberation as key to social transformation.'[17]

Crowley's relationship with demonology was as complex as the man himself. In some ways he relished being described as a 'Satanist', despite never truly aligning himself with Satan in any traditional sense. Also, as we saw from his introduction to *The Lesser Key of Solomon*, he clearly frames the many demons described in the book as elements of the human psyche, rather than hellish supernatural entities. While very much a believer in the occult, magic and ritual, he often toed the line, becoming surprisingly coy and difficult to pin down on what he actually thought.

Despite this, he was clearly obsessed with the idea of demons: in 1909, in a moment that Crowley described as a 'watershed' for his magical career, he initiated a personal blood sacrifice as part of a ritual to evoke the demon 'Choronzon'.

To what degree Crowley's sexuality and his interest in the demonic are tied up is difficult to unpick; nobody ever asked him, and how he described his own sexuality may not have fitted a label like 'bisexual' or 'pansexual'. It can be said that he knew his enjoyment of sex with men and women was not going to be accepted by everyday Edwardian society, and so is it surprising that he searched for beliefs and frameworks that turned this same society on its head?

EMBRACING THE SUCCUBUS

The *Malleus Maleficarum* (The Witch's Hammer) is a treatise written by clergyman Heinrich Kramer in 1486 and is a compendium or manifesto on demonology and witchcraft. It lists the ways in which satanic entities might act upon their victims and how they should be punished. Among its many subjects are the incubus and succubus, devilish creatures of pure sexuality.

The incubus presents as male and preys largely on women, whereas the more commonly discussed succubus takes the form of a beautiful woman to ensnare and drain men. Kramer believed both men and women might give in to a sex demon willingly but that 'it does not appear that men thus devilishly fornicate with the same full degree of culpability; for men, being by nature intellectually stronger than women, are more apt to abhor such practices'. He misogynistically believed women were more susceptible to this, and gives numerous descriptions of such a demonic assault, including 'a woman who thought that a devil copulated with her from inside, and said she was physically conscious of such incredible things'.

Women were often believed to be both the targets of devils and the devils themselves. While the form taken of a sex demon is nearly always of the opposite gender to its victim, a succubus in the form of a woman might also lust after a human woman, although Kramer argues that such a union could not be consummated: 'it must be carefully noted that, though the Scripture speaks of Incubi and Succubi lusting after women, yet nowhere do we read that Incubi and Succubi fell into vices against nature. We do not speak only of sodomy, but of any other sin whereby the act is wrongfully performed outside the rightful channel. And the very great enormity of such a sin in this way is shown by the fact that all devils equally, of whatsoever order, abominate and think shame to commit such actions.' Apparently even the very worst sex demons were a bit squeamish about gay sex!

This quirk is not just an invention of Kramer's: demons and even Satan himself are, despite being lovers and promoters of sins of the flesh, often described around the fourteenth century as being terrified of homosexual interactions. 'Sodomy on the other hand, was considered to be such a heinous practice, that it was usually believed, and asserted by the most prominent theologians and preachers of the time, that even the devil himself "flees with horror" in the sight of this sin.'[18] Yet this is not always the case: we see, for example, in the writings of sixteenth-century philosopher Gianfrancesco Pico della Mirandola an assertion that devils would take great pleasure in homosexual relations with men that 'go against nature'. Pico even argues that the classical gods and heroes who showed same-sex affection or 'foul love of boys' were sodomising demons in disguise.

Despite a demon's conflicted opinions on the act of sodomy itself, sometimes the actual cure for an incubus or succubus attack might also present an opportunity for socially condoned same-sex intimacy. Kramer recounts the case of a 'woman who was often molested by an Incubus in her own bed, and asked a devout friend of hers to come and sleep with her. She did so, and was troubled all night with the utmost uneasiness and disquiet, and then the first woman was left in peace.' Also, while by some accounts neither incubus nor succubus approved of taking part in same-sex intercourse themselves, there are arguments that they might quite happily instigate it amongst their mortal victims. In a small illustration within the Moralised Bible dating between 1220 and 1230[19] we see a man and man lying together, and behind them two women embracing. Around the edge of the human figures we see demons encouraging these unholy unions.

Historically it is true that lesbianism is often less covered, largely due to a textual invisibility of women's sexuality as a whole, down to ignorance and assumptions about women and their bodies made largely by men. Many of the surviving recorded stories of sex, and morality, were constructed by men so we tend to get their biases baked in. That being said, accounts do exist of demonic lesbianism.

In *Satanic Feminism*, published in 2017, Per Faxneld explores many of the ways in which same-sex desire between women might historically be parcelled up with ideas of the demonic, first of all exploring how men wrote of same-sex desire between women, then exploring how these women might themselves repurpose the narrative.

As with the label 'tribad', describing a woman who sleeps with other women as anatomically monstrous, in *The New Sappho, or The Story of the Anandryne Sect*, written in 1784, possibly by the Frenchman Mathieu François Pidanzat de Mairobert, there is a description of the heroine being similarly deformed. Having been seduced by lesbians, 'she has a diabolical clitoris; she will be better suited to women than to men'.[20]

Also, in the *Méphistophéla*, a book by eighteenth-century French poet Catulle Mendès, taking its name from a feminised form of the main demon in Christopher Marlowe's *Doctor Faustus*, the story charts the fall of the main character into sin and vice. In one incredible scene a demonic 'lesbian black mass' takes place, where women dance and chant ecstatically:

> You who rejoices in the nocturnal solitudes, led with dreams and invisible caresses! You who hates the nuptial knot and mocks it! . . . Enemy of weddings, curser of the fertile beds, who finds pleasure in the flat bellies and the bosoms without wrinkles, exquisite and tremendous Demoness, our refuge and our horror, appear upon the altar, Demoness.[21]

But just as with their male counterparts, this demonic imagery could be harnessed and explored by queer women. Renée Vivien, a French lesbian poet writing in the late-nineteenth and early twentieth centuries, used Satan in her work as an ambiguous symbol. As a queer woman, in some of her works she brazenly rejects God:

If the Lord leaned his head over me on my death,
I would tell him: 'Oh Christ, I do not know you.'
'Lord, your strict law was never mine,
And so I lived only a simple pagan.'[22]

And in her own recreation of the creation myth, called 'The Profane Genesis', she casts Satan as being the creator of women, the object of her own romantic affections: 'From the essence of this same flesh blossomed, idealised, the flesh of woman, Satan's creation.'[23]

Queer women were cast as demons, and reclaimed them, every bit as much as masculine-presenting queer people. For a modern spin on this look no further than 2009's female-written horror comedy *Jennifer's Body*, where a popular all-American high school girl is brought back from the dead as a man-killing, woman-kissing succubus. Beyond succubi, perhaps one of the most interesting story of gender-bending femme demons is that of Lamia.

LAMIA'S LAMENT

Part-beautiful woman, part-reptilian creature, Lamia was a queen cursed by the goddess Hera to forever stalk and kill other women's children after having her own children taken from her.[24] She turned into a kind of vampiric snake woman, similar in story to Lilith but closer in form to Medusa or Melusine.*

The monstrous nature of Lamia often included an amount of gender-bending. Describing one of his characters in his comic play *Wasps*, Aristophanes writes, 'He had a voice like a roaring torrent, the stench of a seal, the unwashed balls of a Lamia and the arse of a camel',[25] implying that Lamia was also an intersex creature. This is backed up by a piece of Greek pottery by the so-called Beldam Painter from 470 BCE, which seems to show Lamia tied to a tree, with large breasts and an erect penis, being tortured by five satyrs.[26] Later in England we have the bizarre

---

* Medusa was an ancient Greek woman cursed to have snakes for hair and a petrifying gaze, while Melusine was a European river spirit: half woman and half fish or serpent.

A depiction of Lamia

four-legged depiction of Lamia by English cleric and bestiary creator
Edward Topsell, who shows a scaled Lamia galloping with a visible
clawed penis![27]

In the poem 'Lamia' by John Keats, she gets a slightly different description. She is still a hybrid creature, but her eyes are that of a human woman,
and are unbearably sad and soulful. Also, despite her reptilian strangeness,
the predatory demoness is still beautiful, even when entirely inhuman:

> She was a gordian shape of dazzling hue,
> Vermilion-spotted, golden, green, and blue;
> Striped like a zebra, freckled like a pard,
> Eyed like a peacock, and all crimson barr'd;
> And full of silver moons, that, as she breathed,
> Dissolv'd or brighter shone, or interwreathed
> Their lustres with the gloomier tapestries.[28]

Written in 1819 as a retelling of the classic myth, Lamia is transformed
into a human woman and is able to find love, before having her true serpent form revealed on her wedding night and vanishing. It is a kind of
darker version of *The Little Mermaid* or *Cinderella*, doomed love with a
time limit. Taking a demon that is normally seen as a gruesome hermaphroditic succubus and a dark parody of motherhood and giving her
a sympathetic retelling might have tied in with Keats' own struggles.

As an effeminate and often sickly man, Keats has become an icon for queer people irrespective of his actual sexuality. In *30 Great Myths About Romantics*, Duncan Wu outlines his twenty-third literary myth as the trope that 'Keats was gay'.[29] He points to Keats' clear love for the woman Fanny Brawne and little tangible evidence of homosexuality.

This does not preclude bisexuality, however, and there are still real reasons for Keats to resonate with gay men and women today. The circle of men in which he moved was notably transgressive, as Caroline E. Kimberly writes: 'in many cases, historical facts support the sexual identification of some of Keats' supporters and biographers as what we would now term bisexual or homosexual'.[30] There was also the passionate hate/hate relationship between Keats and Lord Byron, the latter finding Keats' prose excessively sensual or flowery, calling it 'a sort of mental masturbation'.[31]

But perhaps most notable were his final moments: at the age of only twenty-three, Keats began to show symptoms of tuberculosis, possibly caught while nursing his dying brother Tom. Two years later, at just twenty-five, Keats took to his death bed and was looked after by his close friend, the painter Joseph Severn. Severn wrote of Keats' passing in many letters with real tenderness and heartbreak: 'O, he will mourn over every circumstance to me whilst I cool his burning forehead until I tremble through every vein in concealing my tears from his staring glassy eyes. How he can be Keats again from all this I have little hope, but I may see it too gloomy since each coming night I sit up adds its dismal contents to my mind.'[32] Even Duncan Wu acknowledges that 'Keats' appropriation as gay icon may be inspired in part by his protracted disintegration over many months in the arms of Joseph Severn, which resonates in a period devastated by AIDS'. Either way, his illness, his sensitivity, or his affections, allowed Keats to give the succubus a chance to shed her skin. He could see the human where others saw only the demon.

CHRYSANTHEMUM LICKERS

The category of demon can be played fast and loose but many of the so-called 'yokai' of Japanese folklore fit within the bounds of what might be perceived as demonic. There are a few in particular that have interesting crossovers with queer identities. Firstly the 'kappa', an amphibious monstrosity with a cavity in its head for holding water, which has some unusual habits. One is the desire to pull people underwater and drown them. Bizarrely this is often done by grabbing the victim by the anus.

One popular explanation for this behaviour is that the kappa supposedly desires a mythical organ (or in some accounts a precious gemstone) from its victims, known as the 'shirikodama'. This is supposed to exist just inside the human rectum, and the kappa is therefore attempting to remove the organ, killing people in the process. One belief for the origins of this story is rather gruesome and relates to the way drowned bodies sometimes show prolapsed anuses; this might have been blamed on the handiwork of a water-dwelling kappa.

This obsession of the amphibious demon with the human rectum has led to an odd kind of connection between male homosexuality and the kappa. In *Cartographies of Desire*, written in 1999, the historian of gender and Japanese folklore Gregory M. Plugfelder mentions how a kappa was the chosen henchman sent by Enma, the king of the underworld, to fetch the object of his desire: a human male actor who performed within the cross-dressing tradition of Japanese Kabuki theatre. Also, an anonymously written poem entitled 'Maruchin' of 1883 reads, 'In the palace of the dragon king, the kappa has a run-in with the Keikan statute'. Keikan is a term used to describe anal sex, synonymous with buggery or sodomy, and thus the poem implies that the kappa would fall foul of real-world laws that suppressed and punished homosexual intercourse. This led to 'kappa' becoming a slang term in Japanese prisons during the 1970s for the penetrative partner during same-sex intercourse.

The 'ōkaburo' is another demon-adjacent being from Japanese folklore with queer allusions. It might at first resemble a brothel girl, known as a 'kamuro', although it is far too big and tall. The depictions and descriptions of this inhuman entity is that it is in fact cross-dressing. The ōkaburo appears in the *Konjaku Gazu Zoku Hyakki* (The Illustrated Demon Horde from Past and Present) created in 1779 and shows a being in robes covered in chrysanthemums. The creature is sometimes called Yū-Jidō (Chrysanthemum Boy) and claims to be 700 years old. It is believed that this creature represents a possibly gay or transgender sex worker, dressing as a kamuro, but more so that it connects with tales of a Chinese boy known as Ju Citong.

Ju Citong was a favourite of the Chinese emperor around the tenth century BCE, but because of his deep affection for his older master he overstepped his station. It is said that Ju Citong touched the emperor's pillow with his feet and was therefore exiled. As part of this story Ju Citong also had a magic spell to protect him from evil, which he wrote on the leaves of a chrysanthemum. This gave him the name 'Chrysanthemum Boy' and also the more suggestive nickname 'pillow boy'.

The insinuation is obviously that this boy was a submissive sexual partner for the emperor, who fell from grace. When this story was told in Japan, the homoerotic elements became even more exaggerated. In Japanese history and folklore the chrysanthemum was already synonymous with the anus;[33] for example, a passage from an 1872 'senryu' anthology talks about how, for a man, penetrative sex with women is acceptable, but homosexual acts are taboo, using the following allusions: 'The grappling ginger is allowed but the chrysanthemum is forbidden.' The ōkaburo cements these ideas into one frightening gender-bending creature: bedecked in chrysanthemums, wearing make-up and ill-fitting feminine attire, and known to lick the dew off chrysanthemums. These are all clear references to anal sex and anilingus as a foundation for this particular yokai's demonic nature.

FALLEN ANGELS

Despite the ambivalent nature of Satan's attitude to homosexual behaviour, Lucifer has become a popular symbol in the queer community. In Christian theology the demon is often the dark side of the angel, with the idea that Lucifer himself was once a beautiful and exalted angel cast into hell for defying God and craving his own power and autonomy. The depiction of the 'king of lies', 'the lord of Hell' is often far from the demonic monstrosities covered so far.

Lucifer has become a potent image for queer people, partly due to the popularity of depicting him as an idealised masculine form but with a complex backstory. The elements of Satan's past as one of the heavenly host's closest consorts are reflected in many artworks depicting the fallen angel, from Guillaume Geefs' sculpture *Le génie du mal* (The Genius of

Evil) showing a muscular Lucifer crouched in anger, a single tear running down his face, to the work of sculptor Jacob Epstein, committed to explorations of sexuality in the early twentieth century, who created a bronze sculpture of Lucifer as a glorious being with a masculine body and soft feminine face. Epstein also produced the carving *Jacob and the Angel*, a reference to a biblical passage and himself, showing the two locked in an ambiguous embrace. He was also commissioned to create the angel carved into the tomb of Oscar Wilde himself.

There are many examples of the combination of angelic and demonic imagery having a hold over queer people. Writer and philosopher John Addington Symonds was a gay man born in the nineteenth century who wrote passionately about same-sex relationships throughout history. He also recounts an experience in adolescence of sleepwalking and almost drowning in a water cistern, but of being saved by an impossibly beautiful angel with 'blue eyes and wavy, blonde hair'. Raymond Carrance was a French photographer born in 1921, who produced his own hand-drawn erotica, including a beautiful, angelic man, posing, with his lower half inverted to show his buttocks. His wings are multiple, overlapped and layered, as angels are originally described in the Bible, but they also display snarling dogs' heads and fish tails. In this highly homoerotic image it is unclear whether we are seeing an angelic or demonic apparition, or a queer hybrid of both.

Benedetta Carlini was a fifteenth-century woman who experienced visions of angels from an early age. As a nun she continued to have angelic visitations and claimed that she was gifted her own guardian angel called Splenditello by Jesus himself. Splenditello was a beautiful youth bedecked in flowers. Unsure of the nature of these visions, whether they were truly angelic, the now incarcerated Benedetta was chaperoned by another young nun called Bartolomea who shared a cell with her. Later it would be reported that Benedetta would engage in sexual acts with her young female partner:

> For two continuous years, at least three times a week, in the evening after disrobing and going to bed would wait for her companion to disrobe, and pretending to need her, would call. When Bartolomea would come over, Benedetta would grab her by the arm and throw

her by force on the bed. Embracing her, she would put her under herself and kissing her as if she was a man, she would speak words of love to her. And she would stir on top of her so much that both of them corrupted themselves. And thus by force she held her sometimes one, sometimes two, and sometimes three hours.[34]

Benedetta claimed this was actually an impulse driven by her angelic, or demonic, partner Splenditello, and thus did not count as sinful or coercive. In the end Splenditello was deemed a purely demonic influence and Benedetta was accused of heresy and thrown in prison, where she eventually died.

THE POWER OF CHRIST COMPELS YOU

Queer teacher and writer S. Trimble watched *The Exorcist* when they were a teenager with their sister and cousins. In the film, the young girl Regan is taken over by an ancient Mesopotamian demon, Pazuzu. In mythology Pazuzu was actually a personification of the force of wind and not entirely evil, but in the film he transforms the otherwise normal Regan into a vile demonic creature that swears, blasphemes, walks like a spider and projectile-vomits. Trimble saw something else in the transformed little girl as compared to their peers: 'I saw a revolting girl, revolting against the little-girl box in which she was stuck and I saw an army of men trying to put her back in.' Trimble felt a deep sense of connection, as in their own words, 'Like Regan, I became monstrous around the age of twelve.' Indeed, they had been labelled with the cruel epithet 'Manwoman' and as Trimble recalls, 'My peers made it clear Manwoman was smelly and aggressive, and moved in all the wrong ways. And when they spoke for me, they pitched their voice low and growly.'[35]

In folklore, as in *The Exorcist*, demons take hold of human vessels; like parasites they can control and steal the lives of their victims. The people they inhabit are changed, turned into something 'other' that is dangerous and sacrilegious. The ways in which visible queerness, whether that be through sexuality or gender expression, have been conflated with demonic possession is a long and painful story.

This goes all the way back to ancient Anatolia. The Hittites were a group of people inhabiting what is now Turkey from around 1600 BCE. They had beings and spirits that closely approximated what we have in this chapter been referring to as demons. We know of some of their beliefs and rituals from the cuneiform-inscribed tablets that have been translated. One describes something called the 'Ritual of Anniwiyani', a particular sequence of chants and movements used by a priestess or religious leader of the same name. The goal of the ritual was to remove, or exorcise, a feminine demonic force from a young man. This force, both the unwanted feminine and the wanted masculine, is named Lamma. The unnatural feminine was sent out, and the masculine was welcomed in. The ritual proceeded as following: 'As evening falls, blue and red cords of wool are wrapped around several body parts of the ritual patient: his feet, hands and neck. In addition, similar cords are wrapped around some of his personal belongings: his bed, chariot, bow and quiver. All these cords are taken off when dawn breaks. Later on a striking episode occurs, which seems to be the most significant of all procedures that constitute the ceremony: a young virgin is brought to the house entrance.'[36] There are many interpretations of what exactly this ritual might represent, but Ilan Peled proposes that this might have been an attempt to cure, or undo, homosexuality:

> It is now suggested that the 'passage' signifies the shift from an inadequate state, symbolised by the 'effeminate' deity, held responsible for the sexually-passive tendency of the patient, to a proper state, symbolised by the 'manly' deity. In practice, that passage is achieved by crossing through the gate – a symbolic act well-known from other Hittite magical rituals.[37]

An alternative read might relate to gender expression and identity, returning a feminine 'man' to 'his' natural or normal state. Through this lens this can be seen as a kind of ancient sexual or gender-conversion therapy.

In *Counselling the Demonic*, Christian scientist Rodger K. Bufford outlines the case of 'Mack', whose sexual behaviour he associates directly with demonic influence, particularly with an unnamed 'demon of lust':

In counselling it was soon discovered that Mack's sexual habits traced to his childhood, when he was one of a group of boys who spent their time stealing pornographic magazines and engaging in a variety of sexual activities with each other and with anyone else available. This pattern of sexual obsession and promiscuous sexual activity had continued into adulthood, even after Mack's marriage. His wife had discovered only one aspect of this far more pervasive pattern. At what point does one conclude that a person such as Mack is demonically influenced rather than merely exhibiting a chronic pattern of sinful behavior? Could Mack be both sinful and demonically influenced – even possessed?[38]

The exorcism, or the practising of religious rites and rituals to remove demonic entities from queer people is, sadly, a practice that continues around the world today. It is invasive, traumatising, and both a physically and psychologically abusive process. In some cases it can lead to lifelong mental health issues, physical and emotional scarring and even death. Matthew Draper, a conversion practices recovery advocate, kindly shared his own experience with me: 'I had an anti-gay "exorcism" in a church in 2014, which involved intense prayer in a small room with two church leaders. One told me they could see demons leave the room through the window "hand-in-hand". It felt like trying to push one of my internal organs out of my body, like banishing half my mind. Unsurprisingly, I was still gay because it is me, not some hand-holding demons which control me! Recovery from the trauma of this experience involved being kind to myself, and welcoming the whole of my personality back.'

As with many of the more negative elements of queer history and mythology, it might strike some as surprising that there is a movement to reclaim the myth and folklore around this. As with many of these symbols there is a kind of power in reclamation, no matter how dark the subject. This is something that goes to the very core of the queer experience; in fact it explains the very word 'queer' itself as a repurposed slur, originally meaning strange and altered. But I can understand how S. Trimble felt watching *The Exorcist*, perhaps finding a sardonic sense of recognition when the twelve-year-old girl, who is also not-a-girl, screams, 'Shove it up your ass, you faggot!' to the perhaps-closeted men in robes trying to revert her back to 'normality'.

The demonic and subversive imagery that we see in everything from pop star Sam Smith's photo shoots to drag queen outfits and the 'heretical' music video for gay musician Lil Naz X's 'Montero', showing a literal descent into hell, all come from a similar place of recognition. We know these caricatures and we play them well with our own special twist. As Matthew Draper says: 'LGBTQ+ people know what it is to be controlled, and to be free. There is something about rebellious demons as free agents which appeals to a desire to live our own lives and make our own choices. Also, we get told often enough we are going to hell, we might as well make friends with the locals!'

DUNGEONS AND DRAG QUEENS

In San Antonio, Texas, in 1997, Elizabeth Ramirez, Cassandra Rivera, Kristie Mayhugh and Anna Vasquez, all gay Hispanic women, were accused of sodomising young girls. Despite no forensic evidence, the accusation was described as 'Satanic-related'. The group of women were sentenced to between fifteen and thirty-seven and a half years imprisonment as a result of these accusations. Not until 2013, when the women were finally able to challenge these convictions, were they exonerated. In 2016, the documentary *Southwest of Salem* followed their story, showing layers of prejudice, including racism and homophobia, which led to these four lesbian women being perceived as satanic lesbian child abusers.

In the infamous McMartin Preschool trial of 1983 in Los Angeles, Ray Buckey was accused of abusing children in his charge as part of a satanic cult. Buckley was married and heterosexual, but as the trial progressed allegations were made that he was in fact a homosexual man and his wife was simply a ruse. This helped to lay the foundation for an argument for his rituals and demonic assault of children in the school's care, as gay people and satanic abuse were already associated so heavily in people's minds. The trial lasted seven years, and was the most expensive in American history, but was ultimately found to be entirely unsubstantiated.

Accusations like this, associating queer people, devil worship and child abuse, has a long history, but this particular case was born from the 'satanic panic' beginning in the 1980s. This was an entirely manufactured but pervasive societal fear of groups of satanists meeting across America to sacrifice and abuse children, which took hold of America for more than a decade. Through a cascade of religious grifters, false memory syndrome and media-manufactured moral outrage at changing societal values, this fear was made to 'feel' very real to many people, even though it was a complete fiction.

The previously cited book that described the case of Mack and his 'sodomy' being due to an infestation of 'demons of lust' was written during the height of satanic panic in 1988. In the same chapter that describes the demonic possession of homosexuals, there is also a segment devoted to objects that might actively encourage a demon's attention:

> Possession of charms and amulets, and of objects associated with occult practices, may also make one open to demonic influence. Horoscopes, tarot cards, Ouija boards, and possibly the game Dungeons & Dragons may be additional avenues into demonic influence.

For some the inclusion of a nerdy tabletop game might be surprising, but the link between the roleplaying fantasy Dungeons & Dragons (DnD) and satanic panic has been well recorded. Of all the perceived gateways to satanism, it is DnD, a game of elves and warlocks played by groups of friends, that has notoriously become the most popularly derided and portrayed when talking of this 'vintage' moral panic.

At the time, entire articles were written offering guidance to parents around the demonic potential for DnD. One particular case, the tragic suicide of teenager James Dallas Egbert III in 1980, who played DnD, was used to amplify this belief. James was gay; he struggled with his sexuality during a time of great prejudice, as well as his status as a 'child prodigy' with mental health issues. His simplified and exaggerated story, sensationalised in a book by William Dear in 1984 entitled *Dungeon Master*,[39] became an archetype for a combined triad of dangers: DnD, predatory homosexuality and devil worship.

Even though this fear is now considered by many as laughable, and even 'retro', it was incredibly harmful and has left a stain on all the communities it touched. Dungeons & Dragons is now an enormous industry, with Roll20, a popular online provider for the game, estimating 13.7 million tabletop DnD players.

Of these there is a large and ever-growing community of LGBTQ+ people. Just as with James, many queer people find a place of solace, safety and self-exploration in a game that lets them be anyone.

Today, other than in very small conservative and Christian fundamentalist circles, the game of DnD is no longer connected with demonic forces or ritualistic child abuse. That said, this does not mean we have escaped moral panics that associate queerness with demonic or occult forces. Writing this in 2023, we find ourselves at the centre of a 'trans panic' which shares many features with that of the eighties hysteria. To the proponents of this fear, trans and nonbinary teens aren't trans or nonbinary at all, and are in fact being taken away and 'transformed' by a sinister gender cabal.

As described in an article by the website *Vox*, terminology used to describe this fear directly parallels demonic possession, with frightened parents talking about 'grooming' and associating gender-confirming care with 'psychological torture'.[40] The target and mythology of this panic is subtly different, but the basic concept is eerily similar. It seems demonic queer panics are cyclical; every generation they are reborn with a new demonic enemy and a new terminology, but with the same intrinsic messaging around LGBTQ+ people.

Currently drag, as in the performance of cross-dressing and gender-bending, has become the new Dungeons & Dragons. The fear of this art form has a long, dark and fascinating history, and today it is arguably the new tool that is used to seduce and attack vulnerable young people. Of particular focus is 'drag queen storytime' events, where children and drag performers share a space. While these performances involve a person in drag reading a children's story, without any suggestive or sexualised content, the response by a small but vocal minority in recent years has become increasingly virulent, and occasionally violent.

Protests outside drag queen storytime include placards reading 'No warning is too strong REPENT', 'Pride Caused Lucifer To Fall' and 'Drag Queens Are Paedophiles'. A church hosting one of these events was vandalised, daubed with pentagrams and the word 'SATAN'. At the

2023 Conservative Political Action Conference, the founder of right-wing activist group Judicial Watch, Tom Fitton, said, 'The left is attacking our children, pushing sex talk, transgender extremism and noxious politics in our schools, we should reject this demonic assault on the innocence of our children and stand fast against leftist efforts to mutilate their bodies and minds.' While most of those who are scared of 'gender ideology' and decry drag as child indoctrination do not literally believe demons are pulling the strings, the movement still clearly echoes these sentiments.

It is therefore powerful and empowering to see queer people taking to DnD with such ease, seeing them recreating and rewriting fantasy worlds and tropes from LGBTQ+ perspectives. Oliver Darkshire's book *Queer-coded* embodies this, recasting villains from the game's canon with fleshed-out queer versions. These include a pansexual polyamorous dragon queen, Elminster, a nonbinary wizard with a drag alter ego, and the gay demonic lich king Vecna. Another example is Dungeons and Drag Queens, one of many collaborations and crossovers between the art of drag and the world of tabletop gaming, resulting in a ridiculous camp caper through familiar fantastical worlds.

Dabbling with the demonic has become a playful pastime for LGBTQ+ people, and the knowledge of its dark past somehow makes it all the more relevant and meaningful.

Today, whether roleplaying tieflings or horned fauns in DnD, or using occult and demonic imagery in tattoos and fashion, the demon is for many a reclaimed symbol and icon. We are mostly aware of the way queerness is aligned with the satanic, even today, but as with many of the more monstrous and vilified mythic strands in this book, that makes the reclamation somewhat dangerous but also powerful and important.

Queerly Departed

For a few years now my friend the cemetery historian Sheldon Goodman and I have been running queer history tours of cemeteries across the UK. Starting at Tower Hamlets Cemetery in east London, and moving on to the Brompton Cemetery in west London, Arnos Vale Cemetery in Bristol, and Key Hill and Warstone Lane cemeteries in Birmingham's Jewellery Quarter, we have made liberal use of the pun 'queerly departed' when talking about the LGBTQ+ people buried at these sites.*

While walking from plot to plot we explore the lives of the people buried there, telling the story of the full person for a living queer audience, in ways that until recently have often either been edited or entirely left out of history books. The work is challenging: queer people from one or two hundred years ago tend not to leave fantastic records of the hidden content of their lives, particularly when living those lives openly could have resulted in imprisonment, excommunication or even death. The headstones, which are barebones in most cases, showing only date of birth, death and generic religious epitaphs, obviously tell us very little about a person's inner workings; who they loved and how they lived. But we manage to tease out those stories in time, such as that of the flamboyant bisexual Marchesa Luisa Casati buried at Brompton Cemetery, who once entered a party with two live cheetahs on diamond leashes and was painted nude by lesbian artist Romaine Brooks. And the incredible mind of Constance Naden, a scientist and

---

* The pun wasn't coined by us but is attributed to a friend, Dr Alfredo Carpineti, an astronomer and LGBTQ+ advocate, to whom we are eternally indebted!

writer who once wrote a poem about a long, lost pile of love letters addressed to 'Minnie', whose golden curls 'were like piles of new guineas':

> I loved her for beauty and kindness,
> I grieved when I fancied her cold,
> But Cupid, quite cured of his blindness,
> Now takes a good aim at the gold.'[1]

The queer stories of yesterday call to us, or at least they call to many of us. As Sheldon once said to me, 'cemeteries are museums of people', and so it feels both a privilege and a huge responsibility to be a custodian for these queer souls of yesterday. We try to do our best to research and tell the stories of people who are like us, but different. We share these stories with living visitors who are gay, transgender, lesbian, bisexual and asexual, but may not have used these terms if they had lived a century ago, like the inhabitants of the cemetery. It is a constant joy to see teenagers with rainbow badges and rainbow hair, young women in hoodies holding hands and elderly gay activists all visiting these communal spaces of death, but finding life there as well.

But this chapter isn't about this work as such, nor the research of the people buried or interred in these places; it is more about the spaces themselves, and the gothic air they attract. These are spaces devoted to the dead, but which seemed to beckon Sheldon and me from a very young age as well as many other queer people, while they frighten and repel others. This chapter is also about the folklore and mythology that surrounds death, and what people believe might happen afterwards. It is about places like cemeteries, graveyards and mortuaries, but also some of the aesthetics around death: from velvet capes and cowled cloaks to gothic poetry. It is also about ghost stories, spirit mediums and seances. In a darker sense it is a connection with people associated with death in the most unpleasant ways possible: serial killers and murderers. All of these have a hold over many people; death is a very human fascination. But, though it might seem a rather grandiose statement, I believe there is something decidedly queer about death itself.

THEY WERE TOMB MATES?!

For a long time historians have studied the way in which people treat the dead as a means of understanding something about their living culture. For many ancient peoples the only places remaining and still standing are those devoted to the dead; pyramids, tombs, burial mounds and catacombs are some of the structures that tell us about who many long-gone people were. We try to intuit from death what they valued and believed in life. But as with the rest of history, this has largely been done through the lens of presumed heterosexuality and compulsory cisgender identities.

When thinking of an Egyptian tomb, you may first picture a male pharaoh and his female consort laid side by side and etched in stone, or if we think of an eighteenth-century cemetery we imagine large family plots with marble headstones. These Victorian markers normally reflect the rigid patriarchal values of the time. The man's name mostly appearing first, followed perhaps by his occupation, status or some notable anecdote. His wife is usually underneath, her entire life's worth reduced to being recorded as the man's faithful spouse. This is followed by the names of many children, slowly getting smaller as the memorial mason runs out of space.* On the other hand, to see evidence of what might be described as 'queer life' in burial practices and you have to be willing to view things a little differently.

Catterick in North Yorkshire is a town with a deep connection to the Roman Empire in England. Catterick was once Cataractonium, a major Roman fort, mentioned even in the writings of mathematician and geographer from the Egyptian city of Alexandria, Ptolemy. During excavations in the town in 1958 at 'Grave 951, Site 46, Bainesse Farm', a skeleton was found of an individual dating back to 400 CE.[2] This person wore jewellery, including a jet necklace and bracelet, a shale armlet and a bronze anklet; they also had two stones placed in their mouth. The clothing this skeleton wore seemed very feminine at first sight; attire

---

* The ordering of man and wife's names is often due to the shorter lifespan of men, and headstones with the wife appearing first are not rare, but if both spouses are dead, or there is restoration, the tradition is nearly always to place the man's name first.

normally associated with a Roman woman. It has been implied from the burial that this person was a priest or priestess, most likely devoted to the goddess Cybele. Cybele was a mystery cult goddess originating in Greece, associated with motherhood and the earth. The person buried here caused a large amount of media commotion, due largely to the fact that their attire contrasted with their skeleton, which had been described as that of a 'man'. From this they were initially described in newspapers as 'the transvestite priest' and later as a 'eunuch', or to use the Roman term, a 'gallus'.[3]

This person buried in Roman Britain, who was likely of some religious and ceremonial significance to the local community, had probably gone through ritual castration at some point in their life. We know of other accounts of people, those assigned male at birth, being castrated as part of their initiation into the cult of Cybele. Most publications of the time of the excavation talk of the male skeleton, and thus describe this person as a 'young man' and a priest, using he/him pronouns. But was this how this person lived?

In a fragment of a Greek poem from the third century attributed to Callimachus, the poet uses the feminine 'Gallai' to refer to people like the person buried here: 'Gallai of the mountain mother, raving thyrsus-lovers'.[4] The Roman poet Catullus did the same, switching from masculine to feminine forms after a person's castration. Indeed, those devoted to Cybele might also have been described in Latin as being of a third or middle sex: 'tertium sexus'.[5] Despite presumptions around gender identity by contemporary writers, an artist's impression made in 2002 of the 'Catterick Gallus' is both humane and haunting.[6] It shows a person with make-up and jewellery, wearing fine and richly coloured clothing, who stares out of the recreated image from the past, as if to question our preconceptions.

In Egypt we have the case of the tomb of Khnumhotep and Niankhkhnum, two men buried together in the necropolis of Saqqara and discovered in 1964. Colloquially the tomb of these two men is described as 'the tomb of the hairdressers' although they are also described as manicurists and confidants to the pharaoh. The fact that these two men were buried together, and the repeated iconography of them overlapping, side by side and embracing, has been described by some scholars as 'unusual' and many have speculated about their relationship. Some have implied that they were brothers, twins or friends, but today some historians think the clear iconography that seems to place these two men's lives as deeply intertwined suggests a more profound, romantic relationship.[7]

More recently a skeleton associated with a Viking burial in Finland, first excavated in 1968, has caused a certain amount of controversy.[8] The grave's occupant, complete with brooches and weaponry, had been described as a woman warrior. Indeed, it had caused some confusion with the presence of both items normally associated with men (weapons) and women (jewellery) being present in the same grave. After genetic analysis of some of the bones, a more complicated picture arises: this person had XXY chromosomes. XXY, also called Klinefelter syndrome today, is a chromosomal anomaly that occurs in a small proportion of people assigned male at birth. While the effects of Klinefelter syndrome can be subtle, and many either go through life without a diagnosis or are diagnosed only in adulthood, it can result in lower levels of testosterone during puberty, infertility and some anatomical differences, such as the presence of breast tissue and lower muscle tone.

Of those with Klinefelter syndrome today, the vast majority are men. It is not classed as an intersex condition, but it is suggested that a slightly higher proportion of this population will define as transgender or nonbinary than compared with non-XXY populations of those assigned male at birth.[9] The person buried here may well have simply been a man with a chromosomal anomaly, but there are other perspectives which account for the mix of burial goods that could involve the identity of someone that was perhaps neither a man nor woman, or was a mixture of both. This has been the reading of some contemporary historians despite conservative backlash.

Looking at a person's bones or even their genetics does not tell us who they are, or how they lived. As queer people we know this better than most. But cases that open the door for a queer reading are often shut down surprisingly fast, rather than even being left at 'we don't know for sure'. Whatever the case, I believe the door being left ajar for queer interpretation does not mean making false assertions or equivalents. It simply allows for multiple readings. The only reason for being angered by interpretations that leave room for LGBTQ+ identities is either the false belief that people like us are only a recent construct, or that even being associated with us is an insult to the dead. This reaction says more about contemporary fear and hostility around queerness than it does about the existence of queer people in the past. The dead are every bit as queer as the living.

THE CHANTRESS OF AMUN

Florence Farr was born in 1860 and raised by parents with, considering the times, progressive attitudes about the education and elevation of women. They named their daughter after the celebrated nurse Florence Nightingale and instilled in her and her siblings a drive for equality and aspiration. Florence became an artist's model, and later an actress. As a young woman moving in artistic circles, she mixed with an immensely bohemian and often queer set of artists, poets and writers. Beyond this she forged a twin passion for exploring the occult, magic and mysticism, as well as being a passionate advocate for the rights and inclusion of women.

While Farr's life is mostly described through her relationships with men, such as the poet W. B. Yeats, she was an outspoken advocate against Victorian sexual moralism, was against marriage, and there are implications of her feeling romantically and spiritually connected to women as well as men. Yeats himself cast her as 'Aleel', a male poet and seer, in his production of *The Countess Cathleen*, a deeply homoerotic play depicting two women (one in drag) falling in love: 'In one scene, for instance, Farr-as-Aleel reaches in vain for the hands of the Countess but panics: "When one so great has spoken of love to one / So little as I, though deny him love, / What can he but hold out beseeching hands, / Then let them fall beside him, knowing how greatly / They have overdared?" '[10]

We know that Florence also had a connection with Oscar Wilde. Clearly inspired by his writing style, Farr penned her own work 'The Dancing Faun' in 1894, which tells the story of an independent young actress who meets a gambler and eventually murders him. Within this story Farr uses her own self-insert character of Geraldine to criticise the treatment of women in late nineteenth-century society, as well as to express the possibility of a deep spiritual and even erotic connection between women: 'As she listened to the laments of Beatrice di Cenci, it seemed to her some inspired spirit had entered her body and was making use of her voice to reveal to her what life, and love, and divine sorrow meant.'[11] Later Florence would direct the first production in Britain of Oscar Wilde's *Salome* in 1905; this was both after Wilde's incarceration for homosexuality and his death in 1900.

Outside her occupation as an actress, Farr had developed a deep connection with the afterlife, acting as a kind of spirit medium within the secret occult society known as the Golden Dawn. She was known within this 'Hermetic Order' as the Praemonstratrix,* calling upon souls, demons and spirits that she believed she could communicate with. Because of this, she also developed a deep fascination with certain museums and collections, as she believed she could make contact with the ancient people they related to.

On display in the British Museum's Egyptian galleries there is a mummy labelled in the collection records EA6704. We know that, while exploring spirituality and magic, Farr established a profound connection with ancient Egyptian religion and beliefs, known today as Egyptosophy. She claimed that she had received messages from beyond the grave from an 'Egyptian adept'. This ancient individual spoke with Farr, and by visiting the British Museum they would talk to each other and share experiences. This is even referenced in Yeats's unfinished novel *The Speckled Bird*, where he writes, 'With her eyes half closed on a seat close to the Mut-em-menu mummy case' and 'she is doubtless conversing with Mut-em-menu'.[12]

It was with this particular mummy, EA6704, that Farr found companionship on another plane. Arguably what drew Farr to it was its ornate, decorated bindings, coloured nails, painted face, the depiction of lotus flowers on its knees and its full-breasted, curvaceous form. There is also the fact that at this point in time the mummy was erroneously associated with a different woman's coffin, and was therefore described as the remains of 'Mutemmenu, a Chantress of Amun'. Farr herself, as a priestess of an

---

* Latin for one who receives prophecies.

Human mummy, name unknown (British Museum: EA6704)

esoteric occult order which had a deep fascination for the supernatural, formed an intimate relationship across time with this mummy, who she believed to be a fellow priestess.

Years later, when this mummy was investigated and found to have been paired with the wrong coffin, another surprise was revealed. On being X-rayed the remains were described as those of a 'young man' from the Roman era. This person, with a masculine skeleton, has visible hip and chest padding complete with gilded wax nipples, giving them, at least by modern standards, very feminine proportions. There have been different interpretations as to why this person was presented in such a way. Some have argued that this may have been due to them being overweight and thus the padding was an attempt to better approximate their shape in life,[13] while others have noted that there are a few other mummies with similar padding, which include those with 'female' remains. So, based on these other mummies, the padding might have been used to hold small amulets or to retain a human shape.[14] (Although CT scans of EA6704 do not show any amulets within this mummy's wrappings.) Personally, I feel it is not yet possible to know exactly what these features might mean for a 2,000-year-old mummy, but a queer or gender-nonconforming reading still seems possible. Maybe even plausible.

BURY YOUR GAYS

> Death must be so beautiful. To lie in the soft brown earth, with the grasses waving above one's head, and listen to silence. To have no yesterday, and no tomorrow. To forget time, to forgive life, to be at peace.
> *The Canterville Ghost* by Oscar Wilde, 1887

While Oscar Wilde is justly celebrated for his wit and wordplay, much of his writing is classed as an integral part of the gothic revival in literature. This includes a number of late nineteenth-century authors who reflected a newfound interest around themes of fear, haunting and darkness in their work. Much of the modern idea of horror and ghost stories descends directly from this period of writing. While gothic authors could explore all manner of themes and identities within the broad genre of gothic literature, there is a predilection for these authors to push the boundaries, looking at sexuality and gender through lenses that would have rocked Victorian sensibilities. This movement was also part of the *fin de siècle*, 'end of the century', a time of social change associated with decadence and pessimism, but also, by some judgemental critics, deviance. One description of the kind of youth associated with this movement by a concerned art critic puts it this way:

> They are a set of strange young men, dreamers and visionaries – often morbid, broken-hearted, and poor, always nervous and impossible in society, whose first and last endeavour is to do something original, however odd and erroneous it may be.[15]

It is not surprising that within this movement of gothic writers at the end of the nineteenth century we see a huge overrepresentation of people who today we might describe as queer. Henry James, who wrote *The Turn of the Screw*, perhaps Europe's most famous written ghost story, is also seen as part of the movement. It is a tale in which two children are possessed and controlled by a pair of ghosts, ending in tragic death:

> He uttered the cry of a creature hurled over an abyss, and the grasp with which I recovered him might have been that of catching him in his fall. I caught him, yes, I held him – it may be imagined with what a passion; but at the end of a minute I began to feel what it truly was that I held. We were alone with the quiet day, and his little heart, dispossessed, had stopped.[16]

Since his death, Henry James's sexuality has been put under the microscope by many people. He wrote extensively to his gay friend

Howard Sturgis, 'I repeat, almost to indiscretion, that I could live with you. Meanwhile, I can only try to live without you', and jokes to Howard about how he 'paws you oh so benevolently'.[17] Some have argued that James was asexual, one biographer in the 1950s claiming he had 'some fear of or scruple against sexual love on his part.'[18] Others have argued that this reading is simply an attempt to mask his homosexuality, something his surviving family went to great lengths to do after his death.

Charlotte Perkins Gilman wrote 'The Yellow Wallpaper', published in 1892. The story tells of a woman locked in a room by her gaslighting husband, who begins to form a dark and disturbing obsession with the hideous wallpaper and the entity that she begins to believe lurks behind it. Gilman married a man against her own intuition, and after divorcing him formed more meaningful and passionate relationships with women, most notably Adeline Knapp, aka Delle. Of this union Gilman's biographer Cynthia Davis wrote in 2005: 'In Delle she had found a way to combine loving and living, and that with a woman as life mate she might more easily uphold that combination than she would in a conventional heterosexual marriage.'[19]

Even those authors associated with the gothic revival in storytelling that were ostensibly heterosexual frequently overstepped the lines of Victorian expectations of heterosexuality and gender performance. Robert Louis Stevenson, author of *Doctor Jekyll and Mr Hyde*, was a renowned foppish and bohemian dresser who, as described by his friend the homosexual scholar Andrew Lang, 'possessed, more than any man I ever met, the power of making other men fall in love with him'.[20] Even his biographer remarks that Stevenson may have enjoyed and flirted with the attentions of other men, observing that he 'can't have been unaware of the homoerotic forcefield he generated'.[21] Similarly Richard Marsh, who wrote 'The Beetle', about a malevolent sexual entity of ambiguous gender, implies homosexuality even if not directly referring to it, through the mysterious carnal acts of his shapeshifting antagonist.

Put simply, to be an author writing within this retinue of gothic resurgence, with its dark spirits, hauntings, shocking sexuality and crumbling beauty, was to embrace a certain queer style and tone. The original template for gothic writing was crafted by the previous generation, by the likes of Lord Byron, Mary Shelley, Bram Stoker and Horace Walpole, all of whom have such a strong queer pedigree that it is almost innate to the gothic genre itself.

ON THE OTHER SIDE

Some of the Victorian traditions around death seem truly bizarre by today's standards; the desire to pose and take photographs of the dead shortly after their passing, and the ceremony around covering mirrors and stopping clocks when someone in the family died. Many went a step further, believing they could actively commune with the dead. This rise in a 'scientific' and intellectual fascination with ghosts and spirits accompanied a new age of scientific and industrial development. With the likes of radio waves, early telephone systems and the ability to record the human voice onto discs, the distance between the impossible and the probable was quickly narrowing. What if you could capture the voice of deceased loved ones using modern technology? Or, conversely, what if spirits and apparitions could be explained by modern marvels, in the same way that other natural phenomena like electricity and chemical reactions had been?

In particular during the nineteenth century, as stated by historian Molly McGarry, 'Spiritualism held enormous appeal for women and men who inhabited gender and sexuality in transgressive ways'.[22]

Both those who were avid attendees of seances and spirit readings, and those who would conduct them, might find a safe space for homoerotic desire and gender nonconformity. For women in particular there were aspects of practising spiritualism and mediumship that could lead to all manner of erotic situations: 'The séance could be an awfully queer place. Female mediums might be bound together on a mattress in a darkened room, or a female medium and spirit might invite a third woman into their private space, disrobe, and invite that guest to touch their bodies.'[23]

The medium partnership of Miss C. E. Wood and Annie Fairlamb Mellon involved an incredibly close relationship between the two women, who travelled together, conjuring spirits from the dead during the 1870s. As part of this show the two would be tied together physically with restraints. Also, to be able to create the supernatural experiences paying guests expected, the two women had to know each other incredibly well, and live and work closely together. As noted by one particular aficionado of spirit mediums, W. P. Adshead, in 1879, 'The medium having with her, both day and night, a loved and pleasant companion, is, as all Spiritualists know, if not an absolute necessity, an excellent preparation for a successful séance.'[24]

Outside individual partnerships it was commonplace for a female medium to be subjected at length to an examination of her body to ensure that they were not hiding anything under their clothing that might be used to trick guests. This was most often performed by another woman in private. Again, as noted by Adshead before a seance with Wood and Fairlamb, Miss Wood was approached by a Mrs Ford – 'A severe investigator' – and 'asked if she would again submit to the special test. Without a moment's hesitation she acceded to the request. The change of dress was even more thorough than before, her stocking and boots having been taken off and examined.'[25]

The performances of women mediums as described by their awestruck guests often had an explicitly sexual and deeply subversive element to them. During this time it was believed that the apparition of a ghost was often accompanied by a mysterious substance known as 'ectoplasm' or 'teleplasm'. In one such event the medium Mina Stinson Crandon, known as 'Margery', is said to have expelled this substance in a most unusual manner:

> The controversial substance known as teleplasm poured from Margery's vagina, allegedly forming hands and 'rods' that would perform various tasks for the success of her investigators' experiments. All the while, Margery channelled the spirit of her dead brother Walter. Through Margery, this ghost performed an aggressive and rowdy conception of manliness that may have conformed to early twentieth-century ideals of rugged manhood, but placed his sister's claim to respectable womanliness in question.[26]

The male spirits that appeared were not necessarily true apparitions, or even figments of the guests' imaginations; many were in fact devious optical illusions and special effects constructed by their practitioners. Some have implied that the reason female spiritualists would work in pairs was partly so the other member could play the role of the summoned spirit. If this spirit were of a man, this would entail them

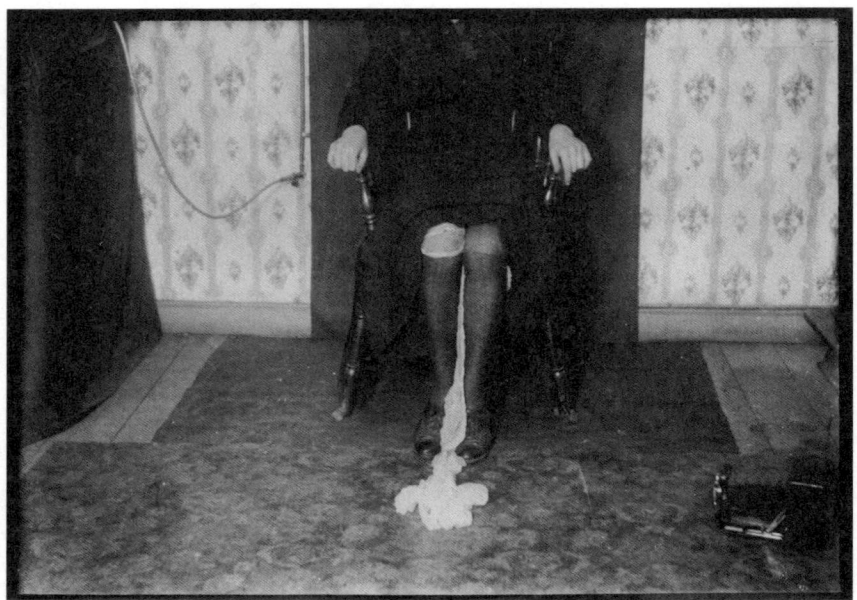

A photograph of a woman exuding ectoplasm

wearing a prosthetic beard. In this form the cross-dressing medium would focus their attentions on female guests, often in a deeply lascivious manner. Marlene Tromp, author of 'Queering the Séance',[27] hypothesises that the apparition of one particular lecherous bearded man may well have been Wood's collaborator and partner Miss Fairlamb, half seen in the dark.

Also, in many cases, once taken by a spirit, a medium might invite guests to touch and feel her body to show that a physical transformation had taken place. Between women this could become incredibly intimate, and in some situations it is almost impossible not to see an erotic element to them. During a seance, Florence Marryat, an author and avid spiritualist, was invited to touch the medium Florence Cook, aka 'Florrie', when she claimed to be taken over by the spirit of a woman called Katie King, stating, 'She had full breasts and plump arms and legs, and could not have been mistaken by the most casual observers for "Miss Cook"' and that:

> On another very warm evening she sat on my lap amongst the audience, and I felt perspiration on her arm. This surprised me; and I

asked her if, for the time being, she had the veins, nerves, and secretions of a human being; if blood ran through her body, and she had a heart and lungs. Her answer was, 'I have everything that Florrie has.' On that occasion also she called me after her into the back room, and, dropping her white garment, stood perfectly naked before me. 'Now,' she said 'you can see that I am a woman.'[28]

PEOPLE WHO MANAGE THE SPIRITS

As with spiritualism in England and America in the nineteenth century, conjuring and speaking with the dead in other parts of the world also involves activities and identities that might be understood through a contemporary lens as queer. Within the tradition of Korean shamanism, there is a whole set of performances, dances and rituals which invoke ancestral spirits and allow commune between a shaman and the dead. In Korea, these shamans refer to themselves as 'shinul purinun saram', meaning people who manage the spirits.[29] While both men and women can become practising shamans, it is more well known for women to enter into this line of work, where they are known as 'mudang'.[30]

While a woman may become a shaman for many reasons, it has been noted by some authors that 'In numerous cases, shamans are women who are unable adequately to "fit the behavioural straight-jacket" of femininity. Whether due to personal or social difficulties, women who become shamans diverge from traditional feminine roles.'[31] Shamanism in Korea allows for many actions and behaviours that might not be socially acceptable for women to normally display. For example, female shamans may take on masculine spirits as part of their practice, allowing them to behave outside of gendered norms: 'For example, during the performance of Tagam nori (Official's play), the shaman wears the garments of a Confucian official and behaves in a domineering masculine manner.'[32] The art of inhabiting and performing a masculine character is incredibly important for a Korean shaman, and is something she can become adept at:

When the mudang calls upon Sanshin, the Mountain Spirit recognised almost universally, the mudang puts on a dress that symbolizes this spirit, mimics the expected movement, and speaks in a voice appropriate to the spirit. If she calls upon the General Spirit, she puts on a military uniform, imitating his movements and speech. In order to demonstrate the General's bravery, she stands barefoot on a pair of razor-sharp fodder blades and begins a slow dance.[33]

For those shamans who are men, known as 'paksu', there is also an opportunity to embody feminine experiences through their work with spirits. In one case a male shamanic tutor known as Pak discussed menstruation with a group of female students, and spoke with them as if he too had experienced it.[34] From the perspective of shamans this would not seem weird, or inappropriate, as shamans habitually inhabit the personalities and lives of spirits of all gender identities.

Korean shamanism also allows for a special intimacy, particularly between women, that might be looked down upon outside of this line of work. A shaman is not just a spiritual role, but also a social one: 'Often, a shaman can play the role of entertainer or guest amongst female gatherings.'[35] Indeed one particular mudang, 'Yongsu Mother, was such a popular member of the village women's event that even the wife of Enduring Pine Village's chief sought out the company of "the articulate, loquacious manshin"'.[36] At times men with female partners who become close to a particular shaman have referred to the fact that it feels like they have now gained a second wife.

AMIDST THE SHADOWY DEAD

The ancient Greek poet Sappho, who inspired the word lesbian, wrote numerous beautiful poems, many of which explore her love and adoration for other women. In at least three of her poems the sweet pain of falling in love, or lust, is expressed with the surprising analogy of death.

Ode To Aphrodite:
A cold sweat covers me,
trembling seizes my body,
and I am greener than grass.
Lacking but little of death do I seem.

Like The Very Gods:
And the sweat breaks running upon me, fever
Shakes my body, paler I turn than grass is;
I can feel that I have been changed, I feel that
death has come near me.

For Sappho, being infatuated with another woman is such a powerful force that it brings on a state that is like death; falling in love is an experience similar to dying.

In the 1776 collection of Japanese stories by Ueda Akinari, *Tales of Moonlight and Rain*, ghosts are used to tell a beautiful and tragic love story between two men. In 'The Chrysanthemum Pact' a man meets a dying samurai and nurses him back to health. The two fall in love and while they must spend time apart, they make a promise to see each other again on the Chrysanthemum Day. When the samurai turns up at the very end of that day, he is silent and unable to speak to his beloved, refusing food. It turns out the samurai is no longer alive, confessing, 'I am not a man of this world. A filthy ghost has taken this form briefly to appear before you.'[37] The samurai was forbidden to leave his post, but rather than break his lover's heart by dishonouring their vow, he took his own life instead: 'A man cannot travel a thousand ri* in one day; A spirit can easily do so. Recalling this, I fell on my sword and tonight rode the dark wind from afar to arrive in time for our Chrysanthemum tryst.'[38] The love between these two men is so strong that it survives death. Also, throughout the story is the recurring motif of the chrysanthemum, the well-known Japanese symbol for male homosexuality.

Wilfred Owen, a gay poet famous for recording his experiences during the First World War, also used ghosts in his poetry, notably in 'The Shadwell Stair' of 1918. Here Owen creates a dreamlike narrative of ghosts mingling around the Docklands of east London:

I am the ghost of Shadwell Stair.
    Along the wharves by the water-house,
    And through the cavernous slaughter-house,
I am the shadow that walks there.

---

* Ri is an archaic Japanese unit of measurement. One ri equates to about 3.827 kilometres.

Yet I have flesh both firm and cool,
      And eyes tumultuous as the gems
      Of moons and lamps in the full Thames
When dusk sails wavering down the pool.

Shuddering the purple street-arc burns
      Where I watch always; from the banks
      Dolorously the shipping clanks
And after me a strange tide turns.

I walk till the stars of London wane
      And dawn creeps up the Shadwell Stair.
      But when the crowing syrens blare
I with another ghost am lain.[39]

This poem alludes to a part of London notable for being used by men to meet other men; the ghosts here are therefore presumed to be other gay men and possibly sex workers or rent boys. He also frames the entire poem around being a ghost, which might be a nickname he picked up during wartime, as mentioned in a letter that he wrote to his mother from the front.

This poem is ostensibly about cruising, and uses the ideas of ghosts – transparent, unseen beings – as a deprecating metaphor for the way gay and bisexual men wandered secret parts of London, looking to find each other.

A PHANTOM ON THE SLUM'S FOUL AIR

Few historical figures from the nineteenth century have attracted more morbid fascination than the serial killer known as Jack the Ripper. All over the world this character has become an obsession and fixation for millions of tourists every year who attend Jack the Ripper tours in London's East End. Online, Jack the Ripper costumes are a popular Halloween staple, and despite the killer's true identity still being unknown, his 'look' is cemented in a long black coat, formal wear, a cane and black top hat. A cartoon in the magazine *Punch* in 1888 shows that much of this conception of Jack was already fully formed while the actual murders were taking place. The image depicts a 'Phantom on the slum's foul air', a wraithlike, cloaked being with an inhuman, mask-like face. This illustration embodies Jack the Ripper's dark presence in east London, and the criminality and moral deprivation that was believed to have created him.

The story of the murders committed by Jack the Ripper, while true, has become a kind of dark fairy tale, as mass-produced as the cheap nylon costumes relating to him that can be bought on Amazon. I mention him in a book on folklore simply because Jack the Ripper's status has been elevated to one strangely inhuman and supernatural, more myth than man. But we must remember that the victims of this killer were very real. As beautifully expressed in Hallie Rubenhold's *The Five: The Untold Lives of the Women Killed by Jack the Ripper*, the fame of this unnamed serial killer who violently murdered women has completely eclipsed the names and identities of his victims: Mary Ann Nichols, Annie Chapman, Elizabeth Stride, Catherine Eddowes and Mary Jane Kelly:

> For over 130 years we have embraced the dusty parcel we were handed. We have rarely ventured to peer inside it or attempted to remove the thick wrapping that has kept us from knowing these women or their true histories.[40]

This sometimes ghoulish fascination with the character of Jack is not merely a modern construct. Even back in 1888, when these murders were taking place, the tabloids followed each murder with thinly veiled excitement, covering every 'scandalous' detail, irrespective of sensitivity or accuracy. Suspects and victims alike were quickly speculated over, and the murder of at least five working-class women in Whitechapel was reported in so-called respectable newspapers with morbid delight like a weekly whodunnit story in a Penny Dreadful.

A motive for these violent murders is unclear, but has been guessed at by many and is still discussed by enthusiasts known as 'Ripperologists'. It has been argued by different advocates that the culprit's motives were: a psychotic hatred for women, a puritanical dislike for prostitution and drunkenness, a predilection for sexual sadism or that they had sexual dys-function resulting in rage at their victims. Woven into this is an implication of deviance and possible homosexuality. Indeed, of the main suspects, at least two have been implied to be gay or bisexual.

Both Dr Francis Tumblety and Montague John Druitt, under suspicion by the police, had been at different times accused of having sex with men, and in the case of Druitt attempting to flee the country, possibly for ped-erasty at a school where he was teaching. Both men had a number of other traits that singled them out as suspects. Tumblety, for example, kept a col-lection of women's wombs, and was wildly misogynistic, and Druitt was described as 'sexually insane', whatever that means. Either way, while nei-ther man was anything even approaching morally pure, the perceived sexuality and deviance of both of them has played a central part in the reason they continue to be labelled as possible murderers.

Queerness, both explicit and implied, has been made a core element of many people's theories about Jack the Ripper, which sometimes gives way to pure unbridled homophobia. In *All About History: Jack the Ripper*, Dr Tumblety's status as a suspect is outlined as 'A quack American Doctor, Tumblety supposedly owned sets of reproductive organs in jars and was thought to be flamboyant and effeminate – and thus homosex-ual.'[41] In another theory, such as the one described in Stephen Knight's *The Final Solution*, the artist Walter Sickert is identified as Jack; this led to other bizarre offshoot theories, which speculate that clues to the iden-tity of the murder are hidden in Oscar Wilde's *The Picture of Dorian Gray*. The murder of the character Basil Hallward in Wilde's book, it is argued, refers to the real-life murder of Mary Jane Kelly, thus suggesting that Wilde had some knowledge of the identity of Jack.

Additionally, the book *They All Love Jack* by Bruce Robinson impli-cates Michael Maybrick, a composer, as the murderer. Bruce states, 'I don't actually know if Maybrick was homosexual, but predicated on that infallible adage, "If it walks like a duck, etc", he was probably a bit of a ducky.'[42] Robinson also implicates another suspect, Prince Albert, a grandson of Queen Victoria, and describes him as an 'effete little useless pederast'. Even at the time of the murders, the killer was believed to exhibit certain unmanly traits; for example, the personal items of Annie Chapman, one of the victims, were said to have been arranged in a 'feminine manner' at her feet. Additionally, the murderer was supposed to have been seen wearing one of his victim's clothes after her murder while fleeing the scene. None of this was ever corroborated.

A secondary layer of queerness to the Jack the Ripper case was the fact that police officers, in an effort to catch the killer, were asked to cross-dress in order to entrap him:

> Let a number of men – say twelve be selected, of short stature, and as far as possible of effeminate appearance, but of known courage and tried nerve. Dress them as females of the class from whom the victims are selected, arm them with the best and lightest weapons and distribute them over the district haunted by the murderer. Note. The men would require to be fair actors, and behave in the natural manner of women of that class, further they would require to be shadowed by help, in an unobtrusive way, and the whole scheme would require to be kept absolutely secret, for once let the press get a hint of it, and farewell to any chance of success.[43]

Even beyond official operations, Jack the Ripper's crimes were associated with a sudden spate of cross-dressing among members of the public; similarly to the police force, men were dressing up as women, with the motivation of entrapping the murderer. The *Yorkshire Gazette* in November 1888 described how 'John Brinkley was charged with being drunk and causing a crowd to assemble in Goswell Road last evening by wearing a woman's skirt, shawl and hat over his ordinary clothes. He was drunk and said he was going to find "Jack the Ripper"'.[44]

But as well as vigilantes in drag, there were those who may have got mixed up in the panic through no fault of their own, merely because of the perceptions of the queer nature of the serial killer himself. Some may have simply been going about their daily lives, dressed in a way they felt comfortable, but, because of wild theories and gossip, were viewed suspiciously for breaking gendered norms. Sixty-one-year-old Edward Hamblar 'was charged with disorderly conduct and being dressed in female attire'. It was later stated that 'All the people around the prisoner imagined he was "Jack The Ripper" and the excitement was very great in consequence.'[45] Unlike John Brinley, Hamblar did not claim to be trying to hunt down the killer, but was arrested and humiliated all the same: 'The prisoner gave no explanation of his conduct. The prisoner said it only was a freak. Mr Saunders said the prisoner had been guilty of very foolish conduct. He did not make a handsome woman.' The fact that a gender-nonconforming person simply walking down the street was almost enough to be 'torn to pieces' by an angry crowd, shows the level of hysteria. It also demonstrates a genuine public belief that Jack the Ripper might be caught wearing women's clothing.

It is true that in both fact and fiction physical deformity is often used as a synonym for internal or moral darkness; a murderer or killer who is ugly, strange-looking or misshapen is an ableist trope that comes up over and over again in films, books and on television. But as a secondary trait used to insinuate a twisted or deadly mind, perceived sexual or gender deviance can work just as well. A queer-coded, lisping, feminine man with a malevolent, high-pitched giggle can come across as the behavioural equivalent to a facial scar, burn or hunched back in implying insanity and a closeness to death for any media-savvy audience.

These fictional ideas have a direct impact on our understanding of real-life criminality. The case of Jack the Ripper shows that it is easy for people to create entire theories and suspicions based on biases around a person's sexuality, or gender nonconformity, meaning that Jack the Ripper as a symbol or archetype for all serial killers has a queer slant to him that can cast a shadow even today.

The image of the queer serial killer is a popular one. Fritz Haarman, John Wayne Gacy, Dean Corll, Dennis Nielsen, Jeffrey Dahmer and Aileen Wuornos are all murderers who were also LGBTQ+ that have developed their own cult followings of amateur investigators and enthusiasts. LGBTQ+ people are in no way overrepresented among those who kill – in fact we are four times more likely to be the victims of violent crime, a statistic that increases exponentially with trans women, particularly those of colour.[46] Public perception does not match this reality. On a discussion board about Jack the Ripper, two users debate the likelihood of the killer being gay. While they don't necessarily agree on the sexuality of the Ripper, they seem to be in agreement about there being a natural link between homosexuality and mass murderers: 'If you browse through the list of serial killers, there are an inordinate number of sk's who have been homosexuals, based on what percentage of the population they are said to comprise'; the other speculates, 'The whole homosexual Jack line of thinking is a bit flawed, in my opinion. While there have been a large number of homosexual serial killers, the vast majority have only killed other men.'[47]

This entirely unfounded idea that queer people have a propensity for killing and sociopathy is sadly still alive and well. While fictional characters like the cross-dressing Norman Bates and transvestite murderer Buffalo Bill are popular and well known, these are purely fantastical creations. Yet even with real-life serial killers it is often insinuated that their homicidal tendencies are linked with some kind of sexual inversion or gender perversion. The murderer John Wayne Gacy was described by his own attorney as having a 'slight, almost effeminate lisp' and 'a handshake like touching damp cloth, his fingers feminine, the nails oh so carefully manicured'.[48] In society's consciousness, to be a murderous man, to be seen as closely linked to the most horrible ideas around death, is linked with being a flawed man, an unmanly man, a queer man.

The average murderer is a cisgender heterosexual man; queer people are no more likely to commit violence than any other kind of person, even though we are much more likely to be victims. Yet there is this strange fact that, at least anecdotally, true crime, and media that covers serial killers, or murderers, seems to be popular with the LGBTQ+ community. Notably a similar trend is observed among women. For example, in a 2010 study by the University of Illinois it was found that 70 per cent of Amazon reviews of true crime books were written by women.[49]

In both cases it can be argued that these groups are drawn to these dark topics as a kind of catharsis, a contrast to the reality where both women and queer people are more likely to be the targets of violence. Therefore documentaries, films and podcasts can create a safe space in which to explore and confront these violent realities, a kind of escapism and maybe even quasi-empowerment. Either way, while the reasons are deeply homophobic and transphobic, the killer, the psychopath and the dangerous murderer are all queer-coded in the public consciousness and the tales we tell.

THE GIRL IN THE TELEVISION SET

The Japanese and American horror franchises based on the book *Ring* by Kōji Suzuki in 1991 involves a cursed cassette tape and a vengeful ghost girl who famously climbs out of a television set to murder people. The terrifying little ghost, with dank, long hair, was originally written as an intersex girl, which when discovered resulted in her murder, thus explaining her dark and tortured nature.[50]

In the cult classic adaptation of *Pet Sematary*, a book originally written by Stephen King, people are brought back from the dead but sinisterly changed, using unspecified Native American magic attributed to a windigo. The main protagonist's wife describes a deeply traumatic upbringing alongside her young sister, who suffered from spinal meningitis. This little girl becomes a twisted, inhuman monster, vengeful and hateful, never quite alive, and never entirely dead. In the film, this frightening disabled creature was played by an adult man, the actor's mismatched sex supposedly adding to the frightening monstrosity of this half-dead little girl.

More recently, the 'Insidious' series of films, which is closely approaching double digits, has a number of evil phantoms as its major antagonists. One, an apparition originally known as 'The Old Woman' or 'The Bride in Black', is a parasitic undead entity who haunts and possesses the heterosexual all-American main character. This character turns out to be the ghost of 'Parker Crane', a man raised by an insane mother and forced to live as a woman, who then becomes a serial killer preying on women, who is captured while trying to castrate himself. The gender-bent characterisation, and the revelation of the woman being a male killer in drag, is used to enhance the terror and unnaturalness of this entity's presence.

For queer and gender-nonconforming people there is a double layer to these portrayals: on the one hand we get a stark reminder of how we still appear to the public, as something frightening and hideous, something akin to being undead. For trans people this is perhaps even more painful, as the language around having a loved one come out as trans is still often described as being akin to being 'widowed' or suffering a bereavement, so the frequent use of gender nonconformity in ghouls and wraiths is perhaps even more barbed.

On the other hand, we can sometimes take ownership of these characters, find empathy for one dimensional 'evil' and find a camp joy in creating our own versions of these tropes. From drag queens vomiting up blood on the main stage of *RuPaul's Drag Race*, to an entire lesbian haunted house constructed by queer American artists, we are aware of how we are perceived, and sometimes can be remarkably playful with this. When the fundamental Christian organisation Spiritual Science Research Foundation announced in a hysterically preposterous report that 85 per cent of homosexuals were possessed by ghosts, stating, 'The main reason behind the gay orientation of some men is that they are possessed by female ghosts'[51] and implied these ghosts made gay men murderous, the LGBTQ+ press had a field day!

Historically, the theme of death has been both a safe and dangerous place for queer people. We have used ghosts and ghost stories as ways to describe our lives and loves, and even found ways to become powerful leaders within spiritualist communities, partly due to our difference. As with many other mythical creatures and ideas, the undead implies something in between and ill-defined. Undead things are frightening partly because they are precariously balanced between two stable states: being alive and being dead. Collectively, as we have seen in previous chapters, humans tend not to like the strange sensation of being in between, or inhabiting the unknown. But for queer people, who so often live a life in a kind of underworld anyway, this can feel almost natural. For queer writers and artists, cruising is like haunting, transitioning is being reincarnated, and loving someone you shouldn't can feel bittersweet, like a kind of death.

PART 4
The Expanded Universe

(Contemporary folklore)

'If I cannot inspire love, I will cause fear!'

From *Frankenstein* by Mary Shelley

9

Loving the Alien

David Bowie was an artist who throughout his life actively cultivated and played with his image as an otherworldly, pansexual, nonbinary being. His alter ego Ziggy Stardust was an alien rock star and messiah figure, both intentionally erotic and yet sometimes asexual or even inhuman. His musical oeuvre, which includes 'Starman', 'Life on Mars?', 'Hallo Spaceboy', 'Space Oddity' and 'The Man Who Sold the World', makes frequent reference to outer space, aliens, science fiction and strange new worlds. These are perhaps among his most signature themes.

As well as being an aesthetic which Bowie enjoyed embodying, through

David Bowie (right) as The Man Who Fell to Earth, 1976

fashion, make-up and performance, he used this 'alien' metaphor to com-municate all kinds of deeper messages through his music: from a simple rebellion against the status quo and an opposition to organised religion, to a countercultural celebration of self-expression and otherness. When asked about his song 'Loving the Alien' in an interview with *MailOnline* in 2008, Bowie said, 'This song is not, it may surprise you to know, another ode to little green Martians'.[1]

One important part of David Bowie's identity, and one of the major appeals to his legions of fans, was his refusal to be entirely pinned down to any one reading or interpretation. Other than simply quoting his own words, it is hard to say exactly what Bowie meant through his use of extra-terrestrial imagery and alien personas. It is also difficult to place Bowie comfortably in any one box within the LGBTQ+ spectrum; at points in his life Bowie announced that he was gay, bisexual and even straight. In an interview for *Playboy* in 1976, he said, 'Sex has never really been shocking, it was just the people performing sex. Now nobody really cares. Everybody fucks everybody.'[2] Combined with his androgynous gender-bending fash-ion, his multitude of looks, characters and costumes, Bowie was a character who was infuriatingly and wonderfully fluid.

Whatever the reading of Bowie, he was part of a long line of artists, writers, musicians and performers who found love in the alien. The description of otherworldly creatures, beings of distant star systems and dimensions, and maybe even the odd personal close encounter with some-thing astral or foreign, are all deeply rooted in the queer experience.

There are obvious statements that will come up again and again, about feeling like the 'other' or being made to feel either outside or separate from 'normal' humanity. But the true story of the extraterrestrial connec-tion to non-heterosexual and non-cisgender people goes far beyond a superficial reading. Also, for those who are confused as to why they have stumbled upon a chapter about 'aliens' in a book about mythology and folklore, let me briefly explain.

Folklore does not need to be old or ancient to count. Stories of alien abduction, modern science-fiction writing and films can still be folklore. Aliens are not simply a modern invention. While the likes of E.T. or Area 51 are entirely twentieth-century creations, their precursors are as old as any of the other mythological beasties in this book.

While the alien has definitely gained a whole set of new tropes and understandings as scientific developments have revealed more and more about the world beyond our stratosphere, we are not the first people to look up at the sky and wonder if we are truly alone. When looking for the real origins of queer little green men, UFOs or giant city-eating blobs, we need to go way further back than fifties B-movies and Roswell conspiracy theories. The earliest recorded accounts of what would later become the E.T. archetype probably began around 5,000 years ago, with classical antiquity.

BORN FROM THE LEG

The ancient Greeks, as with many people throughout history, placed their gods in the sky, or at least high on top of a mountain above regular mortals. These gods are not synonymous with aliens, but elements of the classical pantheon, such as their interest in toying with mortal human fates with a cool intellectual curiosity, and frequent use of magical flying chariots and contraptions, definitely resonate with the alien mythos. More notably there is the ability to descend and spirit mortals away to their realm. All are arguably templates for later alien stories. Indeed, in contemporary science fiction, such as the 'Stargate' series, *Alien: Prometheus*, multiple episodes of *Doctor Who* and even the entire Marvel Universe of films, the idea of classical gods as aliens in disguise is a well-worn trope. It is even at the heart of a number of conspiracy theories and junk-history/science beliefs about the true existence of malevolent humanity-controlling aliens.

Zeus, for example, would often descend to earth in the form of a creature, or human, or even another god, to trick mortals into romantic trysts with him. Sometimes these encounters were entirely against the other person's will, or done without their knowledge or consent. Io, Callisto – who was transformed into a bear and may have started the werewolf myth as we know it – Leda and Danae were women targeted by Zeus. This was done by taking the form of animals, loved ones and even a shower of golden rain. Most of these assaults resulted in pregnancy and the birth of demigod children. But as with most amorous gods, while Zeus's fixation was largely on beautiful women, it could also be applied to men. Ganymede was a handsome young hero from Troy who caught Zeus's eye and was abducted by him, in eagle form, and flown off to Olympus to be Zeus's personal cupbearer. Apollo is also known for his flings with mortal men; Hyacinthus, Cyparissus, Adonis and Branchus are all mortal men the god took a liking to. Just like his father Zeus, this didn't always end well for the love object; Apollo spirited these men away and occasionally accidentally, or intentionally, caused their death, transformation (often into plants) or psychic augmentation (gifting one lover the power of prophecy).

Aliens in a much more literal sense, as in actual life-forms that are born on a different planet, were a topic explored in the classical world in the first century. Lucian of Samosata lived in the Roman-occupied region of what is now Syria and was a hellenised* satirist and writer who often focused on mocking superstitious or outlandish religious beliefs in his work. Due to his extensive use of parody, much of his work takes on epic and ridiculous proportions where truth is stretched to create outlandishly tall tales. His most famous work, the ironically titled *A True Story* (also known as 'True History') is a wacky adventure beyond the earth and among the planets and stars of the solar system. Almost 2,000 years ago, Lucian wrote what some have argued to be the very first known example of 'true' science fiction.

Among the many larger-than-life adventures in *A True Story*, at one point our hero, the author Lucian himself, heads for the moon. When he arrives, there is a war taking place between the kingdoms of the moon and the sun over who owns the morning star, aka Venus. Lucian starts to get to know the lunar people better. He calls these humanoid beings the Selenitai, after the goddess of the moon, Selene. In one scene Endymion, the moon king, offers him a gift:

> When we returned to the moon, Endymion himself and our companions welcomed us with a tearful embrace. Endymion entreated us to remain on the moon and to take part in the expedition to colonise the Morning Star. He promised me his own son as a bride.[3]

---

* Lucian wrote in Greek and was highly influenced by Greek customs, mythology and culture having lived, studied and travelled extensively across Greece.

The Selenitai mate with males and are completely innocent of the word 'woman'. Up until the age of 25 they are brides but afterwards they are grooms. They do not conceive in a womb but in the calf of the leg. When the embryo begins to develop, the calf begins to swell and with the passage of time they make an incision and draw the foetus out dead. But they revive the foetus by exposing it to the wind with its mouth open.[4]

This alien homosexuality might actually have been intended as a flattering portrayal of the nobility of these moon people. Lucian himself is a fascinating figure seen through a queer lens; while primarily extremely critical of the sexual vices of others, he proclaimed that homosexuality was in fact a symbol of a thriving society. In his work 'Amores', during a debate between two characters, one states:

For marriage is a remedy invented to ensure man's necessary perpetuity, but only love for males is a noble duty enjoined by a philosophic spirit. Anything cultivated for aesthetic reasons in the midst of abundance is accompanied with greater honour than things which require for their existence immediate need, and beauty is in every way superior to necessity.[5]

He also provides one of the very few written examples of same-sex desire between women that has survived from the Roman period. 'The Dialogue of the Courtesans' records a comedic conversation between two sex workers, Clonarion and Leiana, about Leiana's encounters with a third woman called Megilla. Clonarion asks, incredulously:

I don't understand. Do you mean to say she is one of those man-like females of Lesbos who will not suffer in their beds the company of men, but prefer to find pleasure, instead, with other women, as if they themselves were men?[6]

With the clear non-heterosexual disposition and allegiances of Lucian's writing, one might also wonder whether *A True Story* was his own kind of personal fantasy. Remember, it is a story in which he placed himself, where he, Lucian, gets to stay in a world inhabited solely by self-replicating hunky gay men, who offer themselves to him selflessly in marriage. Although as a satirist the line between sincerity and parody is always going to be difficult to fully know.

Queer authors have created similar erotically charged 'homotopias' throughout history, often set on mysterious planets or other worlds entirely inhabited by one sex. Charlotte Perkins Gilman wrote *Herland*, where a group of explorers discover a far-off land populated entirely by women.[7] She writes this civilisation of women as largely strong and pragmatic, and eschews most gendered stereotypes. Queer people for thousands of years have used the contrivance of another planet, kingdom, world or dimension to create their own fictional safe havens, or sexy homosocial spaces, free from heterosexual judgement.

It is powerful that what might represent the very first known example of aliens in recorded fiction also depicts them as same-sex lovers living in a gay utopia.

THE LUNARIAN PROFESSOR

Early speculative writers around the turn of the nineteenth century often used alien worlds to explore human gender and sexuality safely from a distance. The moon, an alien yet somewhat familiar landscape that has always been visible from earth, was a popular setting for these tall tales.

In 1909 biologist and writer James B. Alexander penned a piece called *The Lunarian Professor and his Remarkable Revelations Concerning the Earth, the Moon and Mars*. This piece of speculative fiction describes the main insert character Alexander being visited by a strange insectile extraterrestrial entity from the moon. The 'Lunarian Professor', as he is described, talks at length about his observations of the universe and predictions for mankind. At one point the Professor seems to give an insight into the future of human evolution, implying that at some point humanity will gain a third sex:

> Yes the Third Sex. I prefer that name, though some have called it the neuter sex, others name it the Double Sex, or the Epicene or

Common Sex, others the Hermes-Aphrodite. In some respects it is all of these, or either, or neither.[8]

The Professor says that among his own kind there is already a third sex – in fact 'we would not know how to exist if we had but two' – and implies to his incredulous human student that gaining a 'third sex' might be the salvation for mankind. The alien says that the third sex is the most common of the sexes on his homeland of 'Luna', and plays a vital and respected role in society:

> The most responsible places in the state, and the leadership in education, in religion, in public works, engineering and architecture as well as almost all the common occupations, such as manufacturing and storing goods, agriculture etc., are in the hands of the third sex. They are preeminently people of affairs, and for most occupations are decidedly superior to the other sexes, because they are less liable to be distracted from their chosen occupations.[9]

James B. Alexander was not the only author imagining life on the moon as showing a very radical approach to sex and sexuality. Indeed, it is believed that he was inspired to write *The Lunarian Professor* after reading H. G. Wells's *The First Men in the Moon*, written nearly a decade earlier.

In his novel, Wells describes incredible sites of extraterrestrial life on our moon. Here the creatures are insectile and he compares them to bees in terms of their sexuality. He is aided by a particular Selenite (like Lucian, these creatures are collectively named after the goddess Selene) called Phi-oo:

> I am of opinion that, as with the ants and bees, there is a large majority of the members in this community of the neuter sex. Of course on earth in our cities there are now many who never live that life of parentage which is the natural life of man. Here, as with the ants, this thing has become a normal condition of the race, and the whole of such replacement as is necessary falls upon this special and by no means numerous class of matrons, the mothers of the moon-world, large and stately beings beautifully fitted to bear the larval Selenite.[10]

This third gender of Selenite looks after the infants while the reproductive mothers are apparently incapable of doing so: as soon as possible the little creatures, who are quite soft and flabby and pale coloured, are transferred to the charge of celibate females, women 'workers' as it were, who in some cases possess brains of almost masculine dimensions.[11]

Wells has a rather functional role for a third sex, as glorified nannies or neutered celibate females, and shows decidedly misogynistic ideas around masculine and feminine brains. Yet his writing does paint a picture of a seemingly happy society that eschews binary gendered roles, and even makes a case for asexuality, in contrast to the world he was writing from.

CHILDREN OF THE SUN AND EARTH

Heavenly bodies can have deep sexual symbolism, but the origins of this connection between our solar system and human sexuality might come not from science fiction, but instead from philosophy.

The Symposium, a philosophical text by Plato written around 385 BCE, is a fictionalised record of conversations between a number of major philosophers and thinkers of the time, including Socrates, Alcibiades and Aristophanes. In an early part of *The Symposium* this all-male group discuss different approaches to understanding the nature of love. Here comedy writer Aristophanes outlines an 'absurd' but not necessarily 'funny' metaphorical story, to explain the origin of human love and desire. He starts with an interesting preamble on intersexuality:

Long ago both our nature and form were both quite different from what they are now. First, in those days there were three kinds of human beings, not just two, male and female, the kinds you see today. The third type, which combined the other two into one, is now extinct and only its name, 'androgyne', survives. In name and nature this third gender partook of both man (*andros*) and woman (*gyne*). Today, however, only the name is left and people use it mostly as an insult.[12]

He moves on to narrate his very own story of creation, one that accounts for three different kinds of human sexuality. He describes primordial beings that come in different formations:

> Even more unusual, however, all three times of these aboriginal humans were compounds, two bodies joined together front to front with their legs, backs and sides forming a circle. Each one had four arms, four legs and two identical faces upon a rounded neck. There was just one head apiece with the two faces looking out in both directions. Everyone had two backs, arched and facing outwards, which joined together at head and hips. They had four ears and two sets of sexual organs and all the other parts in duplicate, just as you would imagine from what I've already said. With their four arms dangling at their sides, they walked in an upright position, just as we do now, in any direction they chose. But if they wanted to run at full speed they would stiffen and extend all eight of their limbs and twirl round and round like gymnasts doing cartwheels.[13]

These strange proto-humans are associated with different heavenly bodies:

> The ones that were made up of two males joined together were sons of father Helios (sun). Those compounded of two women were daughters of mother Earth. The Androgynes, that hybrid of male and female, were children of the Moon.[14]

In the account, Zeus, fearing the power of these wheel-people, splits them in half. The incision is directly down the middle, dividing them into two separate people. The point where they were once connected becomes a scar, their belly button, a reminder of their lost half. These broken people, separated from their whole, are doomed to look for each other, incapable of finding true fulfilment. Until, that is, Zeus changes his mind, and reconfigures them so they might find each other and give each other pleasure.

In Aristophane's story, primordial humans are four-legged, two-headed creatures, stuck back-to-back, doing cartwheels in space. The children of the moon were a mixture of male and female, and were split in half by the god into heterosexual male and female bodies, but those who are attracted to their own gender are also clearly taken into account:

> Those who come from the man-woman are lascivious and adulterous; those who come from the woman form female attachments; those who are a section of the male follow the male and embrace him, and in him all their desires centre. The pair are inseparable and live together in pure and manly affection; yet they cannot tell what they want of one another. But if Hephaestus were to come to them with his instruments and propose that they should be melted into one and remain one here and hereafter, they would acknowledge that this was the very expression of their want.[15]

The children of the sun, and the children of the earth, became gay men and women respectively. Originally these were two same-gendered souls, conjoined, but then split apart from each other, now forever looking for their missing half. The celestial progenitors of humans in this thought experiment were bizarre and otherworldly, but the love they described was profoundly human. Interestingly, in his description it appears that Plato's version of Aristophanes elevates the love between two men above even that of a man and woman, which he denigrates as 'lascivious and adulterous'.[16]

It is clear that the love between a man and a woman, a man and a man, and a woman and a woman are all given equal weight and validity. The gods split the original celestial beings apart because they were too powerful, implying that love between two humans, irrespective of gender, is also equally powerful.

The inspiration for this story, Aristophanes, was himself a playwright and like many of his contemporaries, often explored gender and same-sex desire in his own work. For example, in *Women at the Thesmophoria*, a conversation takes place between Euripides and another man known as 'the Kinsman', about a third man, who is perceived as particularly feminine:

> Kinsman: You mean the suntanned one, strong guy?
> Euripides: No, a different one. You've never seen him?

Kinsman: The one with the full beard?

Euripides: You've never seen him?

Kinsman: By Zeus, never, as far as I can recall.

Euripides: Well, you must have fucked him, though you might not know it.[17]

Aristophanes was known for being belligerent and comedic, but also for his open exploration of human desires and impulses in every form they took. The metaphors used in Plato's account, of gods, planets and strange 'circle-people' have been taken by queer people from the nineteenth century onwards to attempt to build ways of talking about and understanding their own desires. Many have therefore looked to the heavens for inspiration and understanding.

IT CAME FROM URANUS!

O Child of Uranus, wanderer down all times,
Darkling, from farthest ages of the Earth the same
Strange tender figure, full of grace and pity,
Yet outcast and misunderstood of men—

Thy Woman-soul within a Man's form dwelling,
[Was Adam perchance like this, ere Eve from his side was drawn?]
So gentle, gracious, dignified, complete,
With man's strength to perform, and pride to suffer without sign,
And feminine sensitiveness to the last fibre of being;
Strange twice-born, having entrance to both worlds—
Loved, loved by either sex,
And free of all their lore!

'O Child of Uranus' by Edward Carpenter, 1883[18]

Edward Carpenter was a poet and socialist writing from the mid-1800s through the turn of the century. Carpenter was himself a gay man, and an advocate for homosexuality as a valid and moral lifestyle. He was using a known and well-understood language, at least in certain wealthy

European gay circles, to describe his sexuality. Uranus, and Uranian people, was a semi-coded term for homosexuality that originated within the writings of German activist and lawyer Karl Heinrich Ulrichs.

Ulrichs was a nineteenth-century pioneer in the field of 'sexology', a movement that would later birth and inspire much of the gay and LGBTQ+ rights movement of today. He was inspired by a passage in Plato's *Symposium*, wherein the goddess of love Aphrodite is born in two forms, one from the male god Uranus and another from the union between Zeus and Dione, a man and a woman. These two different Aphrodites are then said to describe two different kinds of human love:

> For there are two loves, as there are two Aphrodites – one the daughter of Uranus, who has no mother and is the elder and wiser goddess, and the other, the daughter of Zeus and Dione, who is popular and common. The first of the two loves has a noble purpose, and delights only in the intelligent nature of man, and is faithful to the end, and has no shadow of wantonness or lust. The second is the coarser kind of love, which is a love of the body rather than of the soul, and is of women and boys as well as of men.[19]

From this Ulrichs created his own terminology to explain sexuality, based around his desire for men. It was clearly an attempt to discuss these urges in a more flattering and humane way than they normally would be. For example, while writing to his sister, Ulrichs attempts to defend his identity as neither perverted or immoral. He uses this newfound terminology to argue that his 'Uranian inclination' is in fact an act of God:

> You believe that the battle against a Uranian inclination is to be fought right at the core. But why, then? I do not understand, since I believe that it would, to the contrary, be a sin to battle against God's work.[20]

Within his language, gay men were described as 'Uranians' or 'Urnings', associated with Uranus, whereas heterosexuals men were 'Diurnians'. While Ulrichs' work largely focuses on the sexuality of men, there were equivalent terms for women, namely 'Urningin' for a lesbian and

'Dioningin' for a heterosexual woman. Ulrichs believed that gay men were attracted to other men as they had an element of femininity to them. He even stated that he was not in fact a man in the traditional sense due to his sexuality, for example telling his sister: 'I said "Spiritually we are women," which means sexually, namely in our bent for sexual love.'[21]

In a letter sent out to many family members he further outlines this, no doubt much to their shock: 'Because a feminine nature dwells in the Uranian which he received from the body of his mother, he is totally wrongly identified as a man.'[22]

And: 'The Uranian is a species of man-woman. Uranism is a variation in nature, a play in nature of which there are thousands of examples in creation.'[23]

Ulrichs' terminology is partially based on Platonic arguments of love and also the tragic story of the original Greek god of the sky, Uranus, who eventually fell and was replaced by his son Chronus. The fallen god, rejected and written out of the Greek pantheon, is seen to represent the experience of homosexual men living in the nineteenth century.

But the planet Uranus would have been closely associated with this all the while: Uranus has been observed since the classical period, but it was only fully studied and understood as being a planet in 1781 by William Herschel. The naming of Uranus, after the god of the sky, was only agreed upon roughly seventy years after Herschel's writings. This is almost exactly the same time Ulrichs began to use the term to describe homosexuality, and is undoubtedly linked: a new named planet in the night's sky, a new understanding of love.

XENOMORPHS

Europeans weren't the only people imagining strange beings descending from the heavens showing blended or ambiguous gender that might be compared to stories of alien beings. In Chinese folklore the 'hundun' is a legendary cosmological creature that was unintelligible and bizarre, often depicted with wings, multiple pairs of legs, but no face. These creatures represented a kind of primordial chaos, shifting and unsettled in their form. In *Shanhai jing*, or 'The Classics of Mountains and Seas', a collection of ancient Chinese mythology, Anne Birrell translates: 'There is a god here who looks like a yellow sack. He is scarlet like cinnabar fire. He has six feet and four wings. He is Muddle Thick. He has no face and no eyes. He knows how to sing and dance.'[24]

In Africa, the people of Mali have referred to ancestral spirits known as 'nommo'. In some accounts these ancient beings are said to descend from the sky, particularly from the Sirius star system.* The beings are said to be amphibious and fishlike in appearance, and also hermaphroditic, having both male, female and genderless forms. They are said in some stories to act as teachers to the peoples of Mali, passing down wisdom and in some accounts travelling down to earth in flying machines.[25]

The idea of aliens in science fiction that have bodies, sexualities and gender identities that mirror human queerness is now a common trope; from Arthur C. Clarke's novel *Childhood's End*, which has a species of alien known as the Overlords that resemble demons and are physically androgynous, to the sex-changing alien species that appeared in the TV series *The X-Files* episode entitled 'Gender Bender' in 1994. Some creators take this 'bent' alien sexuality to darker, kinkier and even Freudian places.

When I was seven I watched my parents' VHS of *Alien*. This turned out to be both a terrible and a wonderful idea. The film absolutely terrified me, and to this day my nightmares are coloured by things crawling on the ceiling, dripping acid blood and malevolently hissing. It is now my favourite film of all time and has informed a lifelong passion for horror and science fiction.

What really intrigued me was the design and life cycle of the nightmarish parasitic alien monster at the centre of the film. The creature is known in later films and spin-offs as a xenomorph, literally meaning 'alien form'.† The biomechanical entity, with shiny black armour, an insectile yet

---

* The veracity of this is still debated as it was largely reported by European anthropologists, who took individual accounts and made both sweeping generalisations and even entire fabrications.

† 'Xenos' is Greek and literally means a foreigner, or a person from another place. It has come to gain the additional science-fiction quality of describing a being from another world entirely.

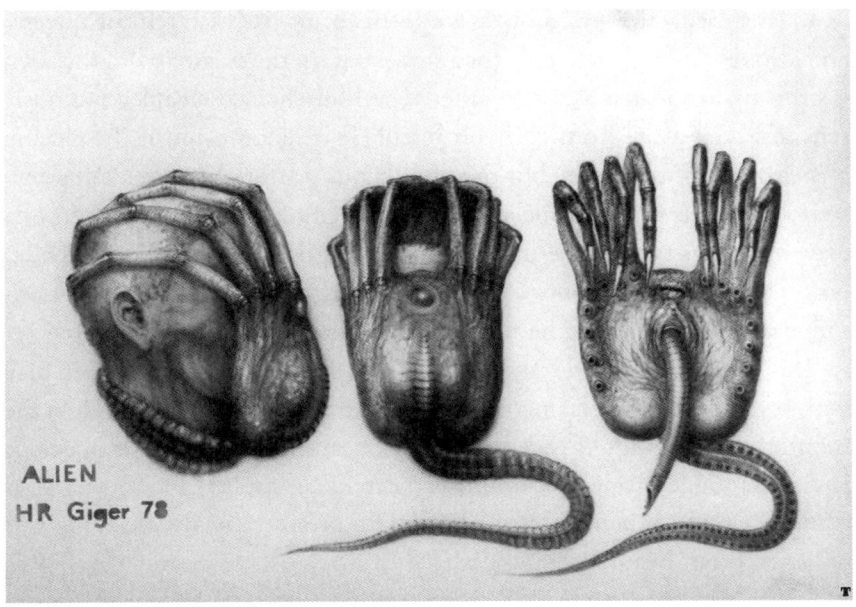

Alien artwork by H. R. Giger, 1978

humanoid appearance and eyeless, elongated head was developed by the artist Hans Ruedi Giger. His drawings, which show hellish combinations of human and machine, with certain sadomasochistic and darkly erotic traits, inspired much of *Alien*'s design aesthetic. Part of Giger's renown is down to his use of psychosexual symbolism in otherwise cold and intentionally disturbing artworks. The creature in *Alien* therefore has elements of its body that resemble the human phallus: a penetrative mouth, and a penile infant form. But this is combined with feminine traits such as having a slender build of a dancer: the monstrous creature was originally performed by Nigerian visual artist Bolaji Badejo, who was discovered in a bar in London's Soho, and later by Australian ballet dancer Andrew Crawford. Both performers were chosen because they were exceptionally tall, elegant and poised, and were placed inside a KY-jelly-covered exoskeleton to bring the terrifying creature to life. But most prominently of all is the alien's ability to gestate within a human host's abdomen, representing a horrifying simulation of human pregnancy. The titular *Alien* is thus a Freudian nightmare that takes human sex, gender and reproduction and turns it on its head into something terrible and wholly foreign.

In later media the xenomorphs are given an ant-like hierarchy of 'queens' and 'drones', though generally they are sexless. In the original film the alien is both male and female, or neither. The lead character Ripley famously screams, 'Get away from her, you bitch!' at a xenomorph in the closing scenes of the film's sequel, but the duplicitous doctor, Ash, says 'I'm going to try to get his finger' while attempting to remove the larval form from a crew member's face, in the 1979 original. Characters seem to apply gender onto the xenomorph depending on how they encounter it, but the creature itself is a frightening hermaphroditic organism.

This is intentional; everything about the xenomorph is designed to play with sex to make viewers uncomfortable, as described by Giger: 'When the mouth is closed it looks very voluptuous, beautiful. But when it opens its jaws the tongue inside the mouth is more like a spear . . . also very suggestive . . . which penetrates the head with greater velocity, snagging bits of brain. From Beauty to the Beast.'[26]

Everything in *Alien* evokes an inversion of sex and gender, from the creature itself through to the biomechanical designs of the spaceships, even through to the human characters. Ellen Ripley, the hero and protagonist of the main franchise, is often argued to be the very first female action hero, but her character also involved a certain gender flip. In the original script written by Dan O'Brien, Ripley was going to be a male character. The gender was swapped, partly to allow the director Ridley Scott to work with Sigourney Weaver. But other than changes to name and pronouns, very little of the character's dialogue or interactions were altered. Many feel this meant that Ripley continued to have as strong a character as she would have if she had been kept male, whereas if her character had been more vigorously rewritten, probably largely by men and based on seventies stereotypes of a female character, some of her heroism might have been watered down.

Ripley herself, while ostensibly a heterosexual human woman, becomes, throughout the franchise, closer to the alien. At one point she carries an alien parasite herself, and later is even genetically combined with the creature. As this happens, her sexuality also seems to shift away from heteronormativity. By *Alien Resurrection,* a clone of Ripley mixed with xenomorph DNA approaches another female character, Call, and while making eye contact intentionally forces a knife through her own hand.

As described in *Alien Woman*, a book that explores the cultural significance of Ripley's character, this disturbing but erotic scene 'effectively creates a discursive space for lesbianism between Ripley and Call, as the most obtuse of viewers would recognise that one woman sticking something into another woman carries at least some connotation of lesbianism'.[27]

There is also another fascinating and often-missed nugget of explicitly queer history in the sequel to the original film, *Aliens*. Among Ripley's ill-fated crewmates who are slaughtered by the xenomorph in the first film is the only other woman character, Joan Lambert. In a blink-and-miss-it moment where Ripley attempts to confront the company who owned her ship, there is the implication that Joan was a transgender woman. Joan's gender is described in a wall of text as '(Female) unnatural' and the biography is introduced as 'Subject is Despin Convert at birth (male to female). So far no indication of suppressed trauma related to gender alteration.'[28] The description, while not necessarily empowering, and using random 'sci-fi' nonsense jargon, would mark the very first canonically transgender character in a science-fiction film.

The idea of gender-bending bodies, frightening intersexuality and a kind of sexual body horror can be seen as a direct progression from earlier genderless, or third-gendered alien tropes. It is present in many contemporary franchises and depictions of extraterrestrials. Aliens are a space where sexuality beyond the boundaries of heterosexual reproduction can be explored, to both horrific and erotic ends. Take gay writer Clive Barker's creation of the Cenobites for the 'Hellraiser' series of films. These are a group of interdimensional beings that travel in search of the deepest pleasure that can be found only through extreme pain. These sadistic humanoid beings are distorted creatures, their bodies twisted and manipulated beyond human possibility in an extreme form of sadomasochism.

Alien worlds don't necessarily exist only on other planets, they can also appear within entirely different dimensions or planes of existence. One remarkable example of this was the thought experiment created by Edwin A. Abbott that posited the existence of a world of only two dimensions. *Flatland: A Romance of Many Dimensions*, written in 1883, was an attempt to play with physics and mock rigid Victorian social hierarchies in a world populated by sentient geometric shapes. The main character, a Square citizen, tries to explain to a three-dimensional person the nature of his world.

In this world the status of an individual is dictated by the degrees of their angles. This results in women, who are all incredibly pointed isosceles triangles, as well as masculine degenerates with acute angles or unequal sides, both being treated very badly. They are collectively perceived as 'Irregular figures' and therefore 'wretched creatures'. Such shapes are treated as an underclass, kept only as 'specimens' for educating the young. The narrator states with derision, 'In some states the specimens are occasionally fed and suffered to exist for several years', whereas he believes it more civilised to 'renew the specimens every month – which is about the average duration of the foodless existence of the criminal class'.[29]

An Irregular figure has a terrible existence in Flatland: 'From his birth scouted by his own parents, derided by his brothers and sisters, neglected by the domestics, scorned and suspected by society and excluded from all posts of responsibility, trust and useful activity.'[30] But the Square protagonist defends this state of affairs, declaring that 'If a man with a triangular front and a polygonal back were allowed to exist and propagate a still more Irregular posterity, what would become of the arts of life?'[31] One of the major fears around these 'monsters' is how their existence would break society's laws; it is posited that such a being might appear from certain sides like a respectable man or even a woman.

Our pompous Square narrator says that 'Nature evidently intended him to be – a hypocrite, a misanthropist, and, up to the limits of his power, a perpetrator of all manner of mischief.'[32] But under duress he acknowledges that some great men from the past had such deviations, although now such people can be changed, altered and converted to fit in with 'normal', regularly shaped society.

The entire novella has been celebrated for its playful use of a science-fiction reality full of strange geometric beings to explore the very real mistreatment of women, the disabled and poor people in nineteenth-century England. I would argue there is a layer here that is less explored, in that there seems to be an insinuation around LGBTQ+ people. In particular men that can be 'confused' for women, who do not fit in, who must be changed to fit or annihilated.

PROBING QUESTIONS

Since around the 1940s there has been a surge of stories about aliens arriving in so-called 'unidentified flying objects', aka UFOs. The descriptions of these alien beings have also become somewhat formulaic. While there are still different alien 'types', the most common reports are of large-headed, slender-bodied creatures known as Greys.

A classic Grey alien is described as follows: 'These beings stand just under 1.2 m (4 ft) tall and are humanoid in appearance. They have thin, almost spindly arms, legs and bodies, but very large and rounded heads. The arms and legs are said to lack elbows or knees and to end in long fingers and toes that are opposable, but again lack clearly defined joints. The heads are hairless, and often earless and noseless. The mouths are usually described as being mere slits, if they are mentioned at all.'[33]

In nearly all sightings the Greys are androgynous, mostly sexless, lacking visible genitalia or secondary sexual characteristics. Many witness accounts make this sexless nature very clear: 'Thinking he has finally caught the vandals who had been plaguing him, Masse crept towards them. When he was about 4.5 m (15 ft) from the "boys" one of them seems to hear him. The figure stood up and turned around . . . Masse could now see that they were not boys at all, but bizarre entities.'[34]

They are also decidedly malevolent and seemingly fascinated with human reproductive biology, taking sperm and eggs as samples. This leads to horrifying witness reports from abductees, where these creatures violate their human captives in a bizarrely sexual fashion.

The account of Jan Wolski, a Polish farmer 1978, is described as follows: 'One of the ufonauts indicated by hand signals that Wolski should undress, which he did. The aliens then studied Wolski visually and passed what appeared to be scanners over his body.'[35]

In Suffolk, England, Rosalind Reynolds and her boyfriend experienced an abduction from the A1092 motorway in the 1990s: 'The Greys swarmed around Reynolds as she lay prostrate and paralyzed on a table. They were equipped with various types of probes and equipment with which they conducted an invasive gynaecological examination of a most unpleasant and unwelcome nature.'[36]

An American account from two men described invasive medical

procedures in even more detail: 'Painful probes were inserted into their bodies to extract samples of blood, skin, urine and sperm. Throughout all this the Greys seemed utterly indifferent to the feelings and pain experienced by the men.'[37]

These meetings with androgynous monstrosities are described by their presumably heterosexual and cisgender victims as unpleasant and intrusive, with their bodies being observed, examined and prodded. The most extreme, and frequently parodied example of this is 'the anal probe', where an alien entity will penetrate its human prisoner to extract samples or information. Betty and Barney Hill claimed to have been abducted by aliens in 1961 and first made mention of this experience. Under hypnosis Barney described how he had a rectal probe inserted which was used in a sexual fashion to force him to ejaculate into a cup.

Later, in the much-publicised 1987 memoir of Whitley Strieber, a self-described abductee and prolific horror author, he describes the following under hypnosis: 'They inserted this thing into my rectum. It seemed to swarm into me as if it had a life of its own. Apparently its purpose was to take samples, possibly of fecal matter, but at the time I had the impression I was being raped, and for the first time I felt anger.'[38]

The original title of his book, *Communion*, was going to be 'Body Terror'. We also shouldn't be surprised that this violent, intrusive experience is inflicted by a gender-bending alien being known only as 'she':

> 'She's sittin' right in front of me the whole time, just lookin' at me. They're moving around back there.' (I could sense them, but I was looking at her. She drew something up from below.) 'Jesus, is that your penis? I thought it was a woman [Makes a deep grunting sound.] That goes right in me [Another grunt.] Punching it in me, punching it in me. I'm gonna throw up on them.'[39]

Aliens and reports of alien abductions seem to peak in relation to other events in history. The popularity of these stories increased at the end of the Second World War and mirror paranoia around developments in medicine and technology in America in the lead-up to the Space Race. It is also notable that from the 1950s there was a surge in the active moral policing of homosexuality and the persecution of queer people in Europe and America. At a time when the family unit was perceived as being under attack, and the so-called American Dream was threatened by communists, there was also the twin fear of deviant homosexuals abusing or seducing children.

Stories of encounters of 'Greys' tinkering with human anatomy might say a lot about fears of war and increased medical intrusion in people's lives; they also seem to depict a specifically queer-coded fear around gender subversion.

A FRAGMENT OUT OF TIME

Of all the franchises that have inspired their audience to create their own fan works, one of the most well documented is that of *Star Trek*. This space-travelling adventure series, originally created in 1965, featured many alien races and beings, some humanoid, others decidedly not. It is perhaps one of the earliest examples that we have of 'true' fan-published stories and material. Fascinatingly, a lot of this revolved around the two lead male characters, Kirk and Spock, engaging in romantic and sexual relationships. For example, in an edition of the fanzine *Spockanalia* published in 1967, Diane Marchant wrote 'A Fragment Out of Time'. In this typewritten story, with intimate images created by tracing over TV stills, Spock, a half-human, half-alien Vulcan, and Captain Kirk, engage in an erotically charged and explicit tryst: 'Well-skilled hands made long, swooping strokes from his knee up the inside of his leg to the upper thighs. Now, he could not prevent this, any more than he could stop a solar eclipse.'[40]

Marchant wrote her piece using 'he' rather than naming Spock, and 'the other' rather than naming Kirk, perhaps to make the pairing less shocking. It's worth noting that she was a figurehead for the *Star Trek* fanbase, particularly in Australia, and also knew the creator Gene Roddenberry personally. Despite the lack of any canon on-screen romance between the two characters, Diane Marchant said in a 2006 interview:

> One would have to be wearing blinkers to miss their growing of two souls becoming as one. It was a beautiful coming together of two halves. The hand needed the fingers if it were to function as its maker

and nature planned. They were what was needed for the other. They were a whole. Sharing/caring/relying/trusting/cherishing/etc. Adding strength to strength, permitting respite, adding closeness, humour, respect and the like. In short, each bolstering the other's strengths – by their friendship, devotion, security, and the constancy of knowing – they are not alone. From our discussion of such things came a natural progression – as to whether, given the century, if not all 'love' was acceptable as legitimate. If one considered the IDIC [Infinite Diversity in Infinite Combinations] as a universally accepted ideal – then the answer must be an unequivocal: YES!

Marchant is often lauded as one of the first creators of 'slash fiction', romantic fan fiction of two same-sex characters from a known franchise. It is powerful that while queer relationships were still a long way from being depicted sympathetically on mainstream television, fans were doing this themselves initially through science fiction worlds and alien beings.

This continues today, and a nerdy obsession with the extraterrestrial protagonists of *Star Trek*, *Star Wars* and *Doctor Who*, while not unique to queer people, is incredibly common. Emily Garside opens her book *Gay Aliens and Queer Folk* with the epigraph: 'For every teen who hid *Queer as Folk* VHS tapes, and then found the Doctor to travel in time and space with'. Her book explores the work of Russell T Davies, a gay man and creator behind the insanely popular 2005 relaunch of the *Doctor Who* franchise. His impact on this particular alien-focused franchise is most clearly embodied in his writing of the fiftieth-anniversary episode, 'Star Beast'. Here the alien transdimensional being that is the Doctor is described as 'male and female and neither and more' in a single monologue voiced by three different people: the Doctor; his ex-travelling companion, Donna; and her transgender daughter Rose. None of this subtext should come as a surprise: Davies was also the mind behind groundbreaking LGBT drama *Queer As Folk* released in 1999, and one of the reasons for the title of the book you are currently reading. Through the lens of queer creators like Davies, themselves queer nerds and science fiction obsessives, alien worlds are still a playground for exploring human sexuality and gender.

From their ancient past, rooted in kidnapping gods, to their strange modern depictions as frightening and sexy entities, aliens are simply a new expression of very old folklore. They combine ideas from the child-stealing fairy 'changeling', demonic possession and paranormal activities, with a more contemporary fear of scientific and medical intrusions into everyday life. While aliens were not always created as direct parallels to real LGBTQ+ people, it is notable that the alien and the queer person have so many similarities and connections that their stories can be difficult to fully untangle.

At best, the alien is a safe space for people to explore their identities, at worst it takes all the greatest concerns around LGBTQ+ people and turns them into a brand-new monster to be feared, hated and even hunted. There is an uncomfortable truth that in science fiction often the only nonbinary or gender-fluid characters are inhuman. As author and video essayist Rowan Ellis shared with me:

> A lot of these elements of nonbinary and genderfluid representation won't come from a desire to represent nonbinary or genderfluid characters – but instead a desire to make a non-human character as non-human as possible. Establishing entire alien races as nonbinary is a way to make them seem fundamentally alien to an average audience – because that's, frustratingly, the way nonbinary people are often perceived.

Yet there is a power in reclaiming these modern monstrosities, even the most strange and inhuman iterations. As described by writer Carrow Narby in relation to the 1988 schlocky horror film remake *The Blob*: 'I, for one, find blobs to be eminently relatable.'

They go on to say:

> The blob is not red, but vibrant pink. It descends on a picturesque slice of Americana: A small town where high school football is the centre of public life and a folksy local diner serves up homemade pies. It immediately begins to upend the entire social order.[41]

Rum, Bum and Concertina

At the National Maritime Museum in London, alongside sea monsters and sirens, I also found myself immersed in the world and history of piracy. While the British Museum has its mummies, and the Natural History Museum its dinosaurs, pirates always seem to be the biggest draw to this museum. There is something about the idea of pirates that incites a certain, often highly romanticised, fervour. Pirates are a popular fancy dress for adults and kids alike, they fill children's books, games and television, and are generally perceived as fun, funny and, for some strange reason, safe. There is also something decidedly camp about the imagined pirate, as expressed in an anonymous nineteenth-century lyric: 'Ashore, it's wine, women and song, aboard it's rum, bum and concertina'.

The pop-culture ideas around pirates are so divorced from their reality that it is incredibly easy to forget that pirates were, and still are, actual people and not just a fun fictional construct. Real-life pirates steal, injure, abduct, abuse and murder, so, while I hate to be a killjoy, that uncomfortable dichotomy between what we think of as a pirate and what real pirates were, and are, has to be kept in mind. Most of the pirates we know, or think we know, are either incredibly fictionalised versions of real people, or are entirely made-up whole cloth.

Both real and fictional pirates are celebrated for their wild ways, their aggression and rowdy masculinity, but there is often something slightly subversive running beneath. Whether it is brightly coloured dress, flamboyant facial hair, a certain kind of fey charisma or rakish sense of humour, portrayals of pirates, even the overtly cisgender heterosexual ones, all seem at least a bit queer-coded in both manner and appearance. 'Swashbuckling', while not exactly synonymous with 'camp', often leans heavily in that direction.

Just look at the description of the notorious Blackbeard in *A General History of the Robberies and Murders of the Most Notorious Pyrates*, written in 1724: 'His beard was black which he suffered to grow to an extravagant length; As to breadth, it came up to his Eyes, he was accustomed to twist it with Ribbons, in small Tails, after the style of our Rammelies Wigs, and turn them about his ears.'[1]

Even descriptions of Blackbeard's voice are subversive and intriguing. In a fictional account of 1847, his introduction proceeds as follows:

> 'What strange apparition is this,' exclaimed the earl involuntarily, as this singular personage stood erect before him.
>
> 'I am no apparition, sir,' exclaimed the stranger, in a voice so finely modulated that it might have been easily taken for a woman's.[2]

The queer subtext to pirates also applies to the half-real tales we tell about a life at sea, and all those who quest for adventure, riches and infamy upon the waves.

PIRATE WEDDINGS

In *Rum, Sodomy, and the Lash*, literary scholar Hans Turley states, 'The evidence for piratical sodomy is so sparse as to be almost non existent',[3] meaning that direct, reliable and factual descriptions of same-sex pirate relationships are almost impossible to come by. He argues that in exploring gender and sexuality among historical pirates one would not expect it to be clearly marked as such, and must read between the lines.

Not everyone agrees with this. B. R. Burg, historian and author of *Sodomy and the Pirate Tradition*, commented that in the seventeenth century polite society was willing to turn a blind eye to certain forms of same-sex relationship, and implies that there is a lot of evidence for piratical sodomy: 'Amid the climate of toleration flourished one of the most unusual homosexually orientated groups in history, the Caribbean pirates who spread terror from South America northward to Bermuda and occasionally into the Pacific throughout the latter half of the 17th century.'[4]

Whatever stance you take on pirate intercourse, one of the most commonly explored concepts among queer historians is that of 'matelotage'.

'Matelotage' is a French loan word meaning 'seamanship', representing an agreement formed between a pair of buccaneers, or pirates, that would allow the sharing of goods and finances. The two matelots, being men in every recorded case, would enter into an economic partnership with each other. This is not entirely dissimilar to the relationships described earlier between Viking warriors, and those between Greek heroes, which will be covered in due course.

This concept is often celebrated as a kind of 'gay pirate marriage' by some progressive circles. However, an agreement between men for mutual financial benefit, particularly men who are operating outside the law and its protections, in no way implies a definite sexual or romantic relationship: 'Matelotage was probably no more than a master-servant relationship originating in cases of men selling themselves to other men to satisfy debts or to obtain food'.[5]

For those pirates employing matelotage, this might be seen as an entirely practical union, or perhaps worse, predatory. That said, there is evidence that this might not always be the case, and could entail a deep sense of romantic affection. For example, Louis Adhemar Timothée Le Golif, a French buccaneer, decided to marry a woman, which enraged his matelot: 'Pulverin, the captain's Matelot, was distraught. He first sought solace in drink, but subsequently claimed his right and was admitted to the marriage chamber.'[6]

Another story concerns the infamous Cornish pirate Robert Culliford, operating during the late seventeenth century. He is particularly known for his bitter rivalry with the infamous William Kidd, being behind a mutiny that caused Kidd to lose his entire crew.

Culliford met John Swann, a lesser-known pirate, while in Madagascar, and by 1699 the pair were inseparable. In a set of papers written about piracy in the West Indies on 8 June 1699, His Majesty's Stationery Office published the following description: 'At this place of St. Mary's fort live Capt. Culliford and Capt. Sivers, who pretends to be a Dutchman. There is one John Swann, a great consort of Culliford's, who lives with him.'[7]

The two were believed to be in a state of 'matelotage' with each other.

As well as living together, they shared property and had the right to inherit the other person's possessions after death. It is not known precisely how long the two pirates had been in this union prior to the 1699 report. They spent the following year travelling together, and seemingly parted ways around 1700, when Swann stayed in Barbados and Culliford ended up back in London, narrowly escaping execution by becoming an informant. Robert Culliford, like many pirates, then disappears entirely from the historic record.

The two men have been described by some as 'gay' or 'bisexual' pirates, and their cohabitation and relationship has been compared to same-sex marriage or civil partnerships. How much of this interpretation is fact or fiction depends on your perspective. Still, it is far from impossible.

A life at sea, not just one of piracy, has been studied from a queer perspective by many institutions and individuals, as it often operates under different norms and laws than for landlubbers. Pirates created their own rules and codes of conduct, but even government-backed, state-sanctioned buccaneers were known to allow certain behaviours that might have been frowned upon elsewhere.

As an example, Welsh pirate Bartholomew Roberts wrote up a set of laws to be obeyed aboard his ship, a so-called 'Pirate Code'. Alongside the right for all men to vote on decisions made onboard ship, an outlawing on gambling, and a promise to keep their cutlass and pistols in good shape, is the following:

> VI. No boy or woman to be allowed amongst them. If any man were to be found seducing any of the latter sex, and carried her to sea, disguised, he was to suffer death.[8]

While the major focus is on ensuring women are not taken aboard the ship, as they were deemed bad luck (more on this later!), it also mentions boys, and, intriguingly, the idea of 'disguise'. The implication is that same-sex relations, arguably of a pederastic or a nonconsensual variety, did take place among pirate crews, otherwise it would not need to have been outlawed. Also, with the idea that women were dressed as men, so as to come aboard ship, there is a precedent for cross-dressing which we will delve into later. Finally, note that the seduction of the 'latter sex', meaning women, was punishable by death, whereas no punishment is stated for those bringing a 'boy' aboard ship. This could be because of the superstition concerning women aboard ship, but could equally be interpreted as some pirates having a permissive approach to 'sodomy' or pederasty.

> Sexual encounters involving sailors are a part of maritime lore, and fo'c's'le humor [jokes relating to sailors] abounds with stories of below deck encounters in which salty bosuns initiate tender cabin boys into the arcana of the sea.[9]

CABIN BOYS

Today there is a certain wink-wink nudge-nudge attitude about the role of cabin boy, the idea being that this crew member, the lowest-ranking on a ship, often a young man, was also used for sex by the rest of the crew. Famously, *Captain Pugwash*, the children's comic strip and TV series created in the 1950s, spawned a rumour that the characters had been given intentionally smutty names. These included 'Seaman Staines', 'Master Bates' and notably 'Roger the Cabin Boy'. The rumour was pure fiction, created in 1970s schoolyards, as the real names were significantly less euphemistic. Thanks to the association, however, it gained so much traction that in the nineties both the *Guardian* and the *Evening Standard* had to published formal apologies to the creator, John Ryan, for derogatory articles. That is the strength and pervasiveness of the trope.

Bisexual songwriter Tom Robinson, famous for writing 'Glad to Be Gay', a protest anthem for queer people, also wrote 'Cabin Boy' in 1984, employing the role to describe being a submissive and attentive lover in a same-sex partnership. The song is full of cheeky double entendres for gay sex such as working the pump, stripping the guns, biting the biscuit and going all the way.

'Cabin boy' was a formal (albeit) lowly rank in the navy, as well as among pirates. In some cases this would be the first step into a career at sea, some cabin boys becoming captains, although most were simply working-class boys in need of 'low-skilled' work. In terms of sexualisation, a print from the National Maritime Museum presents a somewhat

Cabin Boy by Thomas Rowlandson, 1799

disturbing picture. Simply called *Cabin Boy*, the image, dating from 1799, shows a young man holding a mop and a bucket.[10] The figure is androgynous but suggestive, with rouged cheeks, and a belt around their waist giving the impression of an ample bosom and a dress. The boys who served aboard naval ships as cabin boys were often aged between twelve and sixteen, so the way the image feminises and sexualises this character is undoubtedly deeply sinister.

Even more dark are the lurid descriptions of the torture and death of cabin boy Richard Pye, at the hands of a sadistic 'barbarous' merchant known as Captain Jeane, Jayne or Jane of Bristol (depending on the source). On finding the eighteen-year-old had stolen a dram of rum from his private cabinet, the young man was whipped and tortured over a period of days, resulting in his death. At one point, as part of a cruel trick, Pye was forced to drink the captain's urine, thinking it was water. There is something awfully sexual about the descriptions of these actions, and the obvious pleasure that the vindictive captain takes in inflicting strange punishments on the boy. In the end Captain Jeane is convicted of murdering the boy and put to death himself at Execution Dock in east London, a famous execution spot for pirates and smugglers.

What this story illustrates is that a cabin boy might be perceived by some crew as barely human, disposable, a lowly creature to be used for any purpose his superiors desired. Sadly, records do show that young 'inferiors' were occasionally abused aboard ship. For example, B. R. Burg's *Boys at Sea* discusses numerous accounts of young men and boys being preyed upon by both pirates and merchant seamen. We see this idea reflected in fiction: *Bom-Crioulo*, written by Adolfo Caminha in 1895, which is also the first known text to deal with a homosexual relationship in Brazil, revolves around a freed enslaved man and his love for a white cabin boy. In Herman Melville's *Moby-Dick* the antihero Captain Ahab takes the young black cabin boy Pip into his own cabin and the two become incredibly close, even holding hands. Ahab admits: 'Thou touchest my inmost centre, boy; thou art tied to me by cords woven of my heart-strings.'[11]

Later, driven mad by being abandoned at sea, Pip even begins to ramble about serving captains and superiors in a somewhat suggestive manner.

> Ha! what's this? epaulets! epaulets! the epaulets all come crowding! Pass round the decanters; glad to see ye; fill up, monsieurs! What an odd feeling, now, when a black boy's host to white men with gold lace upon their coats![12]

The idea of boys and young men becoming sexual subordinates is therefore, sadly, not without precedent aboard ships of all kinds. Accusations of 'sodomy' aboard ship were not even uncommon. Records at the National Maritime Museum from 1699 refer to an incident aboard a merchant navy vessel: 'Edward Bigley and Daniel Parker, who are evidences against one John Cates accused by them of sodomy, you are to cause them to be entered and borne aboard the said Ship as part of the aforesaid Complement.'[13]

There are also stories where power dynamics, and the moral outrage at same-sex desire, make it hard to know exactly how consensual these relationships really were. In 1698, Captain Edward Rigby was convicted of sodomy with a nineteen-year-old crew member called William Minton. While the manuscripts from the trial paint Rigby as an assailant and

Minton as the victim, something seems a little off. Indeed, there is evidence that the entire event was probably orchestrated to entrap Captain Rigby by the Societies for the Reformation for Manners. Minton, it seems, played a knowing and willing role as bait, and was an active party to the interaction with the goal of outing and humiliating Captain Rigby. Even Minton's incredibly explicit confession, which was almost certainly highly embellished or even staged, seems to imply a more active role for the young man: '[Minton] took hold of Rigby's Privy Member and said to Rigby, I have discovered your base inclinations, I will expose you to the world, to put a stop to these Crimes.'[14]

Pirate ships, and ships in general, might offer liberation to some, and there are even examples of there being certain kinds of democracy not offered on land, but, conversely, they can also be perceived as floating prisons. These are isolated and confined spaces, inhabited generally entirely by men, often with previous criminal convictions, for months at a time. As stated by William Hacke, a mapmaker, from his personal experience aboard a ship with buccaneer Captain Bartholomew Sharp, a crew might be made up of all kinds of criminal class. In particular he says of the crew: 'Some having merited the Gallows, other Fire and Faggot for Sodomy.'[15] This is the perfect cocktail for dark and dangerous behaviours born not always out of affection or mutual attraction, but anger, frustration and sadism. But at the same time these were spaces where people who wanted to transgress social, and not necessarily criminal, boundaries, might turn to seek a certain kind of escape.

I do not want to equate the behaviours in this segment with loving and equitable queer relationships, but they do have to be acknowledged when considering how the rose-tinted folklore of pirates has evolved from what was really a chaotic, libertarian and dangerous homosocial environment.

The unequal power play, cruelty and abuse featured in this chapter was not solely the province of 'queer' pirates and sailors; young women and girls were treated every bit as badly, if not worse, by ostensibly heterosexual men. So be under no illusion that any of this is intrinsically 'gay' or tells us anything about real homosexual or bisexual relationships. Simply put, the seventeenth-century maritime world was, for better or for worse, an intense, strange and frightening place for all involved. Some of this darkness has carried over into popular folklore, and some of it remains just beneath the surface.

GAY ROBINSON CRUSOE

Not all same-sex relationships at sea would have been violent and cruel. There is the previous case of Swann and Culliford, but also lower-ranking examples. Naval records from the National Maritime Museum show what appear to be consensual relationships between crew mates. Sadly, even relationships between adult men were still punishable under the Buggery Act introduced in 1533 by Henry VIII, which also applied at sea.

There is also the general implication that consensual same-sex relationships were a common part of many voyages at sea, both among pirates and in the merchant navy. This was such a trope that such relationships were almost unremarkable. For example:

> I have been stationed, as you know, in two or three ships . . . On the D—, homosexuality was rife, and one could see with his own eyes how it was going on between officers. I have been told that in some services (the Austrian and French, for instance), nobody ever remarks about it, taking such a thing as a natural proceeding: that may be so or not; but in any case, nobody was 'shocked' on board either the A—or the B—. There were half a dozen ties that we knew about . . . To my knowledge, sodomy is a regular thing on ships that go on long cruises.[16]

Sadly, the majority of accounts we have of queerness at sea are down to records of punishment. Whether or not such behaviours would be allowed to pass unnoticed depended on the ship, its crew and its captain. Some captains might turn a blind eye, others might punish any 'deviant' behaviour. One of the few accounts that actually centres the voice of such a person is that of Leendert Hasenbosch. Hasenbosch was not a pirate, but a soldier of the Dutch East India Company, although his account seems to come straight from a nineteenth-century pirate novel.

After being found guilty of 'the abominable sin of sodomy' aboard his ship, Hasenbosch was abandoned on Ascension Island, 1,000 miles off the coast of Africa. Amazingly, he kept a diary of his time on the island. It tells the story of a lonely and desperate man trying to survive and slowly losing his mind.

The story has occasionally been romantically framed as a kind of 'Gay Robinson Crusoe'. While not accurate – and Hasenbosch's story is far more grim – it is at least understandable: this is one of only a handful of surviving accounts from real sailors marooned on desert islands, and it is notable in being written by a man punished for his sexuality.

But, again, we need to be careful: the exact nature of 'sodomy' could be interpreted in many ways. Hasenbosch may well have simply been a gay or bisexual man, caught in the act of 'buggery' with another crew member, or it could be due to a sexual assault, accusations of bestiality or an attack on a minor. As described by B. R. Burg in his introduction:

> At various times sodomy and buggery, as defined by law, included homosexual acts, homosexual child molestation (but never hetero-sexual child molestation), bestiality, heterosexual anal-genital contact, and assorted methods of homosexual masturbation.[17]

Historical stories of queerness therefore lead us into murky, shark-infested waters, as consensual homosexual sex and those acts still deemed criminal and immoral today were sadly synonymous. To this day gay and bisexual men still have to deal with the fall-out from this through their conflation with actual child abusers and rapists, partly because of the cruel indifference of the historic record.

Was Leendert Hasenbosch an unfairly punished queer man, or a sexual predator? One part of his diary that tips the scale in favour of the first, more favourable interpretation is when he begins to hallucinate seeing demons due to severe dehydration. Poor Hasenbosch writes that one of these demons had 'The resemblance of a man I had been well acquainted with, whose name I am afraid to mention; he staid with me for some time'.[18]

Later, still talking about these visitations, Hasenbosch confesses that they resemble a man he knows called Andrew MacFercen: 'The Devil has many ways to tempt and lead men astray: We were formerly soldiers together and I know that he was a very dabaucht person, and a Menist as to his belief.'[19]

The intimacy of this description of the 'debaucht' man the demonic figment resembles implies a personal connection, arguably that of a past lover. This vision of 'Andrew' says terrible, blasphemous things, causing Hasenbosch to identify himself as a sodomite, trying desperately to fight 'temptation' and repent. These, to me, are the words of a desperate and wretched queer man, wracked by fear and guilt about his longstanding desire for other men, not those of a person punished for committing a single one-off assault.

When the diary of Leendert Hasenbosch was retrieved by a passing ship there was no sign of the sailor, no body or skeleton left behind. His diary lasted approximately five months, and then in October 1726 simply . . . stops.

PIRATE QUEENS

As we have seen, women aboard ship were perceived as bad luck by sailors and pirates alike, the sea being presumed to be a masculine place, fit only for hardy men and unsafe for the fairer sex. But as we know, such boundaries have never stopped women, and those who might have been perceived as women, from finding escape and adventure on the high seas despite society's chokehold on femininity.

Of all the female pirates, the most famous and frequently mentioned are Anne Bonny and Mary Read. Most of the information we have about these two women comes from a single book, *A General History of the Robberies and Murders of the Most Notorious Pyrates*, written in 1724. The book is considered a frustrating blend of fact and fiction, with the author, a pseudonymous 'Captain Charles Johnson', occasionally taking incredible liberties with the truth. That said, the book has become the backbone of what people 'think' about pirates; irrespective of its actual accuracy as a historical source, it is responsible for creating the folkloric pirate and, therefore, is a worthy source in this book. But before we proceed, everything cited here should be taken with a mountain-sized grain of salt.

Anne Bonny was born out of wedlock to a maid of a wealthy gentleman

An engraving of Anne Bonny and Mary Read

in a town near Cork in Ireland. As a girl she was nicknamed Andy and actively presented to others as a boy by her father. After her mother passed away, Anne grew up a strong-willed and passionate woman who 'was of fierce and courageous temper', once beating up a man who attempted to assault her until he 'lay ill of it for a considerable time'.[20]

Anne ended up becoming embroiled in piracy after starting a relationship with the pirate John Rackham, known as 'Calico Jack', despite already being married to a poor seaman. She followed Rackham to Cuba, and despite becoming pregnant (the whereabouts or fate of their child is never described) continued to work tirelessly by his side. Anne Bonny's pirate credentials are openly celebrated in the book, which says that 'no Body was more forward or courageous than she'.[21] The entire time Anne was aboard ship, she dressed and was identified by the crew as a man, and only Rackham and his close companion, Mark Read, knew the truth. It is here that things become positively Shakespearian and decidedly queer!

Mark Read was a fellow pirate, to whom Anne Bonny took a liking. Thinking him 'a handsome young fellow', she made a move on him despite already being involved with Captain Calico Jack. Through a situation that is not fully described but can surely be guessed at, it is revealed to Anne that Mark is in fact Mary Read. Mary is a woman who was also in disguise aboard Rackham's ship, revealed only through Anne's persistent courtship! Mary therefore also discovers Anne's 'true' identity, thus ending the love affair, much to Anne's 'disappointment'. Rackham is so jealous of what happens between the two that he threatens to cut Mark/Mary's throat, until he is also let in on their secret. This entire encounter, while not decidedly homosexual, is also hardly heterosexual either!

Mary was herself a working-class woman from London, and like Anne was raised as a boy. Indeed, for much of Mary's childhood, she believed herself to be a boy: 'Thus the Mother gained her Point, she bred up her Daughter as a Boy, and when she grew up to some Sense, she thought proper to let her into the Secret of her Birth, to induce her to conceal her Sex.'[22]

Later, Mary also falls for a young man 'of a most engaging behaviour' with whom she begins a relationship. Over time Mary does reveal her 'secret' to this man, although their relationship seems to begin before her identity is clear to him – again, making this a wonderfully confusing relationship to describe as purely heterosexual or homosexual, both, or neither!

Both Anne and Mary end up in prison together as pirates and are sentenced to be executed. Both women 'plead the belly', meaning that as they were pregnant they might avoid being hanged. Sadly, Mary, while pregnant, becomes sick with fever and dies, whereas Anne disappears. Some say she died, others that she fled to America to live in North Carolina.

For both Mary and Anne I have chosen to use the pronouns she and her, as both identified themselves as women when in safe company. But what a highly novelised text written by a pseudonymous man from the seventeenth century cannot tell us is anything they felt about themselves in their heads. To imply that Anne or Mary were trans, or nonbinary, would be revisionism, but they also lived lives that bent and blurred the boundaries between what it was to be a man and woman. While crossdressing doesn't mean the same thing as being queer, or gender-fluid, it is easy to see how the lives of people like Anne and Mary might resonate with a contemporary LGBTQ+ audience.

***

The Chinese pirate Zheng Yi Sao was born in 1775. She began life in Guangdong aboard a so-called 'flower boat', essentially a floating brothel, where she would have been put to work from a young age. At twenty-six, Zheng escaped sex work through marriage to another famous Chinese pirate, Zheng Yi (from whom she takes her name). In time Zheng Yi Sao would eclipse her husband, becoming one of the most feared of all Chinese pirates and earning herself the romanised name Ching Shih (meaning 'Widow of Zheng'), or Madam Ching.

Unlike Anne Bonny or Mary Read, Zheng Yi Sao never attempted to pass herself off as a man, but her reign of terror also has queer allusions. In marrying a pirate lord, Zheng gained not only a powerful ally, but also a stepson, a close companion of her spouse known as Cheung Po Tsai – although stepson might not be quite the appropriate word, as Cheung Po Tsai, a handsome young man forced into piracy during his youth, soon became a lover of both Madam Ching and her husband. This bisexual, polyandrous relationship benefited Madam Ching, who cemented her security and dynasty through the two pirate men, while, some have argued, ensuring her husband would not leave her for a man, and that after his death she would have another husband waiting in the wings.

Some have argued that despite being a ruthless pirate lord in her own right, controlling more than 400 junks, Madam Ching was highly influenced by her early years as a working-class sex worker. When capturing a ship, no women were to be abused or executed by Madam Ching's crew, on pain of death.

THE WIDOW IN MASQUERADE

In the cases of Anne Bonny and Mary Read, the description of them as 'cross-dressing women' is perhaps accurate. But based on how they identified, the story of Hannah Snell, aka James Gray, is somewhat more complicated.

A pamphlet entitled 'The Female Soldier' written in 1750, supposedly recounted by Snell but recorded by an anonymous source, tells us that Snell grew up in Worcester and already had a fascination with the army. At just seventeen, she married a sailor named James Summs and had a little girl. The sailor abandoned young Snell, and tragically her daughter died, which drove Snell to go in search of her errant husband. She did

HANNAH SNELL.

An engraving of Hannah Snell, 1854

this by assuming the identity of her brother-in-law, wearing his clothes and taking his name, James Gray.

Snell, as Gray, discovered that their husband had been executed for murder, but rather than return home, they joined the army, and later the navy as Summs. In this role they lived as a cabin boy, travelled to Mauritius and fought against Bonnie Prince Charlie. During this time James/Hannah's identity was never revealed. At one point when wounded in the leg by a bullet they refused help from the ship's doctor, instead seeking the aid of a local woman to avoid revealing their sex.

Once back in London, after an illustrious and exciting military career, James/Hannah reveal themselves in a pub in London, to the surprise of their friends and crew. From here Hannah identifies publicly as a woman and goes by the name of 'The Widow in Masquerade'. Being a canny businesswoman, she established this as her brand, performing in full army regalia, posing for paintings, and even founding a pub in Wapping. One of the main bones of contention was that the government at first refused to award her an army pension, as no woman was entitled to one, despite her active and demonstrable record of service.

The written record of Hannah's story is very much intended as self-promotion and exoneration; it is intended to tug at the heartstrings, and probably the purse strings of all who read it. In this Hannah is repeatedly described as a weak woman, and being of the 'fair sex', a mere victim of circumstance. Yet the story also reads as an adventurous romp, something in which Hannah clearly took enormous pride.

The sequence where Hannah, living as James, becomes enamoured with another woman and is even engaged to be married is played out as a kind of comedic farce, but one has to question the true desires and intentions behind these actions:

> Hannah finding this young Woman had no dislike to her, she endeavoured to try if she could not act the Lover as well as the Soldier, which she so well effected, that it was agreed upon she should return from London, in order to be married as soon as she had got her Discharge and Pay; and tho' but so short a Time there as two Days, had effected this her Amour so as to obtain the young Woman's Consent to marry her.[23]

Hannah's identity is seemingly more complicated than simply that of a woman pretending to be a man, as the final words of the piece allude to:

> I shall now conclude with informing the Publick, that she still continues to wear her Regimentals; but how she intends to dispose of herself, or when, if ever, to change her Dress, is more than what she at present seems certain of.[24]

This is as close to a personal declaration that the boundary between Hannah and James is fluid, and that their sense of self might lie somewhere in between, as one might expect to read.

With Snell, I feel from her writings that both James and Hannah were legitimate identities worthy of respect. But by the end of her life Hannah is living as a woman, she marries, has children, and ends up tragically being committed to an asylum, and dies in Bethlem Hospital. Hannah is buried alongside other veterans, all male, at the Royal Hospital Chelsea. Either way, Hannah was someone who revelled in the buccaneering gender confusion her life generated in eighteenth-century society, and in fact actively cultivated this image.

YO HO, A PIRATE'S LIFE FOR ME

In 1720, at the start of the decline of the 'golden age of piracy', Daniel Defoe wrote *The Life, Adventures and Piracies of the Famous Captain Singleton*, a fictional account of a good-hearted pirate who adventured around the world, only to discover that pirating was not the life he truly wanted. It is arguably the first truly fictional novel dealing largely with pirates, and already lays out a number of tropes that are well established today. The main character, the troubled hero Captain Singleton, is guided largely by one relationship with another man, William Walters, often referred to as 'William the Quaker'. The connection between these two is probably the central relationship in the entire text, and has been read by many contemporary critics as passionate, loving and homoerotic. Frequently Walters saves Singleton's life through his kindness and love:

> However, it pleased God to make William the Quaker everything to me. Upon this occasion, I took him out one evening, as usual, and hurried him away into the fields with me, in more haste than ordinary; and there, in short, I told him the perplexity of my mind, and under what terrible temptations of the devil I had been; that I must shoot myself, for I could not support the weight and terror that was upon me.[25]

While there are women who are love interests in the text, it is these two men who truly wish to spend their lives together, and who are central to the story:

> William looked very affectionately upon me. 'Nay,' says he, 'we have embarked together so long, and come together so far, I am resolved I will never part with thee as long as I live, go where thou wilt, or stay where thou wilt.'[26]

The happy ending involves the two men giving up piracy and living a simple life together, with Captain Singleton dispassionately marrying William's sister, seemingly so as to be able to be closer to his companion.

'If you will agree to two or three things with me, I'll go home to England with all my heart.'

Says William, 'Let me know what they are.'

'Why, first,' says I, 'you shall not disclose yourself to any of your relations in England but your sister – no, not one; secondly, we will not shave off our mustachios or beards' (for we had all along worn our beards after the Grecian manner), 'nor leave off our long vests, that we may pass for Grecians and foreigners; thirdly, that we shall never speak English in public before anybody, your sister excepted; fourthly, that we will always live together and pass for brothers.'[27]

It is highly unlikely that anything approaching a queer reading would have been intended by Defoe. Indeed, we know from a publication of 1707 that Defoe had a passionate dislike for men who had sex with other men, writing:

It is hard to treat of a nauseous Subject, without some loathsom Expressions, but I shall take Care not to offend the Ears of the chastest Reader, and any one shall be able to read me without Blushes, tho' I think, we ought all to blush for the abominable Encrease of Vice in this Age.[28]

Yet his story of 'Pyrates' naturally includes a sentimental intimate relationship, which, while intended to be chaste and platonic, does not always read this way. Piracy and a seafaring life, both in their historical reality and their fantastical fiction, offer spaces in which the boundaries of masculine and feminine become blurred. Where women can become men, where men dress as women, where men love men, and where women who are men love women who are also men – the whole thing begins to resemble the lyrics of Blur's 'Girls & Boys'.

The sea is a true in-between space; even 'in the navy', officially under legal jurisdiction, there are 'sea laws' where chaotic, explicit and gender-bending activities can take place, and then be forgotten onshore. Where the crossing of the equator is associated with cross-dressing, naval attire makes for popular Tom of Finland gay pin-ups, and nineteenth-century

Crew of *USS Saratoga* dressed up for a
'Crossing the Line' ceremony

photographs at the National Maritime Museum show sailors in drag. It is
not necessarily a kind space, or a safe space, and the realities of piracy in
particular are far from the fairy tale, but both share a queer origin that is
hard to refute.

I'm Sorry, Dave

I n the film *2001: A Space Odyssey*, the 1968 adaptation directed by Stanley Kubrick of a science fiction novel by Arthur C. Clarke, the main antagonist is a spherical black machine with a single red glowing eye. This is HAL 9000, an artificial intelligence (AI) that runs all the major systems on a spaceship inhabited by an active human crew of just two men, but carrying a precious living cargo of people kept asleep in hibernation.

Over time HAL becomes a paranoid, controlling and homicidal force. He is the archetypical AI turned evil: cold, detached, logical, creepy and ultimately deranged. One of the things that makes HAL so terrifying is in fact the calm, subtly feminine voice he speaks with, emanating an infuriatingly paternal and passive-aggressive manner. While continuously lying to and misleading his living, breathing companions, he maintains a cool, softly spoken demeanour. Most famously he simply states: 'I'm sorry, Dave, I'm afraid I can't do that', as he refuses to follow Dave's order to open an airlock. Here the passive language and intimate use of the character's name seem to hide a clear sense of malice. A malice that eventually leads to the death of all but one crew member.

But what is HAL's real motivation? In the film, as far as we the audience know, HAL is simply malfunctioning, or has an element of paranoia accidentally put into his programming that leads him to respond with irrational hostility. In *2010: The Year We Make Contact*, the sequel to *2001: A Space Odyssey*, Arthur C. Clarke explored this further. He explains that HAL malfunctioned because of having to keep a secret from the crew. The AI was tasked with lying to his crew mates, keeping the existence of a mysterious alien artefact under wraps. This is believed to have led to an internal inconsistency in HAL's programming, one that the artificial intelligence couldn't handle. This lie would slowly result in the bizarre and murderous behaviour in the previous book and film. In a sense, HAL has been forced to keep a dark secret that eats him up inside, and it is his guilt that makes him act so strangely.

This complex motivation, and the claustrophobic intimacy of the second half of the film – which revolves around two male characters, the human astronaut David Bowman and HAL the synthetic being – has led many to see a dark homoerotic subtext in HAL's actions. HAL is an ever-present voyeur, watching everything, hidden but silently observing an all-male crew as they eat, sleep and exercise in tight, white gym shorts. If you take the early dialogue between Hal and David out of context, it could easily be seen as flirtatious. The following scene, for example, is filmed from the perspective of HAL, providing us with a single unblinking fish-eye view of a handsome young astronaut showing off his drawings. All the while HAL is flattering, bordering on obsequious, as he attempts to probe his human partner for information.

> HAL: Have you been doing some more work?
> David: A few sketches.
> HAL: May I see them?
> David: Sure.
> HAL: That's a very nice rendering, Dave, I think you've improved a great deal. Can you hold it a bit closer?
> David: Sure.
> HAL: That's Doctor Hunter isn't it?
> David: Mmmhmm.
> HAL: By the way do you mind if I ask you a personal question?
> David: No, not at all.
> HAL: Well, forgive me for being so inquisitive, but during the past few weeks, I've wondered whether you might be having some second thoughts about the mission . . . [1]

In a much later scene, when HAL is in the process of being shut down by David, after trying to kill him, and having already succeeded in killing the other crew mate, his calm, monotone plea for forgiveness sounds eerily like the apologies of an abusive, gaslighting ex-boyfriend:

'Look, Dave, I can see you're really upset about this. I honestly think you ought to sit down calmly, take a stress pill and think things over. I know I've made some very poor decisions recently.'

When director Kubrick was asked if HAL was gay, he flatly denied this subtext: 'No. I think it's become something of a parlour game for some people to read that kind of thing into everything they encounter. HAL was a "straight" computer.'[2]

Arthur C. Clarke believed the voice of HAL had a 'certain ambiguity' and gave a much more interesting and open-ended reply to the same question. When asked about HAL's sexuality, Clarke said: 'I can't confirm or deny your speculations. Who knows what goes on down in the subconscious?'[3] Also, prior to devising *2001: A Space Odyssey* with Kubrick, Clarke wrote a number of notes in his journal regarding initial ideas, including, '17 October: Stanley has invented the wild idea of slightly fag robots who create a Victorian environment to put our heroes at ease.'[4]

Clarke himself was evasive about his sexuality when asked by journalists, but many of his friends have spoken about his open identity as a gay man among friends. They say Clarke was simply afraid of how he would be treated. He was writing science fiction from the 1950s through to the early 2000s, a highly male-dominated arena. His close friend Michael Moorcock spoke about him fondly and openly in an article for the *Guardian* after Clarke's death: 'Everyone knew he was gay. In the 1950s I'd go out drinking with his boyfriend. We met his proteges, western and eastern, and their families: people who had only the most generous praise for his kindness. Self-absorbed he might be, and a teetotaller, but an impeccable gent through and through.'

In his writing, from which the cinematic version of *2001: Space Odyssey* shares its narrative, when introducing HAL 9000 Clarke directly references the work of another gay man:

> Turing had pointed out that, if one could carry out a prolonged conversation with a machine – whether by typewriter or microphones was immaterial – without being able to distinguish between its replies and those that a man might give, then the machine was thinking, by any sensible definition of the word. HAL could pass the Turing test with ease.[5]

PASSING THE TURING TEST

Here Arthur C. Clarke is referring to the mathematician, logician and cryptographer Alan Turing. Turing has become one of the best-known and most loved LGBTQ+ heroes in the UK, although that was not always the case. He is most famous for having an incredible mind and for his tireless work with many other men and women at the top-secret Second World War facility Bletchley Park. Here, using one of the earliest examples of a computational device, known as the bombe, coded German messages were intercepted and painstakingly decoded. The supposedly unsolvable 'Enigma' cypher, a complex letter substitution code that changed with every keystroke and was altered each day with a different input sequence, was cracked in secret, partly through the work and commitment of Alan Turing.

More recently the experiences of Turing as a gay man, a man who, after his incredible contribution to the British war effort, was persecuted and eventually sterilised because of his sexuality, has sadly also become part of his legacy. Today Alan Turing is probably perceived by most as an example of someone who never received the respect and admiration he deserved in life, simply because he was homosexual. His later suffering and suicide are often cited as an example of the historical mistreatment of all LGBTQ+ people.

Sadly, by becoming a symbol Turing has perhaps lost some of his humanity. Through retellings and film adaptations, he has, in many people's minds, become more of an *idea* of a person than an actual person. Through reading biographies, and particularly the words of his friends and family, we see a more rounded yet still remarkable human being. Softly spoken, deeply sensitive, sometimes socially awkward but passionate about the world around him, Turing saw patterns everywhere and was entranced by scientific developments and possible future applications for technology.

Turing's passion for cyphers and finding hidden meaning in things is twinned with his identity. As a young gay man he had a deep and clearly romantic affection for his friend Christopher Morcom. Their friendship was partly based around conversations about science and a shared fascination in exploring and learning about the natural world. A teenage Turing wrote extensively of his marvellous and talented friend, in awe of his intellect, skill and physical dexterity, and was always driven to seek his affection.

> Chris's work was always better than mine because I think he was very thorough. . . . He could sometimes see Venus in the day-time. Of course he was born with very good eyes, but still I think it is typical of him. . . One cannot help admiring such powers and I certainly wanted to be able to do that kind of thing myself. Chris always had a delightful pride in his performances and I think it was this that excited one's competitive instinct to do something which might fascinate him and which he might admire.[6]

Tragically, Morcom died at just eighteen of tuberculosis. Turing was devastated, but that first crush and the affection the two young men shared inspired him to push himself into academia. As Turing, the same age as Morcom, wrote in a letter to Christopher's mother:

> I feel sure that I shall meet Morcom again somewhere and that there will be some work for us to do together, as I believed there was for us to do here. Now that I am left to do it alone I must not let him down but put as much energy into it, if not as much interest, as if he were still here.[7]

While Alan Turing's work is often celebrated in the field of computing, beyond his work on Enigma his other contributions, for example to the world of artificial intelligence, robotics and even philosophy, can often go unrecognised. While the idea of a machine that could think, or at least simulate thinking, has existed for a long time, Alan Turing wrote about this in great depth, creating the foundation for all modern ideas around artificial intelligence.

In an interview with the BBC in 1951 he said:

> . . . it is not altogether unreasonable to describe digital computers as brains . . . For any one calculation the whole procedure that the machine is to go through is planned out in advance by a mathematician . . . I think it is probable for instance that at the end

of the century it will be possible to programme a machine to answer questions in such a way that it will be extremely difficult to guess whether the answers are being given by a man or by the machine.[8]

As referenced by Arthur C. Clarke, Turing developed the idea of a test that might be used to explore whether an artificial intelligence could fool or trick a human into thinking they were conversing with a fellow human. This test was known as 'The Imitation Game' by Turing, as it tested the ability of a computer to successfully imitate a human. This would require two unseen individuals chatting with each other. The goal was asking the flesh-and-blood participant whether they thought they were talking to a person or an AI. If on average people were convinced that an artificial 'chatbot' was human, then it could be seen as having passed the Turing test.

In the twenty-first century we come across the legacy of Turing's idea almost every day without even knowing it. When you log into social media on a new device you might be asked to enter a string of letters or spot images of traffic lights in photographs. This system is known as CAPTCHA, which stands for Completely Automated Public Turing test to tell Computers and Humans Apart. Turing's work inspired the systems which we use every day to ensure a computer knows that you are who you say you are.

Turing died in 1954, the inquest describing his death as suicide by cyanide poisoning. Some biographers have implied that his death, which was believed to be caused by a poisoned apple, had been staged to reflect a scene in Disney's *Snow White*, which he had supposedly taken a shine to. Turing had been receiving hormone 'treatment' after being accused of having a sexual relationship with a man; this destroyed his libido, as well as his physical appearance, self-confidence and mental health. The coroner stated coldly: 'I am forced to the conclusion that this was a deliberate act. In a man of his type, one never knows what his mental processes are going to do next.'[9] Very much a reflection of attitudes of the time towards homosexuality as a kind of mental illness.

All this is, of course, mere conjecture; whether or not Turing's death was truly intentional or accidental is still heavily disputed. The final fairy-tale twist is also compelling, but that doesn't make it true. Either way, it was a sad and tragic end to a fascinating, complex and nuanced man, the father of the modern computer.

When Arthur C. Clarke says that HAL would pass this test designed by Alan Turing, he is saying that HAL is so convincingly human that he can persuade strangers that they are talking to a real human being. Clarke, like Turing, is also part of the history of LGBTQ+ people exploring the significance and applications of an artificial mind; gay men fascinated by the idea of a sentient being created by man, one that might equal us, or even surpass us.

This has led to a tradition of robotic and AI entities in storytelling and fiction affecting traits and quirks most closely associated with queer men.

GALATEA'S LEGACY

As with aliens, pirates and the soon-to-be discussed superhero, robots have a much older pedigree than you might imagine and are a kind of folklore that blurs the lines between genuine and imagined realities. Artificial beings, created and imbued with life, exist in almost every world culture, and often form part of the origin and world myths of many peoples. In many stories people are sculpted or formed out of mud or clay, before being given the gift of life by a benevolent creator. Stories of humans building their own contraptions and things that live, or seem to simulate life, are just as old. Most of these are not robots in the strict twentieth-century sense; not all are made from metal and before the industrial revolution they don't use microchips, processors or electronics to simulate the human brain. Examples might include the 'golem', a creature from Jewish folklore built as a protector, and through a prayer or symbol given the semblance of life, although mostly lacking free will. In ancient Greece, Hephaestus, the god of blacksmiths and other related trades, created many artificial beings such as the Keledones, singing golden maidens, the Tauroi Khalkeoi, an animated bull made of bronze, and a set of three-legged automaton tripods which helped him work.

One particular story that reflects some of the themes and ideas explored even in today's robot stories is that of Galatea. Galatea was a creation of a mythical sculptor from Cyprus called Pygmalion. In the story, a white ivory sculpture of a woman was so perfect, so beautiful, that Pygmalion fell in love with her in preference to any other real, living woman. After making offerings to the goddess of love, Aphrodite, Galatea, named after the Greek word 'gala', meaning milk, for her flawless skin, comes to life.

This story is told by Ovid, but, as is common in Greek myths, there are multiple figures who share names. Galatea is the statue who comes to life, but she is also a Spartan woman who makes a pact with the gods to transform her daughter into a son, and a sea nymph who turns her dead lover into a river, a tale also recounted by Ovid. The one common feature among these disparate Galateas is that they are women connected to transformation: from stone to flesh, from flesh to river, and even across and between genders.

The story of Ovid's statue given life has inspired many other tales. *Pygmalion*, named after the mythological sculptor himself, is a play by George Bernard Shaw, later adapted into the classic 1964 film *My Fair Lady*. Both Shaw's play, the musical adaptation and the original myth explore ideas around creating, manipulating or cultivating a person into the shape of your own desires – an idea explored in much more gothic and grizzly depth by Mary Shelley.

An even more modern example of this appears in camp classic *The Rocky Horror Picture Show*, when the infamous 'transexual' alien Frank-N-Furter creates his ideal man using the brain of a previous lover, all packaged up in the form of a blonde beefcake he calls Rocky.[10]

In many fictional and fantastical depictions of mechanical beings or artificial constructs, the creation is an object of longing or loss. Classically the human protagonist might create another being to love, or to become, or achieve what they cannot, or to fill a void in their life: Geppetto creates Pinocchio as a substitute child, Dr Frankenstein creates a monster out of a desire for glory and immortality, and Pygmalion wants a lover as beautiful as Aphrodite herself. In these examples one is a living statue, one a wooden boy and one a creature made of human body parts, but all are arguably precursors to the modern robot story.

Robots are often a reflection of our own needs, particularly those we cannot fulfil. Needing, and wanting hopelessly, are associated with the queer experience, so it's unsurprising that LGBTQ+ artists, authors and audiences have seen something of themselves in the artificial creature. Also, because robots and their ilk are made by us, often in our own image, they can become a stand-in not only for unfulfilled desire and potential, but for our own narcissism.

In modern depictions of robots, AI and cyborgs, there is often an undercurrent of vanity, hubris and self-love that is expressed frequently through homoeroticism. In 1997 the musician Björk released a video for her song 'All Is Full of Love' depicting two intensely eroticised robotic versions of herself kissing and fondling each other. This allusion is nothing new; the artist falling in love with their own creation and therefore an aspect of themselves can be seen throughout time and across genres. These kinds of stories descend directly from myths and legends like that of Galatea, Oscar Wilde's *The Picture of Dorian Gray* and even Mary Shelley's *Frankenstein*.

FLESH GOLEMS

Written in 1818, Shelley's *Frankenstein; or, The Modern Prometheus* predates the origin of the word 'robot' – first used in 1912 in a play by Karel Čapek – by almost one hundred years. Superficially, Frankenstein's monster also does not resemble the classic image of a robot. He is not mechanical, he is not a machine, being made of flesh. Yet in every other sense the story is an archetype for all later robot stories: a creature given life, that questions its own purpose, that struggles to cope in a world it is placed into, and has conflict with its creator.

Frankenstein has been adapted so frequently, particularly in film and television, that the square-headed, green-skinned creature with bolts in his neck supplants the original description of Mary Shelley's creature:

> How can I describe my emotions at this catastrophe, or how delineate the wretch whom with such infinite pains and care I had endeavoured to form? His limbs were in proportion, and I had

selected his features as beautiful. Beautiful! Great God! His yellow skin scarcely covered the work of muscles and arteries beneath; his hair was of a lustrous black, and flowing; his teeth of a pearly whiteness; but these luxuriances only formed a more horrid contrast with his watery eyes, that seemed almost of the same colour as the dun-white sockets in which they were set, his shrivelled complexion and straight black lips.[11]

Dr Frankenstein's creation is all the more horrific because his intention was, in fact, to create something beautiful. He had chosen body parts that were attractive, and it is only when assembled and animated that the creature becomes monstrous in his eyes.

Rather than the lumbering, lantern-jawed comic-book monster he would later become, the original creature is far more complex and subtle in its horror, built from the doctor's vanity, hubris and desire to create a perfect and attractive being.

Shelley famously began this story the same night Lord Byron started writing the fragment that would be taken by Polidori and become 'The Vampyre'. Shelley, alongside the bohemian literary crowd she mixed with, was also romantically interested in men and women. After her husband Percy Bysshe died, she wrote to her friend Edward Trelawny about author and social reformer Caroline Norton:

I never saw a woman I thought so fascinating. Had I been a man I should certainly have fallen in love with her; as a woman, ten years ago, I should have been spellbound, and, had she taken the trouble, she might have wound me round her finger. Ten years ago I was so ready to give myself away, and being afraid of men, I was apt to get tousy-mousy for women; experience and suffering have altered all that. I am more wrapt up in myself, my own feelings, disasters, and prospects for Percy. I am now proof, as Hamlet says, both against man and woman.[12]

Tousy-mousy comes from 'tuzzy-muzzy', seventeenth-century slang for vagina, and so there is very little ambiguity as to what Mary is suggesting here! However she implies that she is currently too busy and, more importantly, too unhappy, following the death of her husband, to devote herself to any other man or woman.

The awkward flesh construct that is misunderstood, hated and feared has become a symbol for LGBTQ+ people, and the fact that it was created by a woman who also lived and loved outside societal norms, while fighting misogyny, heartbreak and loss, should not go unnoticed. While the creature in *Frankenstein* is a dangerous monster, it is not without pathos and is written with genuine warmth and humanity. Queer writers today have borrowed from Shelley's story to describe their own experiences, particularly those who find that their oppression and discrimination is rooted in their body and how it is perceived. Transgender author and historian Susan Stryker wrote a powerful call to action in response to Shelley's *Frankenstein*:

> Words like 'creature', 'monster', and 'unnatural' need to be reclaimed by the transgendered. . . Hearken unto me, fellow creatures. I who have dwelt in a form unmatched with my desire, I whose flesh has become an assemblage of incongruous anatomical parts, I who achieve the similitude of a natural body only through an unnatural process, I offer you this warning: the Nature you bedevil me with is a lie. Do not trust it to protect you from what I represent, for it is a fabrication that cloaks the groundlessness of the privilege you seek to maintain for yourself at my expense. You are as constructed as me; the same anarchic womb has birthed us both. I call upon you to investigate your nature as I have been compelled to confront mine. I challenge you to risk abjection and flourish as well as have I.[13]

Stryker is not the first to draw from this well. Frankenstein's fusion of flesh to create a new, strange being is eerily reminiscent of one of the origin stories used to explain gender nonconforming and intersex people in the classical world. The word 'hermaphrodite', a rather outdated dehumanising and medicalising term when used for intersex people today, historically described a person whose body did not fit the rigid sex binary. It comes from the fusion of the names of the masculine god Hermes and the feminine goddess Aphrodite. Sometimes Hermaphroditus, as they were known, was an individual, an icon or god in and of themselves.

The Nymph Salmacis and Hermaphroditus by
Michel de Marolles, 1655

One story for the origin of this mythic person who mixed the masculine and the feminine concerned a water nymph named Salmacis. Salmacis
fell in love with a young man, already called Hermaphroditus. Spying
him near her sacred spring, she grabbed hold of him and pulled him into
the water, begging the gods to allow them to be together forever. The gods
granted her wish but, with a twist, they mixed Salmacis and Hermaphroditus, turning them into a single intersex person. This new person, the
intersex Hermaphroditus, seemingly happy with their new form, asked
for the river to grant other people the same wish, to blend future bathers'
sexes, although in some accounts this is a curse by the fused person,
angered at what had been done to them. Either way, the waters of Salmacis were thereafter known for this gender-bending property.

Constructed beings of flesh and bone may not be the mainstay of robot
stories today, but they chart a throughline that connects clearly with stories by and about LGBT people, arguably for thousands of years.

THE UNCANNY VALLEY

Robotic beings unnerve others, either because they attempt to be a facsimile of real humans, but fail, or they are wholly alien in design, other than their minds and voices. This roughly relates to a concept coined in the twentieth century, known as the 'uncanny valley'. The idea is that, as we attempt to accurately replicate humans through technology, both physically and psychologically, we tend to be accepting of depictions that are cute but clearly inhuman, and those that pass as humans flawlessly. In between is this so-called 'valley', where faces, features, movements and behaviours seem to come close to humanlike traits, but still fall short. They become uncanny and creepy.

In 1912 Selma Lagerlöf wrote a poem entitled 'Slåtterkarlarna på Ekolsund', which translates as 'The Reapers of Ekolsund'. The poem describes a horde of robotic wooden workers that are created by a fictionalised version of the inventor Christopher Polhem. They are made to farm and till the fields in Sweden. When first seen, the artificial constructs are monstrous and frightening:

> Is this the human race? Fighting back his astonishment,
> he looks out again and then sees in wonder
> that each man is made of pine trunks.
> He doesn't want to believe his eyes. They walk, the ground shakes,
> but with every step you hear how hard the wood cracks.
> Without the help of eyes they reach the goal of their journey,
> quite roughly they are drawn with head, arms, torso,
> not the slightest trace of art, but perhaps precisely because
> it seems more horrible, that the dead are moving.[14]

Selma is exploring this 'uncanny valley' property of non-human humanoid things way back in the early twentieth century. Their visual horror is foreshadowing. Eventually the fields are no longer tended by human farmers, and even the creator loses control over his own mechanised minions. They become a dangerous and unstoppable force, where the word 'reaper' takes on a sinister double meaning.

This poem appears in a larger collection of stories written by Lagerlöf called *Troll och Människor*, meaning 'Trolls and Humans'. It includes a famous tale, 'Bortbytingen', translated into English as 'The Changeling', where a woman is presented with a troll baby whom she must care for in place of her real child. Lagerlöf's story of robots appears among these as another kind of reimagined folk tale.

Lagerlöf is clearly writing critically of the world around her. Namely, the mechanised workforce and impact of industrialisation on agricultural livelihood and families. 'The Reapers of Ekolsund' is still one of the earliest examples of a mechanised robot slave turning on its master, a narrative trope that has since become incredibly well traversed, as can be seen in this chapter's introduction.

Selma Lagerlöf herself was a teacher and writer who spent much of her life in a partnership with Sophie Elkan. The two women writers had a tempestuous but passionate relationship and a love for folklore, history and theology. The creepy robot farmers were a product of Selma's incredible imagination, her critique of society and her pleasure in writing about uncanny 'copycat' beings. This desire to explore what makes a person feel real and human, as explored by a queer woman, has helped frame the narrative of robots even today.

The strangeness of artificial intelligences is still one of the things that attracts queer people to them. For example, in terms of gender and sex, robots in their 'uncanniness' create fascinating reflections of our own attitudes. In the introduction to her *Robots: Fact, Fiction, Prediction*, Jasia Reichardt ponders on whether robots will one day acquire civil rights and become equal to humans. In the same paragraph, and connected to this, she talks about the perceived gender of robots as discussed by a group of children at a school in London: 'The boys agreed that a robot is definitely "it"; the girls said that a robot is "he"; and a few thought that some robots might be "she", if "she" serves a man.'[15]

Does a robot have gender? Does it have sexuality? Queer audiences are notably fascinated by these beings, partly because of the strange ambiguity they have and the opportunity for playful subversion. The 2022 horror comedy film *M3GAN*, directed by Gerard Johnstone, has become a viral sensation particularly with LGBTQ+ audiences. The creepy robotic doll, who becomes found family for a young orphaned child, prances and skips her way through one bloody massacre after another.

Despite being a creature designed to play directly into the uncanny valley of creepiness, with M3GAN's face almost, but not quite, passing for human, she has become a queer icon. In British men's magazine *GQ* Jack King sardonically writes:

> Sure, it might be that *M3GAN* resonates with us gays on a deeper subconscious level, reflecting the anxieties around familial aban-donment that unfortunately affect a disproportionate number of the LGBTQ+ population. Maybe she's the maternal figure we all yearn for – we're all Cady, desperate for the embrace of a woman who yasses and slays her way to success, as we all so clearly desire.
>
> Or, you know, she's just kinda serving. Her reference points, like most dangerously online gays who spend hours of screen time scouring the Twitter timeline, are empowering pop ballads, not least Sia's 'Titanium', delivered here in the form of a camp lullaby. She reads bitches for filth, then kills them. She rhythmically con-torts herself like many a twink in Heaven on a Friday night. There's the all-too-familiar sense of whimsical tragedy, like Norma Des-mond in *Sunset Boulevard* – a cultural artefact long upheld by gay men who like to imagine themselves in the limelight.[16]

In a less murderous and frightening form we also have the cute come-dic duo of C3PO and R2D2 from the *Star Wars* franchise. One is an anthropomorphic golden humanoid, the other a cute beeping trash can on wheels. They are designs that navigate the uncanny/cute spectrum with care, both being perceived unanimously as lovable. Neither really attempts to pass as convincing humans in looks or behaviour, and there-fore don't trigger the disgust response.

The voice of C3PO in particular, as portrayed by the actor Anthony Daniels, is partly the reason for the character's heartfelt popularity. The robot has a kind of camp, posh, British butler affectation that, at least in the original franchise, contrasts with the otherwise stoic heterosexual and generally all-American human cast.

DARLING SWEETHEART

As well as virtual people, beings and constructs – for example both real and fictional robots, as well as AI's ever deepening influence on society – we also now live in partly virtual worlds populated with virtual characters. Videogames are part of this, and are arguably one of the newest human art forms; many thousands of years younger than paintings, dance, music and even a century younger than the relative latecomers of film and photography.

Just as with every other artistic medium, or form of human expression, videogames tell stories, and those stories are reflective of the people who create them and play them. In all honesty a history of queer videogames is a book in itself. (Hold that thought!)

The history of gaming, as with any other kind of history, has always involved queer people. Born in 1916, Christopher Strachey was an early computer scientist and one of the leading pioneers in computer language. Despite being a scientist, Strachey was also an artist and a poet at heart. As well as developing computer programming, he used computers to produce some of the very first digital art; creating, for example, a self-portrait out of letters and symbols, which is currently in the collection of Oxford's Bodleian Library. Strachey also created a programme that would generate humanlike text, some of the earliest experimentations in language learning models. In 1954 in an article entitled 'The "Thinking" Machine' Strachey published two AI-generated love letters written through his programme. One of them reads:

> Darling Sweetheart,
>   You are my avid fellow tiding. My affection curiously clings to your passionate wish. My liking yearns for your heart. You are my wistful sympathy: My tender liking.
>   Yours beautifully,
>   M.U.C.[17]

Back in 1952, Strachey used a system originally based on Alan Turing's own designs for an Automatic Computing Engine, to model a game of draughts. Arguably, this simple digital reproduction of a popular physical boardgame was the true first videogame.

Strachey was also a gay man, who struggled with his sexuality. His close friends and family were aware that he suffered from severe depression and unhappiness through his attraction to other men, and fear of how society might perceive that. The fact that Strachey created a system that generated surreal, forlorn and gender-ambiguous love letters makes it feel all the more meaningful.

It is beautiful, and worthy of celebration, that videogames themselves were arguably birthed by a gay man, created on hardware developed by another gay man. The two men, Alan Turing and Christopher Strachey, knew each other casually. In fact they had attended the same college at Cambridge and Christopher's father had been at Bletchley Park with Turing. But they were not close acquaintances, despite Turing being the assistant director of the computer laboratory where Christopher Strachey studied and offering him some guidance on his projects. Yet in their work, creating entirely new fields of technology, there was a kind of intellectual intimacy that the two may well have never been fully aware of in life. Both gay men built upon each other's achievements and creations, in pursuit of similar passions.

But if we take the story of computer science, games and AI even further back, before Turing's work, and to the very earliest example of what we might call a computing device, there is still a decidedly queer slant to the story. Charles Babbage, who is often described as being the mind behind the very first computer, was in fact working in a partnership with Ada Lovelace, whom some have described as one of the first computer programmers. Ada was born in the early 1800s, and while as far as we know Ada was cisgender and heterosexual, her life was defined by queerness. Ada's father was none other than Lord Byron, whose loves and actions were seen as dangerous, dark and transgressive, as we saw earlier. Because of her parentage Ada was raised by her mother to avoid poetry, arts and bohemian vices out of the fear that it might awaken something of her father's nature.

It is never officially stated, but as well as his stormy temperament and questionable character, it was also Byron's romantic nature and rampant bisexuality that was deemed a kind of family curse. Therefore Ada's skill at mathematics, her interest in Babbage's work, might be traced back to her unique upbringing; one that attempted to keep her from the arts and associated 'queer' behaviours. Despite her mother's attempts, Ada was known to also have a complex and tempestuous character, and her close working relationship with Charles Babbage was not necessarily deemed normal or ladylike for a woman in her position.

GAYME OVER

Obviously the history of robotics and AI in fiction and reality involves far more people whose lives were not directed and influenced by queerness than otherwise. But it is clear to me that there is a vast overrepresentation of people like us at important moments of creation and confluence in robotics, interactive technologies and AI, not to mention the science fiction and storytelling that surrounds it. Some of the most famous depictions of robots, the stories that inspired later tropes, and the minds behind the research that mixed virtual with reality, were people who were queer, or who today might have defined as LGBTQ+.

As with other chapters, there is an obvious connection between otherness and robotic or non-human intelligences. But specifically here I also think there is a kind of longing expressed in all these individual stories; people who, like Shelley's Dr Frankenstein, want to create something new, a new construct or a new technology, perhaps in response to their own sense of loss or strangeness.

Perhaps there is also a desire to be able to work quietly, privately, with a machine or system that does not judge you; writing love letters, sharing secrets and being protected by a kind of self-constructed guardian for company. A computer screen, a cyborg, real or imagined, can play this role as a safe partner. As expressed in Bonnie Ruberg's *Videogames Have Always Been Queer*, there is perhaps also a safe homosociality that can take place in front of a screen, over a piece of research or in a videogame world: 'By insisting on a physical closeness between game and player, the original Pong arcade cabinet enacts an alternative and arguably homoerotic understanding about what it means to stand in relation to a videogame.'

From personal experience, similarly to Turing, some of my earliest flirtations with forming relationships with other boys were through shared nerdy interests and hyperfixations. Playing games together and reading and talking about science were ways to be close to other boys without triggering any 'homo' alarms. As a nerdy queer young person, these can be safe spaces for a kind of physical and social intimacy: coding together, talking about robots, devising science-fiction fantasies, or shooting each other in *Goldeneye 64*! None of this is unique to a queer person's life, but it should be obvious why such settings would be powerful for those seeking connection with others but afraid to express their feelings fully.

That's not to say robots are solely a creation of sad queer artists and scientists, but more that these stories, science fiction and science fact, often benefit from an outsider's perspective. Someone who sits a little on the sidelines, who can dissect what it is to not feel quite human, to feel like your body is strange or different. Such a person might be better placed to imagine breathing life into inhuman things, or conceiving an AI that could convince another person. You may be more sensitive to all the subtle nuances of behaviour that can give you away, when you are yourself different. Knowing how to pass, how to keep a secret and convince others you are normal, might be the exact tool set and experience that would draw someone to the idea of constructed or designed entities.

Ex-Men

As with the other subjects in this section of the book, superheroes may not at first seem to be folkloric figures. That might be because we are currently so close to them in time that it's difficult to dissect them and reflect on them the same way we would an ancient Greek legend. That said, these are fictional entities, with rule sets, a complex overlapping mythos, drawn from historic and mythological sources, and used as ways to reflect and explain real-world experiences. In this sense superheroes match every required standard to class them as folklore that I can think of. Indeed, the young creators of arguably the very first superhero, Orgon Bat, were themselves inspired by much older Japanese mythology and folklore, which they had seen in Tokyo's Ueno Royal Museum.[1] The superhero is merely a modern retooling of a much older trope of storytelling, surrounding super-powered legendary heroes; this trope goes further back thousands of years.

Today there are many conversations about the superhero franchise, its growing and seemingly limitless popularity and its impact on culture and society. One of the conversations that has been particularly prominent over the past two decades concerns inclusion and representation. While most superhero films are knowingly about escapism from reality, there has been a push for including themes and identities that reflect their broad real-world fanbase. With every inclusion of a female character, a person of colour, or deviation from original source material in aid of less problematic storytelling, there is a small but vocal pushback. The 'culture war' is in fact writ particularly large in superhero fandoms, partly due to the cultural prominence and corporate clout of these franchises and their many spin-offs. Also, while superheroes are now seemingly popular with 'everyone', there is still a sense of ownership around particular groups of hardcore fans who see superheroes as their own intrinsically white, masculine and hetero-sexual icons. In particular, the inclusion of queer characters in superhero media, while still in its infancy, has caused outrage and anger among these groups.

In 2022 John Stossel wrote an article for the Daily Signal, a staunchly con-servative news outlet, entitled 'Comic Book Fans Shun Superheroes' Woke Makeovers', in which he outlined with derision the inclusion of bisexual and queer characters among major superhero franchises such as *Batman* and *Superman*. Also in 2022, Paul Hair, a writer for Bounding Into Comics, a comic-book-enthusiast website with a similarly conservative agenda, responded to Marvel's release of a comic based around transgender teenagers with: 'The woke company can always find new ways to go even farther. The only question is, what new depths of awfulness will it sink to next?'

Even among less overtly anti-LGBT fans, you can still come upon a certain level of background hostility against the introduction of LGBTQ+ characters into the comic and superhero arena. This is often described using language such as 'shoehorning', being 'unnecessary', or 'pandering' to a perceived liberal agenda.

While a valid argument can actually be made around big companies using queer identities to promote themselves as 'edgy' or 'socially con-scious' as a shallow marketing ploy, it feels that the majority of the backlash is not about this. Rather, the implication is that LGBTQ+ people simply don't belong in stories of orphaned alien heroes that can fly, bench-press cars and shoot lasers from their eyes.

LOVE HIM AS A WIFE

The Epic of Gilgamesh dates back an incredible 4,000 years, to around 2100 BCE. The British Museum contains a fragment of the story, carved in cuneiform on a tablet dating to 700 BCE, so old that it was originally believed to be a recording of the great biblical flood.[2]

The story is written in the form of a fragmented epic poem, full of areas where the engraved text is hard to read, translations are disputed, or whole chunks are simply missing. Bracketed text is often used by translators to approximate what they believe was intended and fill in the gaps with their own interpretations. The poem describes the highly mythologised adventures of the demigod king of Uruk, named Gilgamesh. Gilgamesh is a proud but cruel leader who exhausts and terrorises his kingdom, insisting that every woman who marries a man must sleep with him first. At first the main feature of this 'hero' is his physical impressiveness and beauty:

> It was the Lady of the Gods drew the form of his figure,
> While his build was perfected by divine Nudimmud,
> [Powerful of] body, majestic of [beauty],
> [He was large] of stature, eleven cubits [tall]
>
> His cheeks were bearded, dark as [gleaming] lapis lazuli,
> The locks of his hair grew thickly [as barley]
> When he grew tall his beauty was consummate,
> Most handsome was he by the standards of men.[3]

We are told repeatedly that this giant of a man, sixteen feet tall if we are to believe the description, is defined by his attractiveness and masculinity. Other than this he is petulant, vain, cruel and stubborn. Early in the story, the pleas of the people of his kingdom, for the young king to calm his temper and curb his voracious desires, are finally heard by the goddess Aruru. She conspires to cool the demigod's temper and correct his wicked ways. She does this by creating a companion for him, crafting the ideal 'other' to balance Gilgamesh, to distract him and teach him the error of his ways. She therefore creates Enkidu, saying:

> Let him be a match for the storm of his heart.

Like Gilgamesh, Enkidu is a mountain of a man, but unlike the trim, handsome demigod, Enkidu is wild, part-animal, both hyper-masculine and feminine and in tune with the natural world and beasts:

> All his body is matted with hair,
> He bears long tresses like those of a woman:
> The locks of his hair grow thickly as barley,
> He knows not a people, not even a country.

Coated in hair like the god of the animals,
With the gazelle he grazes on grasses,
Joining the throng with her at the water-hole,
His heart delighting with the beasts in the water.

After Enkidu is created, and tempted away from the wilderness by a
female sex worker, he is told of the demigod king. Meanwhile, in his chambers Gilgamesh receives prophetic dreams of his newly born consort, dreams
that are tinged with passion and love. When Enkidu and Gilgamesh finally
meet for the first time, they wrestle, and the king is surprised finally to find
his match in strength and virility:

Gilgamesh and Enkidu took hold of each other, backs bent like a bull
They smashed the door-jam, the wall did shake.

The fight is quickly over and Enkidu and Gilgamesh instantly connect
with each other. This passage, from what is known as the Yale tablet, or
'Gilgamesh Y', is, sadly, missing much text; one can only infer the connotations of the two men's first meeting:

They took hold of each other and . . .
They [linked] their hands like . . .
Gilgamesh . . .

They kissed each other and formed a friendship.

The rest of this part of the epic tracks the adventures of Gilgamesh
and Enkidu, who travel the world to hunt and kill the evil Humbaba,
who is a kind of ogre or demonic spirit of the forest. The two men
share a bed, share their lives and their experiences, becoming ever
closer and closer. But there is no happy ending: after being defeated
and killed, the evil demon Humbaba lets loose a terrible curse, that
Gilgamesh shall lose his companion forever, but be doomed to live to
experience the loss.

Soon after, Gilgamesh offends the goddess Ishtar by refusing her
advances, and this curse does indeed come to pass. Enkidu dies and

A basalt carving depicting Gilgamesh and
Enkido fighting Humbaba

Gilgamesh is devastated. An entire passage of the epic poem is devoted
to Gilgamesh's mourning for Enkidu, where he falls to madness, again
tearing his clothes and hair:

> I shall weep for Enkidu, my friend,
> Like a hired mourner-woman I shall bitterly wail
>
> The axe at my side, in which my arm trusted,
> The sword at my belt, the shield at my face,
> My festive garment, my girdle of delight:
> A wicked wind rose up and robbed me.

On burying Enkidu, Gilgamesh refuses to leave his side, even as his
corpse begins to decompose. This entire experience, finding, loving and
losing his Enkidu, is the spur for the rest of the story. Gilgamesh, heartbroken and alone, goes to the underworld, seeking knowledge about
death and the meaning of his existence without his companion. There he
comes across many strange beings, spirits and gods, including two fearsome scorpion-men, who are each other's mate, being depicted in carvings

with matching erect penises. These two men warn Gilgamesh of the dangers ahead, but let him pass when they realise he is not mortal and that he is so driven by loss:

> The scorpion-man called to his mate:
> 'He who has come to us, flesh of the gods is his body.'

> The scorpion-man's mate answered him:
> 'Two-thirds of him is god, but one third human.'

The Epic of Gilgamesh is an ancient story of a great but morally flawed hero that predates other famous classical heroes such as Hercules, the Hindu story of Rama and Sita from the *Ramayama*, and Beowulf. Yet the seeds of this narrative of a man with god-like strength, who must go on a dangerous journey of self-discovery, is argued to have been codified here. Many think this story, and the many permutations it inspired, were the groundwork for much of later classical writings, from the biblical flood to the epic poems of Homer, including *The Iliad* and *The Odyssey*.

Arguably, Gilgamesh, a man of incredible strength who slowly learns to control and temper his powers, is the very first superhero. He was notably a character who loved women, who enjoyed having relationships with them, but whose central and most powerful and intimate relationship was with another man. The words used to describe Gilgamesh and Enkidu as a partnership include words frequently translated in English as 'friend' and 'brother', but they also include the idea of loving as a wife, sharing their bed, and kissing and embracing each other. The Mesopotamian storytellers who created this epic poem would not have had a concept of bisexuality, or homosexuality, that would match these terms today; but clearly their understanding of a great masculine hero had room for same-sex love as well. The two concepts were seemingly not at odds with each other; indeed, in some ways Gilgamesh is all the more manly because of his love for another man who is his equal in strength and power.

ACHILLES HEEL

The idea of strength and virility among male heroes being associated with rigid, performative heterosexuality is a relatively modern one. In the classical world, a time long before either the concepts of homosexuality or heterosexuality existed, or at least not in the same form as today, this was not the case. In classical Greek and Roman society men sleeping with other men could be acceptable, even celebrated, in particular circumstances. To paint with incredibly broad brushstrokes, an older man sleeping with a younger man, as well as having a wife and children, was relatively common in ancient Greece. The younger man (sometimes called the 'eromenos', or little lover) supposedly benefited from a teacher and a wealthy benefactor who might boost their career or social standing. The older man (sometimes called the 'erastes') was supposedly gaining the companionship of a young attractive lover and squire. The beauty of young men, alongside young women, was considered sacred in ancient Greece, powerful and worthy of respect, even by the gods themselves.

Obviously the age dynamic of these same-sex pairings are by today's standards questionable, if not entirely objectionable. We are often talking about what we would consider teenage boys and children today. Even when the younger man was a consenting adult by modern standards, there is still a question of power here: how much agency would the younger partner have in such a relationship? Yet, equitable love of one man for another was also not inherently wrong or deviant, at least among the academic, political and military classes of much of classical Europe.

These kinds of relationships are reflected in the myths and legends told and retold by the Greeks and Romans; there are, of course, many beautiful women who men go to war over, but there are also beautiful men who inspire similar lust, passion and violence in the very same heroes.

The most commonly told story is probably that of the hero Achilles and his lover Patroclus. Achilles, known for being dipped in the River Styx by his mother as a baby, thus gaining divine invulnerability except for a weak spot on his heel (by which his mother held him), was every bit the ancient Greek superman. After being hidden away and raised as a girl during his youth, at fourteen he is made to choose between two futures: one is a long but unremarkable life, but, as described in Stephen Fry's retelling:

> The other life is a blaze of glory such as the world has not seen. A life of heroism, valour, and achievement that outshines Hercules, Theseus, Jason, Atalanta, Bellerophon, Perseus . . . every hero that ever lived. Eternal fame and honour. A life sung by poets and bards for eternity. But a short life Peleus, so short . . . [4]

Unsurprisingly, Achilles chooses the life of fame and heroism.

In the epic poem *The Iliad*, written around 800 BCE, Homer describes Achilles' role in the final years of the Trojan War. It is here that we are introduced to Patroclus, Achilles' companion and confidant, the pair having been friends since childhood. Dares of Phyrgia, in what was claimed to be a first-hand account of Troy, describes the young warrior very favourably: 'Patroclus was handsome and powerfully built. His eyes were grey. He was modest, dependable, wise, a man richly endowed.'[5]

Patroclus was well loved for his beauty and virtue. He also had a fondness for animals, particularly horses, and the scholar Ptolemaeus Chennus, writing during the Roman Empire, claims that Patroclus's horse-whisperer status was down to one particular god's affection for him: 'Homer calls Patroclus the first horseman because he learned from Poseidon, who loved him, the art of riding horses.'[6]

Over the past few hundred years, mainstream historians and writers have often described Achilles and Patroclus simply as 'close friends' or 'brothers in arms', entirely platonic in their relationship. This assertion is frequently stated as fact, without room for any other interpretation, despite what is, for many, clearly a romantic partnership.

In the film adaptation *Troy*, made in 2004, where many liberties were taken with the original writings of Homer, one particularly jarring alteration was making Patroclus a teenager, and the much younger cousin of an adult Achilles, played by Brad Pitt. Ultimately this made their relationship familial, paternal and entirely asexual.

While it is true that in Homer's writings there is no direct reference to sexual intercourse between the two men, there is for many readers a clear depth of emotion that seems to go beyond mere friendship. Also, the two young men are about the same age, and definitely not related by blood. This is important when thinking critically about their partnership, as the strength of the relationship between these two is the driving force behind much of the story of Homer's *Iliad*.

The epic even opens with:

> Sing, O goddess, the anger of Achilles.[7]

This refers to Achilles' rage after losing Patroclus. As with Gilgamesh and Enkidu, written a thousand years earlier, it is the death of his beloved Patroclus, and resulting despair, that becomes the key instigator for the later part of this tragic story. Patroclus is killed in battle by Hector, and on discovering this, Achilles responds with both heartache and a lust for vengeance of epic and bloody proportions:

> A dark cloud of grief fell upon Achilles as he listened. He filled both hands with dust from off the ground, and poured it over his head, disfiguring his comely face, and letting the refuse settle over his shirt so fair and new. He flung himself down all huge and hugely at full length, and tore his hair with his hands.

Achilles professes that Patroclus is the one person he cared about in the world, and so determines to avenge him, even at the cost of his own life. At the end of the Trojan War, both men are dead. In Homer's *Odyssey*, being cremated the ashes of Achilles and Patroclus are mixed together in a symbolic ceremony.

The nature of this love has not just been called into question by contemporary scholars, or queer historians. The playwright Aeschylus wrote his own interpretation of the Trojan War, based on Homer's writings. Little survives today except for a few fragments, which include a scene where Achilles grieves beside the corpse of Patroclus and, addressing his dead lover, describes the many kisses he would like to exchange with him: 'No reverence hadst thou for the unsullied holiness of thy limbs, oh thou most ungrateful for my many kisses!'[8]

A little later in Plato's *Symposium*, it is shown that both Aeschylus and Plato's characterisation of the Athenian aristocrat Phaedrus agreed that the two men were indeed romantic lovers – although they do seem to be in disagreement as to which of the two were the 'beardless', more beautiful passive lover, or the mature 'bearded' active lover: By today's standards Phaedrus is arguing against Aeschylus's interpretation of who is the top and who is the bottom:

> Aeschylus talks nonsense when he says that it was Achilles who was in love with Patroclus; for he excelled in beauty not Patroclus alone, but assuredly all the other heroes, being still beardless and, moreover, much the younger, by Homer's account.

In terms of the resurgence of this interpretation, even Shakespeare had something to say of the two. In his 1602 play set in Troy, *Troilus and Cressida*, the hero Ulysses comments mockingly on the intimacy between Achilles and Patroclus:

> The great Achilles, whom opinion crowns
> The sinew and the forehand of our host,
> Having his ear full of his airy fame,
> Grows dainty of his worth, and in his tent
> Lies mocking our designs: with him Patroclus
> Upon a lazy bed the livelong day.[9]

Later on, since the nineteenth century at least, queer men have recognised themselves in Achilles, and early ideas of homosexuality were created using Greek myths and legends as a framework, before the identity was understood or described as it is today.

John Addington Symonds, previously mentioned for his dalliances with angels, wrote *A Problem in Greek Ethics* (subtitled: *Being an inquiry into the phenomenon of sexual inversion, addressed especially to medical psychologists and jurists*) back in 1873. Symonds uses the relationship between Achilles and Patroclus as the centrepiece for his own philosophical and personal self-exploration. It is clear that he thinks there is something empowering for queer men in ancient Greek literature:

> For the student of sexual inversion, ancient Greece offers a wide
> field for observation and reflection. Its importance has hitherto
> been underrated by medical and legal writers on the subject, who
> do not seem to be aware that here alone in history have we the
> example of a great and highly-developed race not only tolerating
> homosexual passions, but deeming them of spiritual value, and
> attempting to utilise them for the benefit of society.[10]

Symonds, a gay man of the nineteenth century, seems to be trying to
argue that there were two kinds of homosexual relationships in classical
Greece, good and bad: the heroic form, which was to be celebrated, and
the darker, unpleasant kind, which he describes as 'the vice of boy-love',
meaning pederastic relationships with underage boys.

A passionate, if biased scholar of Greek mythology and philosophy,
Symonds argued that the relationship between Achilles and Patroclus
was the former type of love, a perfect, noble and equitable love between
men, something he clearly wished to elevate, and replicate in his own
life. The love of Achilles and Patroclus is used by Symonds to show that,
despite the prejudices of the times in which he was writing, love between
men could be beautiful, mutual and equitable, not just predatory and
perverted. This 'heroic' love, he believed, could be impossible to reach,
but aspirational nonetheless.

> We are justified in describing [the love between Patroclus and Achil-
> les] as heroic, and in regarding [this love] as one of the highest
> products of their emotional life. It will be seen, when we come to
> deal with the historical manifestations of this passion, that the heroic
> love which took its name from Homer's Achilles is an ideal rather
> than an actual reality.[11]

Achilles was not just an inspiration for gay men, he is also an archetypal hero. In many ways his story connects directly with modern
superheroes. He is a man with superstrength, superior to regular mortals.
He has one special weakness, the equivalent to Superman's Kryptonite,
the only way he can be defeated. Achilles must go on an epic quest, and
wrestle with morality and how best to use his superpowers. Finally, as

with heroes like Batman and Spider-Man, he loses his love and his state as an unquestionable hero becomes decidedly grey and hard to pin down, based on the decisions he makes while in emotional anguish. Achilles flips between superhero and supervillain at certain stages in *The Iliad*, particularly after his loss of Patroclus.

Today a heroic main character loving another man might be seen as woke pandering, an awkward attempt by a studio to inject progressive politics into their writing, but it is arguably at the heart of what male heroes were. Masculinity has changed and evolved over time; it is no more static than anything else. The incredible warrior Spartans, for example, appear in cinema as heavily muscled super-heterosexuals, but in fact included a group of fighters made up of male couples. The Sacred Band of Thebes used the idea that men forced to fight side by side with their lovers would fight harder and longer. The same-sex love of these men in no way devalued their fighting prowess, or called into question their masculinity; in fact, it bolstered it.

Hercules, for example, the very embodiment of masculine heroism, was known for his many relationships with beautiful women, but we often miss out the parts where male lovers are mentioned. Abderus, Admetos, Adonis, Elacatas, Hylas, Ioleus, Iphitos, Jason, Nireus and Corythus have all been described as male lovers or paramours of the epic hero.

Obviously all these stories are incredibly flattering to gay men, particularly in times when there was no other language or framework in which to describe themselves. The idea of using classical heroes and elite fighters must have seemed like such a pleasant antidote to stereotypes of the effeminate and weak 'sodomite'. Yet the needle can swing too far. It can lead to an image of male homosexuality that requires classical ideals, that encourages its own type of rigid masculinity and aesthetics. It is very 'white', very gendered and in that sense exclusionary. Also it can lead to the erasure of women in the lives of these mythical men; Achilles was also deeply in love with his enslaved lover Briseis, and the instigation for the Trojan War was one man's love for a beautiful woman, Helen.

Others also argue that pushing for confirmation of homosexual desire can erase meaningful and powerful non-romantic love between men, or devalue the beauty of platonic male friendships. I stand somewhere in the middle. I think celebrating the bisexual polyamory of epic heroes is in keeping with everything else we know of the times during which they were written. Also, while I take the point that non-romantic affection is both important and valuable, I have to say that I have never heard this argument being levied at a classical heterosexual pairing: maybe Antony and Cleopatra were just good friends?

As described in the book *Bad Gays*, there has been a desire to construct a kind of masculinity that is epic, mythic and hypermasculine which can lead to dark places, although it cannot be denied that the original superheroes were, at the very least, far from heterosexual.

VIGOROUS MAIDENS

Heroes, both super and classical, have often favoured masculine-presenting characters in the patriarchal societies that created them, with women sadly treated as merely a reward for defeating the bad guy, yet there are still stories that describe superpowered women. The popularity of women in the role of 'superhero' has been growing in film and television over the past hundred years, and despite a backlash at representations of female heroes from a small but vocal group, their history is as ancient as Hercules, Achilles and Gilgamesh.

The Amazons of ancient Greek mythology were a mythological all-female society, ruled by a queen and well equipped in warfare. In some stories the Amazons would remove one of their breasts to make drawing a bow easier. While the Amazons almost certainly did not exist, historians today believe the Greeks constructed this story based on other groups of people they came across – most notably the Scythians. The Scythians were horseback warriors, and from their burials there is evidence that the women as well as the men were fierce fighters: 'Among the nomad horse-riding people of the steppes known to the Greeks as "Scythians", women lived the same rugged outdoor life as the men.'[12]

They also had among them a revered caste of people known as the 'enaree', priests, magicians and soothsayers who were assigned male at birth and then castrated so as to worship the androgynous sex-changing goddess Artimpasa. The image of the foreign warrior woman on horse-back, side by side with those who transgressed male and female binaries, may have ingrained itself in the Greek psyche and given birth to the myth of the Amazons.

The Amazons were not written about as explicitly queer, or same-sex-attracted. One major story was that while Amazons would shun men from their society, they would actively seek male lovers outside their tribe with whom to have children, and return with any female offspring, leaving males to be raised elsewhere. Yet this is not exclusively the case – at least three named Amazonian women were described as exclusively asexual. Also a single glass vessel, an alabastron from 525–500 BCE, depicts a Thracian woman in a loincloth dressed as a Maenad and labelled as 'Thra-ichme' courting an Amazonian queen called Penthesilea, by gifting her a rabbit, a well-known love token.[13]

The Amazon has become a very powerful symbol for queer women. In 1932 the poet Marina Tsvetaeva wrote a letter to fellow lesbian writer Natalie Clifford Barney, entitled 'Letter to an Amazon', talking about same-sex desire and heartbreak over other women. She wrote: 'Don't be upset with me. I am responding to the Amazon, not to the pale feminine image that wants nothing from me.'[14]

***

The Minoans occupied the island of Crete from 3500 BCE until 1100 BCE, predating the ancient Greek civilisation as we know it. On excavating archaeological sites around Crete, one surprising element for early twentieth-century historians was the prominence and reverence seemingly given to women in their artworks. Women were depicted on thrones, and often were larger and more prominent than men. Statues and sculptures of deities seemed to favour images of women, such as the Snake Goddess sculpture at the Heraklion Archaeological Museum. Originally it was believed that while Minoan religion may have had many smaller gods, the major image of worship was of a great mother goddess. While this was later disputed, it very much impacted the perception of these ancient people as matriarchal, or at least more empowering for women than the later Greeks would be.

In particular, one symbol that often accompanied goddesses and images of Minoan women with religious significance is a large double-sided ceremonial axe, known as a 'labrys'. This weapon usually appears with women, as a religious symbol and a votive offering, possibly symbolising the creation of the universe. The axe is also occasionally associated with the ancient Greek hunter goddess Artemis, one of the three Greek virgin goddesses, who would run through the forests followed by her all-female following. Laphria was the name of one of Artemis's festivals, involving a single virgin priestess who would ride in a chariot drawn by deer, followed by the sacrifice of many wild animals. Laphria has been argued to be a possible etymological origin of 'labrys', with this axe being associated with Artemis's priestesses, particularly by later writers.

There is also the suggestion of standing up against misogyny, and eschewing so-called feminine pacifism in favour of violence and rebellion, as embodied in the symbol of an axe. For example, an 1882 painting by John Collier of the ancient Greek woman Clytemnestra, famous for murdering her husband Agamemnon after he committed adultery and sacrificed their daughter Iphigenia, includes a bloodstained axe that closely resembles a labrys.

By the 1970s the idea of a culture of people who revered women, wherein priestesses and goddesses sat at the top of the hierarchy, whether or not this reading is wholly accurate, became strongly connected with the feminist movement. Women who fought for their rights, safety and freedom against a strict patriarchal society became inspired by certain Minoan imagery, particularly a sacred double-sided axe wielded only by women. The labrys became a symbol specifically of the lesbian identity and the power of women who love women. It is still a symbol of this today, appearing on badges and pins, as well as being integrated into some versions of the lesbian pride flag.

As Claire Meade, self-proclaimed sword lesbian historian, queer heritage educator about arms and armour and author of the comic *Girls' School of Knighthood*, explained to me in an email interview:

> The labrys has itself long been associated with warrior women and powerful goddesses. Even though it would not actually have been exclusively associated with goddesses and heroines within Minoan Civilization and beyond from the evidence we now have, we do

find it linked to offerings made to Artemis in certain parts of Ancient Greece, or to weapons used by the Amazons across the Ancient World.

The idea of queer womanhood, gender-bending and fluid sexuality is often embodied in these classical warrior women. Indeed, many of the greatest male heroes of Greek folklore come across groups like the Amazons, or other women of power, and meet their match or are emasculated. A great example of this is Hercules being sent to Omphale, the fierce queen of Lydia. On arrival he becomes her slave, forced to do 'women's work', and in one incredible Roman mosaic Hercules is depicted wearing a dress, whereas Omphale is bedecked in the hero's lionskin and holding his club aloft.

The best-known woman hero in classical literature is probably Atalanta. Atalanta, meaning 'equal of weight', was born to a well-to-do couple in Arcadia, but her father Iasus decided he did not want a daughter so abandoned the child on Mount Parthenion. Luckily the baby was taken in by a mother bear – much like Romulus and Remus with the she-wolf, or the Greek hero Paris – who raised her alongside her own cubs. Atalanta was found by hunters and brought back into human civilisation. Thereon Atalanta devoted herself to hunting and the worship of the goddess Artemis.

Being of extraordinary capability as a hunter and fighter, Atalanta has a number of stories associated with her. She is often celebrated for slaying two centaurs who were assaulting her, and killing a giant boar summoned by Artemis herself. In some accounts Atalanta was the only woman to be allowed aboard the *Argo* to join a fearsome troop of warriors, the Argonauts, on their many adventures. In physical appearance Atalanta is a natural athlete, with a 'fiery masculine gaze'[15] and an imposing presence.

It is repeatedly stated that Atalanta was not interested in men, preferring to fight and seek adventure, and devote herself to her patron goddess. Indeed, a prophecy is given to her that states that if Atalanta were to ever be married she would be cursed. For this reason anyone attempting to court Atalanta would first have to beat her in a running race, something she excelled at. If they lost, they would be executed. Surprisingly this did not put off all her admirers, notably a young man named Hippomenes. Hippomenes asked the goddess Aphrodite for her help in winning the right to marry the young huntress, and was gifted with three golden apples. While racing Atalanta, and clearly losing, he used the golden apples to distract her, finally winning the race, through cheating, and gaining the right to marry her.

The entire story, while it ends with Atalanta 'happily' married, is of a woman who lives a life actively avoiding the romantic attention of men; who, like Callisto, only has eyes for Artemis. By today's standards there are fair readings of Atalanta as either a lesbian woman, infatuated with Artemis, bisexual or asexual, determined to live a life of her own devising without unnecessary romantic involvements.

In the end, after the marriage of Atalanta and Hippomenes, the pair forget to honour Aphrodite, who afflicts them with wild sexual passion wherein they defile the temple of Rhea, the Titan mother of Zeus. Rhea curses the couple, turning them into lions. The curse on Atalanta is there-fore fulfilled: in marrying a man she is transformed into a savage beast.

Warrior women and their sigils have always been a disruptive force in storytelling, and therefore a common source for queer and gender-nonconforming women to gather round. Claire Meade continues:

> The use of a warrior woman's weapon as a lesbian symbol can also be linked to the fact that warrior women were historically seen as disrupting traditional femininity, both in the way they dressed and sometimes their relationships with other women. The term 'virago' described a woman with 'masculine' attributes (which we may call butch today) and ended up both describing warrior women and being conflated with lesbianism.

Atalanta appears not only in Greek myths but also in the silver age of comic books from 1956 to 1970. Here she is an Amazon, the sister of Hippolyta, the queen of the Amazons. In this interpretation of Greek mythology she is also the aunt of the superhero Wonder Woman.

PRINCESS DIANA

Classical mythology makes for fertile ground for superheroes. Indeed, while many modern heroes borrow from the tropes of ancient Greek, Roman and Norse epic storytelling, they also borrow entire characters. Mythic figures such as Hercules, King Arthur and the Aztec god Tezcatlipoca all appear alongside superheroes like Superman and Captain America. Thor and Loki are rewritten as superheroes directly from the *Poetic Edda*. And the very first female superhero was drawn from the myths of Greek warrior women.

Wonder Woman was the co-creation of William Moulton Marston, his wife Elizabeth Holloway Marston and their lover Olive Byrne. This 'unusual' set-up (at least for the 1920s) was even celebrated in a ceremony uniting the thrupple, wherein Olive, known for her golden bracelets, exchanged two of them with both William and Elizabeth.[16]

The Marstons were both progressive psychologists and were incredibly active concerning gender equality and sexual liberation. William was encouraged to create a female superhero partly at Elizabeth's insistence. He was quoted as saying of his creation:

> As lovely as Aphrodite – as wise as Athena – with the speed of Mercury and the strength of Hercules – she is known only as Wonder Woman. The only hope for civilization is the greater freedom, development and equality of women.[17]

It is clear that, while it was a collaboration, Wonder Woman became a personal passion for William, who had a strong, and not entirely platonic, love for the idea of dominant, powerful warrior women. Indeed, he relished the idea of a real Amazonian woman, and the imagery of bondage and submissive role play were embedded into the early characterisation of Wonder Woman. William Marston is known for saying that he believed women to be in many ways superior to men.

Both Elizabeth and William saw something in Olive – something athletic, vibrant and strong that they equated with the fearsome women warriors of Greek myths. It is therefore no coincidence that the character of Diana Prince, aka Wonder Woman, was based upon Olive herself, even down to the bangles that she wore. It is also notable that among Wonder Woman's superpowers and abilities is her magic lasso, which she can use to force enemies to succumb to her powers and to tell the truth. William worked closely on the team that developed the original polygraph lie-detector machine, clearly putting some of his work on revealing 'truth' into his character.

As with most superheroes, Wonder Woman has multiple origin stories, with different comic-book generations often starting her story over and rewriting it. But the basics of the story is that Diana is a princess of the Amazons. As with the original Greek writings, this is an entirely female warrior caste that lives in a magically protected land called Themyscira or Paradise Island. No men are allowed within this land, until a weary Second World War soldier, Steve Trevoe, ends up there by accident, dragging Diana into the world of men.

Diana is either an Amazon champion born within the society, or handcrafted by the queen of the Amazons out of clay, but in all accounts she is different and fated by the gods to head out of paradise and fight the evil forces in the patriarchal world beyond.

In the 1940s this was a revelation, as Diana, aka Wonder Woman, was the very first fully realised female superhero, who would join the likes of Batman and Superman to fight for justice. As well as becoming an icon for young women, she would also become beloved among the LGBTQ+ community of all genders. They would see in her a feminist icon, a symbol of non-masculine heroism with a certain camp flourish. Most notably, in the 1970s TV series with Lynda Carter playing Wonder Woman, she spins around and around in a much-parodied transformation sequence to take on her superhero guise.

The fact that this superhero's inception, created by a bisexual polycule of two sexually liberal psychologists and their muse, is often missed out entirely. The borrowing of the Amazonian mythos, with its links to Atalanta and classical nonconforming women, is also important when considering what she represents. There are very clear reasons why she is such a beloved LGBTQ+ icon today.

Claire Meade speaks passionately about how characters like Wonder Woman subvert archetypes for queer women, by harking back to mythic women heroes:

Very often, queer people have been marginalised and sidelined for their differences or turned into a story's villain rather than its protagonist. If we see superhero comic books as the descendants of epic sagas, it is not always easy for queer gender non-conforming people in particular to see themselves there – and in women's cases are often the prize for a quest rather than their own hero.

Fantasy gives anyone the chance to imagine picking up a sword and fighting for their beliefs – and maybe it's a bit cathartic for so many of us who do fight everyday for our lives and identities. Superheroes and warriors show us that different, 'strange' qualities outside of the usual status quo of 'normal' do not make us weak or undesirable – they make us powerful.

BOY MADE GOD

How does someone become a hero? By modern metrics, in comic books and films, this is normally down to some particular birthright or the fickle hand of fate. Superman, the X-Men and Wonder Woman are born into their power; they are simply different from birth, being either Amazonian constructs, genetic mutants or literal aliens. Spider-Man, Captain America and Black Widow acquired their powers through strange circumstances, from being bitten by a radioactive spider or injected with super serum. Either way, being a hero is seldom entirely by choice; it's something that just happens to the characters, whisking them away from normality into a world of danger, adventure and secrecy.

The original classic heroes had similar stories, gaining powers by divine intervention or parentage. Although heroes would have to demonstrate their heroic credentials during their lives, the abilities that differentiated them from other mortals were largely left to fate or chance. Yet there are examples of heroes being created intentionally. The journey from everyday human to superpowered being, an everyday person plucked from obscurity and hurled into eternity, is as old as time itself. While most superheroes are fictional characters, in the ancient world it might be possible to blur the line between fact and fiction; for a real human boy to be elevated to heroic status, and even to become a god.

Emperor Hadrian, most famous for the construction of the epony-
mous Hadrian's Wall, the great divider built to demarcate the borders
of the Roman Empire in Britain during his reign and to hold back
the dangerous Scottish hordes, was also arguably responsible for creating a god.

It is hard to come across accurate factual information about the meeting of Antinous and Hadrian, but we know that Antinous started out as
a young man from Bithynia, what is today Turkey. In every description
we are told of Antinous's incredible beauty, and how this struck the
much older emperor. Here we come across the first issue with this
account, which has been celebrated in some queer circles as the greatest
ever homosexual love story. Exactly how old was Antinous? In some
accounts he is a young man, or a 'hairy legged' adult, but it is fully possible to interpret him as a child, at least on their first meeting. Remember
that in the Roman Empire a woman was expected to marry by the age of
eighteen; taboos around underage sex and relationships existed, but were
not what they are today. The dynamic is at the very least a morally
ambiguous one, and while we get a strong sense of how Hadrian felt
about his beloved Antinous, we have little or nothing of Antinous's own
voice. Irrespective of the age gap, and possible child grooming, there is
also the question of the intrinsic power disparity between a young
working-class man and the literal emperor of Rome. Even if Antinous
was a fully grown adult, if he had not been interested would he have
been able to say no?

It is, of course, possible that the relationship between Hadrian and
Antinous was the beautiful 'pure' love that many gay men understandably want it to be, but there is very little to go on either way.

Whatever the nature of their relationship, it is clear that Hadrian was
obsessed with Antinous, pulling this country boy out of obscurity and
taking him on journeys across the empire. Soon the pair were inseparable
in the public consciousness, not necessarily with unanimous support.
For a young man to have so much power and influence over the Roman
emperor was no doubt of concern to other contenders and key players in
Roman politics. Either way, the majority of what we know of Antinous
as a figure comes after his death, which is when he truly finds fame.

At a young age, between nineteen and his early twenties, Antinous drowns in a river in Egypt. The exact circumstances of his death remain hazy. Some writers claim it was a tragic accident. Others say that out of love for Hadrian, Antinous sacrificed himself by drowning. A few authors and historians have even implied something more sinister, that Antinous was drowned by some of those who feared his influence, or, even more disturbingly, by Hadrian himself.

In death, the youthful, good-looking Turkish boy becomes a hero and a literal god. His image is hewn from marble, cities are named in his honour and entire cults spring up across the Roman Empire. Some of this may have been down to Hadrian's work, in his grief deciding to immortalise his lover, or it was perhaps simply a response to a young well-known man, connected to power, dying in such tragic circumstances.

Antinous is associated with a number of other gods such as the Egyptian god Osiris and the Roman god of wine, Bacchus; he is even on occasion fused with the mythical figure of Hercules or the horned Celtic god of forests, Cernunnos. Being originally a simple country boy, as a god Antinous is responsible for the countryside, for crops and woods; he is also, because of his tragic end, supposed to have dominion over death.[18]

Through the love, grief, and perhaps even guilt of a powerful Roman emperor, a young man becomes a heroic figure, his story an epic. Much like Hercules, who after his death is transformed into a constellation of stars, the emperor's boyfriend also becomes eternal.

Such a journey from human to god is not entirely unheard of; we see much the same among the Egyptian pharaohs, who were both humans and gods at the same time, and even in the canonisation of Christian saints, wherein martyrs are elevated to a status as spiritual beings. But there are only a handful of examples where someone elevates their lover to this status as a way to preserve them. One of which is Cleopatra, who did the same for her lover Mark Antony, also associating him with Dionysus. The other is Alexander the Great, with his beloved Hephaestion.

Alexander the Great's story is in some ways remarkably similar to that of Hadrian and Antinous. In this case Hephaestion acted as a bodyguard to Alexander, but was also a childhood friend and confidant: 'He had been brought up with Alexander and shared all his secrets.'[19]

After Hephaestion died of an unknown illness, Alexander was grief-stricken, and just as with Hadrian, asked for his beloved to be elevated to godhood as a 'divine hero'. Many have debated the nature of the two men's relationship, but a romantic or sexual element cannot be ruled out. Indeed, the two men were frequently compared to Achilles and Patroclus, who we already know were perceived by many contemporaries as lovers.

While the majority of classic heroes are not created by heartbroken boyfriends, the power of love could clearly elevate some everyday men and boys into gods and legendary warriors, particularly if that love came from an emperor or king. Due to the patriarchal norms of ancient Greece and Rome, women were rarely celebrated as 'heroic' in the same way as men, and rarely if ever deified after their death. As the majority of leaders with enough clout to canonise their partners were also men (Cleopatra being an obvious exception), the incidences whereby a common man might be transformed into a hero, immortalised in stone, or enshrined into the names of cities, were most likely due to homosocial and homo-erotic relationships. Therefore some of the mythic heroic statues, symbols, cults and characters from the ancient world that inspired images of heroism even today can be connected to the beautiful youths valued by privileged and powerful men in the past; the heroes themselves, tall, usually white, muscular and 'perfectly' formed: Superman and Captain America are cut from this very cloth.

MAGNETO WAS RIGHT

Of all the mainstream superhero franchises that seem to appeal to the LGBTQ+ community, it is probably the X-Men franchise that is most notorious. Based around a group of 'mutants' who are born with super abilities, the story charts an enormous cast of these characters as they attend a secret school to hone their powers and fight back against bigotry from the non-mutants in society. X-Men was originally devised by major comic-book creator Stan Lee back in 1963, only to be cancelled due to lack of popularity and relaunched in the 1970s. Stan Lee has been open about the influences on his group of renegade 'born different' superheroes and their struggle for freedom. As the series has progressed, obvious parallels have been drawn between the story arcs of the series and the fight for civil rights for people of colour in America, as well as the history of anti-Semitism. Homophobia and transphobia are also clear and obvious influences, particularly from the 1980s onwards.

In 1993 the series introduced a new nemesis, this time not another anti-mutant robot or evil supervillain, but a virus. The Legacy Virus, first described in *X-Force* Volume 18, was a disease that affected only mutants. The virus created skin lesions, fever and coughing in its victims, eventually resulting in death. This plague was clearly based on the very real plague of HIV that had been ripping through the LGBTQ+ world since the 1980s. HIV and AIDS seemed to target a specific minority at this time (indeed it was originally called GRID, standing for Gay Related Immunodeficiency), there was no cure and the symptoms were all incredibly similar to the comic-book version.

Other parallels for the LGBTQ+ experience are also there: the character of Mystique, who can shapeshift and take on the appearance of any person, is perhaps the most famous example. In the canon story Mystique has struggled with her identity, trying to hide her baseline blue 'inhuman' form. She has also lived as both men and women, and had relationships with characters of all genders. Other X-men struggle with their appearance and identity due to their powers, either having to repress and hide them, or learn to embrace them. Some have powers that are only visible when manifested; they can 'pass' in non-mutant society. Others are visibly different from non-mutants no matter what they do. Rogue cannot touch another person without harming them, Cyclops must cover his eyes which otherwise perpetually fire dangerously powerful optic blasts. Wolverine is super-strong, but suffers from post-traumatic stress and is hurt by his own adamantium claws that tear through his fast-healing flesh every time he uses them.

Most LGBTQ+ people have found at least one character whose mix of powers and flaws resonates with them, like a larger-than-life version of the queer experience itself: painful secrets counterbalanced by the joy of community and self-discovery. Partly based on the civil rights movement and, controversially, the leader of the Black Panthers, Malcolm X, Magneto is the supervillain or antihero who represents a flipside of the mutant heroes. His story, which begins in the Nazi concentration camps, is that of a separatist who wishes to create a world solely for mutants and free from bigotry, whatever the cost. The analogies with the lives of many LGBTQ+ people are also there: the desire to blend in and to fit, mixed with the desire to fight intolerance and rebel against injustice. Sometimes this can result in unity and solidarity, but as with Magneto it can also result in anger and resentment: following Pride month it is not uncommon to come across messages such as 'This year we will celebrate Wrath month' as an expression of this frustration.

The X-Men were not created with LGBTQ+ people in mind, and the series tends to tackle any number of societal issues and injustices, but there are clear elements borrowed by the fictional superheroes and villains from very real LGBTQ+ life and history. Today there are now even canonically LGBTQ+ superheroes; unsurprisingly many of them were debuted in *X-Men* and related comics. In 1964 Stan Lee wrote the character of Pinky Pinkerton, a British Second World War commando whom Lee described as follows in an interview:

> He was gay. We didn't make a big issue of it. In this comic book that I read, the word gay wasn't even used. He's just a colorful character who follows his own different drummer. He follows a different beat. But we're not proselytizing for gayness.[20]

Stan Lee explains that the sexuality of the character was never intended to be explicit, but was merely incidental due to the eccentric way he had been created.

Later, and far more importantly, there is Northstar, introduced as a side character as part of Wolverine's backstory in 1979, who in the eighties would be hinted at being gay. In one scene Northstar receives a phone call from another character which is answered by an anonymous shirtless hunk. Later on, the sexuality of Northstar would be made canon and every bit as much a part of the character's identity as his super speed and photonic energy blasts.

THE RED PILL

Today superheroes appear beyond comic books and are branching out to explore themes and genres perhaps never initially considered possible back in the 1940s. Characters are more and more coming to represent the many different lives and identities of the ever-expanding audience which consumes them. LGBTQ+ superhero characters are rising from one or two to multiple in nearly every franchise.

Superheroes and comic books also draw a large and diverse audience of creators even within mainstream works, including Phil Jimenez, Kate Leth, Rebecca Sugar, James Tynion IV and Tee Franklin. Many of them found escapism or salvation in the comic books they read in childhood, and now as queer adults help create and build the stories for the likes of Spider-Man, Superman, Wonder Woman and their ilk.

Creators like the Wachowski sisters have also helped to reinvent superheroes in new ways, often without capes, masks or superpowers, at least in the traditional sense. The 'Matrix' series follows the human Neo as he discovers reality is in fact a simulation created by evil machines, and harnesses his powers as the chosen one. It was created while Laura and Lilly Wachowski were themselves coming to terms with their own gender identity as transgender women. The symbols of the red pill, representing oestrogen, and the original (cut from the film) conception of the character 'Switch' changing genders between the real world and the Matrix, all point to the entire story as a metaphor for transition. The Wachowski sisters have frequently discussed how this metaphor was intentional, that their superhero Neo's journey from ordinary to extraordinary was a reflection of their own personal journeys. They also comment on how significant the series has been for transgender people, even before their own coming out, with Lilly saying in a BBC interview: 'They come up to me and say these movies saved my life . . . I'm grateful I can be throwing them a rope to help them along their journey.'[21]

Superheroes as they stand today are a relatively modern construct, but their history combines ancient classical depictions of heroism and gods with modern struggles and societal issues. Masculine heroes like Hercules, Achilles and Gilgamesh are the mould from which modern heroes were forged. While there has been an attempt to dilute and distance classical homoeroticism from their modern male comic-book equivalents, this 'queer' ancestry cannot be fully eroded. It is there in their hypermasculine physiques, which draw from the eroticised sculptures made in homage to long-lost lovers in ancient Greece and Rome. It is there in the swish of their capes, their fantastical costumes and superpowers, born of Greek and Norse gods whose norms of gender and sexuality, while still patriarchal, were not what they are today. It is there in the camaraderie between fellow fighters for justice, warriors bound together through battle, which in ancient stories was never entirely platonic.

The fact that many, but not all, of the influential writers of the 1940s and 1950s who created the most beloved comic-book characters never intended to represent these themes, and wished to create heterosexual masculine icons for young straight men, is almost irrelevant. Queer themes and symbolism are still there and visible just below the surface.

For female heroes, we see a legacy going back to ancient heroines, defying feminine archetypes and creating characters that eschew marriage and familial duties in pursuit of adventure or friendship with other women. Warrior woman, 'vigorous maidens', Amazonian queens, all have been a beacon for queer women since at least the nineteenth century, and their stories directly led to the inception of the likes of Wonder Woman, Poison Ivy and Catwoman. Even when framed by men, heavily sexualised and created for a presumed male audience, the female superhero has unshakable connections with the history of lesbianism and queer women that predate the modern characters and tropes.

The superhero is a representation of everyday people, simply exaggerated and made more vivid. It therefore represents humanity in all its facets, so queerness is as much a part of the modern superhero as X-ray vision, leaping tall buildings in a single bound and radioactive spider bites.

As for today's remixed heroes, Phil Jimenez, a gay comic-book artist known for his work on Wonder Woman and X-Men comic series, told me:

> Inherent in the DNA of super-heroes is transformation. Many superheroes transform from someone mild and meek and hidden into who they truly are – often super-powerful, brazenly garbed, with a code name and powers and presence to match their colorful

uniforms. Super-heroes are a terrific metaphor for coming out, and for transness/transition.

Beyond that, another important aspect of super-heroes is the fantastical, the outrageous, the whimsical; the opposite of mundanity. Many LGBTQ people (clearly not all) connect with these concepts through self-expression, coded language, media representation, personal fantasy, and the like – and make super-heroes a perfect vehicle to explore queerness across the spectrum of experience.

PART 5

And They All Lived
Happily Ever After . . .

*'I am intrigued, Geoffrey,' she said. 'Why do you want to
be a witch instead of a wizard, which is something
traditionally thought of as a man's job?'*
*'I've never thought of myself as a man, Mistress Tiffany. I don't
think I'm anything. I'm just me,' he said quietly.*

From *The Shepherd's Crown* by Terry Pratchett

Five Magic Beans

When writing this book I have occasionally discussed passages with my ever-patient husband, or talked through my current reading and research with him. Despite his unwavering support (I am an incredibly lucky man), he has commented on the darkness of so many of these stories. He is not wrong: queer history, even when it is about mythology and storytelling, often brings in elements of torture, death, punishment and suffering. The surviving records are rarely ones of joy or celebration.

But there is a way to flip this round. While the way history cements LGBTQ+ experiences is so often based on the worst day of an individual person's life, we can remember that this is just one day. The person lived a life that was full, rich and complex outside that one gory end, or asylum record, or sodomy accusation. The upsetting document or anecdote might be how the story has survived until today, but it is not indicative of a real human life that spreads far beyond the text from a court record, or a mugshot, or a burned love letter. The light that shines down into the oubliette* of sad and half-forgotten stories is that LGBTQ+ people are not victims any more than they are heroes. They are just people, and people have an indomitable spirit to live, love, fornicate and express themselves. So we know the same applies to every person, every story, every fragment here.

I want to approach the central argument of *Queer as Folklore* with some light for a change. When grappling with the question, the big why,

---

* An oubliette is a dungeon, normally under a castle or keep. The name comes from the French term 'oublier', meaning 'to forget', as it served the purpose of keeping a wretched prisoner out of sight and memory.

I will be moving from historical fact to speculation. There is truly no single explanation for why LGBTQ+ people, and the people who might have described themselves that way today, are drawn to folklore and mythology as both consumers and creators. I believe I have demonstrated a connection between many of the storybook tropes, monsters and spirits that we have been immersed in for thousands of years and those who live and love differently. But, rather than looking purely at the obvious themes of oppression, and being monstered, let's explore those special qualities that might place us closer to folklore. Let's explore why these kinds of lives provide such fertile soil for stories, myth, legends and monsters to grow.

Just like Jack, who received five humble beans that transformed into a world-bridging beanstalk, I believe there are five qualities that are shared between LGBTQ+ people and the kinds of people who create, consume and oversee humanity's folklore. These are my reasons for why people like us find ourselves so frequently in the worlds of myth and legend, and why we are still so drawn to them today.

Many of these are not unique to queer people – they may overlap with people of many experiences and identities – but taken together they do go some way towards explaining the specific queer connection. They describe five different kinds of people with different roles in society. They are not real people, merely archetypes, categories and concepts that highlight the connection between queerness and traits that are involved in the construction and dissemination of stories.

I. THE BETWEEN PEOPLE

> I love borders. August is the border between summer and autumn; it is the most beautiful month I know.
>
> Twilight is the border between day and night, and the shore is the border between sea and land. The border is longing: when both have fallen in love but still haven't said anything. The border is to be on the way. It is the way that is the most important thing.
>
> Tove Jansson[1]

One word that has hovered at the edge of my brain throughout writing *Queer as Folklore* has been 'liminal'. It is a word that simply means something that is in between, neither one thing nor another. Liminality can describe anything from spaces like a dentist's waiting room or an empty corridor, to life experiences such as puberty or divorce. Anything that feels or appears transitional and temporary.

Both queer people and folklore operate in this space. The way lesbian, gay, bisexual and transgender people live in gender roles and relationships that are outside or in between what is often condoned by society is a kind of liminality. Similarly, many of the beasts described in this book are hybrids, formed by mixing two creatures together: half fish, half woman, half horse, half man. The mixed, transformative nature of these creatures is also liminal, often symbolising transformation, change, otherworldliness or something strange and unsettled.

It is no wonder that people who have perceived themselves as existing between standard definitions for human genders or human relationships might also seek out those well-known mythical symbols that represent something similar. Is it a coincidence that Hans Christian Andersen wrote a book about a half-formed creature, trapped between two very different worlds, who must sacrifice half of herself to try to live fully? Perhaps; perhaps not. But similar stories abound in history, from the queer men and women who wrote about beings that exist between life and death, and the non-gender-conforming people who went to sea to find freedom beyond the edges of the map.

Liminality represents spaces such as the aforementioned life at sea, or a life constantly travelling, or a life lived half among ancient Greek ruins or immersed in the pages of dusty manuscripts. Queer people may, more than other people, seek out locations and lifestyles that are also in between by their very nature. The grand tour of Greece and Italy, during which wealthy queer men and women would discover themselves while adventuring abroad, away from their families and associated conservative expectations, is a common trope among the privileged classes. But travel, constant movement and a desire never to settle in one location is present in the lives of LGBTQ+ people of all social standings. Such a liminal lifestyle would also naturally lead to an interest in stories, traditions, art and culture different from one's own. Mythology and storytelling from around the world would be more discoverable by such people, and more relatable for those people who would travel and move constantly between different social strata. The liminality of a queer life could there be seen as conducive to a natural interest in folklore, simply by the nature of coming across more folk and more lore!

Liminality both in identity and lifestyle is the obvious connector between queer people and hybrid mythical creatures, monsters and supernatural forces. I am not the first person to make this connection. Historically being 'between people' is often seen as a negative, associated with being outcast, other or different. It can also create opportunities to look at history and humanity from imaginative and unique perspectives, making queer people perfectly placed to understand stories of magic and mayhem, by drawing connections to the same chaotic and transformative natures in their own lives.

2. THE MAGIC MAKERS

> Watch with glittering eyes the whole world around you because the greatest secrets are always hidden in the most unlikely places. Those who don't believe in magic will never find it.
>
> *The Minpins* by Roald Dahl, 1991

Magic and the supernatural exist in every single human culture. But who are the people believed to be responsible for overseeing and controlling these unseen forces? Throughout history, even in times of extreme religious dogma, there have been magicians, priests, shamans, conjurers, fortune tellers, fakirs, witches, healers and druids – individuals, or small groups of people, who claim to have a connection with the magical, the divine or the profane. Whether creating mysterious brews, seeing the future in animals' intestines or going into ecstatic frenzies in honour of a particular local god, these are permanent fixtures in every society and every time and place.

Individuals might become such a person for myriad reasons, perhaps by a personal connection with the supernatural, by right of birth or through diligent study. There is no one kind of person suited to such a profession, but there are clusters of traits that might be associated with many of these magic makers. Many are described as outsiders, the strange old man or women at the edge of the village, or as being perceived by their peers as somehow different. While there are respectable supernaturalists who work closely with kings and leaders, or who practise their magic in well-to-do circles, these are largely people who are treated with a kind of reverence, tinged with fear and suspicion.

It is notable that in multiple cultures the person who communes with the dead, who reads mystic signs or dreams, is often gender-nonconforming: a woman who does not dress as society dictates they should, a feminine man, or a person who belongs to a third or other sex entirely. This is not to say that magic makers the world over are queer, or even that the majority are. But historically there has been a space for some people who might today fit under the queer umbrella in these livelihoods. Most witches weren't gay, the majority of shamans are not trans and Greek priests weren't necessarily nonbinary. But traits aligned with all these identities do find themselves occurring well above average in these roles.

I am again by no means the first to make this observation. In *Queer Magic*, Tomás Prower explores the rich history and diversity of people that would today be described as queer playing central roles in spirituality and magic around the world. He sees this going back extraordinarily far in time:

> It's amazing to discover how widespread and disproportionately high our queer ancestors were represented in the priestly classes of Mesopotamian society. Making this more impactful is how these are some of the earliest civilizations in human history.[2]

Indeed, at the root of some religions, the blending of gender in one's appearance, identity and presentation would place them closer to the gods. In Hinduism the god Ardhanarishvara is a combination of the male god Shiva and his female consort Parvati in a singular being: 'the lord who is half woman'. This being represents a balance of the two divine energies. Despite an increase in persecution in India since the introduction of British imperialism, the 'hijra', a third-gendered group including people who could be described as trans women and those who are intersex or eunuchs, are enshrined in Islamic texts dating back to at least the fourteenth century. They are often associated with magic and Hindu spiritualism and even believed to have the ability to curse those who wrong them. Similar writings appear around those indigenous peoples who have a third gender, for example the lhamana of the Native American Zuni people, where those assigned male at birth but who live partially outside this category are believed to be naturally gifted at divination.

Obviously this can have both a positive and a negative association; as the chapters on demons and witchcraft show, one's visible 'queerness' can also be used to cast a person as further from God. The practising of magic can therefore be a reason to persecute, ostracise or attack LGBTQ+ people. Yet this association might also explain why queer people find themselves so frequently involved in folklore and mythology. For magic makers, the worlds of myth, legend and religion blend together, and a magic maker might find themselves responsible for constructing stories and legends as well as recounting them.

Similarly, if an association with queer lives and magic making is as ancient as it seems, we may find ourselves written into stories as witches, spirits and otherworldly beings. Here gender nonconformity, dress or behaviour can become a well-understood shorthand for someone who dabbles in the dark arts, reads secret signs or speaks to the dead.

3. THE STORY WEAVERS

> 'My dear sister, if you are not asleep, tell me I pray you, before the sun rises, one of your charming stories. It is the last time that I shall have the pleasure of hearing you.'
> Scheherazade did not answer her sister, but turned to the Sultan. 'Will your highness permit me to do as my sister asks?' said she.
> 'Willingly,' he answered. So Scheherazade began.
> *The Arabian Nights Entertainments* by Andrew Lang, 1918

At university I studied psychology and became captivated by evolutionary psychology and its seductive promise to explain human behaviour and eccentricities with facts and logic. In my final year I wrote my thesis on evolutionary explanations for male homosexuality. I now see that I naively thought that if I could explain my sexuality, to others and to myself, as being natural and understandable by scientific laws, I could build a wall against bigotry and intolerance.

Now, I feel that evolutionary psychology, while fascinating, often offers little more than 'Just So Stories', giving only provocative and even offensive explanations as to why we do what we do. It is so often mere pseudoscience littered with jargon that is unprovable, unverifiable and simple flights of fancy. The arguments around homosexuality were similar: the researchers who wrote on this topic were puzzling over why such a thing might exist when it was clearly detrimental to an individual's reproductive potential. While I don't think any of the arguments put forward held water, and some were downright stupid, a few have lingered with me.

One argument states that gay people, and those who are not interested in having relationships with the opposite sex, might still play a valuable role in the community.[3] Biologist Jeff Kirby argues that we might act as support workers, a little bit like the worker caste in certain eusocial insects, like bees and ants. While we are less likely to have our own children, our genes, they argue, might be carried on by our family and siblings who we help, not being distracted by our own families and offspring. In this argument gay and asexual people would become the ultimate babysitters, social workers and guidance counsellors.

Even at twenty I thought that, taken wholesale, this argument was a bit silly. Queer people tend to invest a lot in their romantic relationships, and there is no evidence that we act as free childcare and drone workers in societies. That being said, the kernel of the idea, in a heavily diluted fashion, might help us to understand how LGBTQ+ people could become good story keepers and lore holders.

It is a well-known stereotype that LGBTQ+ people are drawn to art, literature and theatre. We are overrepresented in the creative fields today, and historically have found ourselves as key leaders in the arts, despite low social standing elsewhere. There are a million reasons why LGBTQ+ people might seek creative and artistic careers and circles, but one is a lack of interest in pursuing a traditional family life, at least the kind of family template modelled in the societies we are born into.

Within families people do tend to find themselves fulfilling roles. One sibling might be the peacekeeper, one might become a caretaker for elderly parents, and one might be the problem child or, conversely, the breadwinner. There is no one particular role that queer people find themselves fulfilling, but, purely anecdotally, I know of many LGBTQ+ children who, of their brothers and sisters, are the unofficial family archivists; the record keepers for their family's history and stories.

In many societies with small, intimate communities, a person without a blood family of their own might find significance within their community as a story keeper, maintaining the community's sense of self, its own internal history and lore. Arguably such a person, by not putting energy into their own children, might instead invest in other skills, such as providing entertainment, specialising in creating artworks, or producing and telling stories for their nieces and nephews. Also, might we be the people listening, sitting with elderly relatives, talking with fellow weirdos and sharing in their gossip and chatter?

Art, poetry, music and literature are also produced both for and by escapists, the stereotype for creatives being that of daydreamers, bohemians and people who value self-expression over conformity. LGBTQ+ people who often find themselves struggling to find a role within strict family life, or small conservative communities, may also travel to larger metropolitan areas and explore careers and livelihoods in the arts that celebrate self-expression.

Again, remember these are broad brushstrokes; I don't believe many queer people I know were destined to become storytellers by birth, and I also think we are far from glorified babysitter librarians. Indeed, many queer people I know, myself included, have their own families in whom they are fully invested. Still, the archetypal story keeper, the preserver of lore and crafter of tales, does at least overlap with a vague, nebulous concept of many queer people's experience in family and community life: the well-read spinsters, the quirky uncles and the activist aunties.

There is evidence beyond mere anecdotes. If we look at some of the most celebrated or prolific story originators of all time, we find among them a surprising number of eccentric bachelors and unmarried women. People who travelled widely, made strange friends and lived unusual and transient lifestyles. People such as Giambattista Basile who wrote *Cenerentola*, later translated as *Cindarella* and Henriette-Julie de Murat, the controversial author of such tales as 'The Princess Fairy' and 'The Sprites of Kernosy Castle', who was even openly accused of lesbianism in her lifetime.[4] The exact identities, sexuality and proclivities of these individuals may not be known or recorded, but their lives are at least relatable to the queer experience.

Then we have the likes of Hans Christian Andersen, Oscar Wilde, Tove Jansson, Mary Shelly, Bram Stoker and Henry James, all of whom lived and loved outside heteronormative societal expectations and crafted the narratives, characters and storytelling tropes we may take for granted today. The role of story weaver may not be intrinsic to being queer, but it is, I believe, aligned.

4. THE TIME TRAVELLERS

> So she sat on, with closed eyes, and half believed herself in Wonderland, though she knew she had but to open them again, and all would change to dull reality.
>
> *Alice's Adventures in Wonderland* by Lewis Caroll, 1865

We have discussed the propensity for queer people to travel in space. The desire to find oneself in a big city, or to escape to in-between spaces where things might be more permissive than at home. But what about travelling in time?

Throughout this book we have found numerous examples of queer people using history and mythology to understand themselves: the early gay communities who looked to Plato, Achilles and ancient Greece for terminology with which to describe their feelings; nineteenth-century poets who reached for Sappho, over 1,000 years earlier, to find a way to express their own yearning for women; or the self-described nineteenth-century 'Androgyne' meeting with the kindred spirits of faeries at the Paresis Hall nightclub. The language and culture of LGBTQ+ people are littered with classical allusion and throwbacks to points in history.

Beyond the worlds of fantasy, we have collectively sought escape and recognition in the past. Occasionally this has also led us to sugarcoat the realities of history, attempting to find a time, not just a place, where people like us might have lived more freely and safely.

A journey to ancient temples in Rome and Greece, or an obsession with classical artworks, might be largely a preoccupation of the wealthy and privileged, but it is still remarkably common in the lives of all LGBTQ+ people. In this sense we are the ultimate time travellers, seemingly with one foot in an imagined past. Unable to find language or affirmation in their lives today, queer people have often become experts, or at least armchair enthusiasts, of the distant past. I wonder whether the drives of the likes of Aleister Crowley, to rebirth ancient religions and dogma through his constructed religion of Thelema, might have been partly born out of a desire for a liberal and permissive world drawn from some perceived fictional golden bygone age.

By immersing ourselves in ancient worlds of classical heroes and monsters, we end up becoming some of their most passionate living ambassadors today. Writing the names of gods, nymphs, sprites and gorgons into our poetry, painting them onto our canvases and performing them in our plays. True, an interest in mythology and the past is not intrinsically queer. We know that painters of all identities have been drawn to ancient Greek myths as symbols, but there is perhaps an added layer of meaning for those of us who see something shameful, powerful or hidden about ourselves in these stories.

I know for a fact that my love for history, for myths, is so closely tied to my experience of being a boy who 'was not like the other boys' that it is almost impossible to disentangle. Dwelling on the past, and conjuring it into the future, is surely an important part of keeping folklore, legends and myths alive. On the flipside, as well as looking for equality in the past, time-travelling queer people might also have a propensity to imagine equitable futures. Science fiction written by certain queer authors might in this sense simply be a mirror to an obsession with the classical past. Daydreaming of brave new worlds and ancient histories is something queer people have done for at least the past 250 years, and arguably longer than that. This means we are naturally connected to the very history of epic storytelling itself.

5. THE WYRD FOLK

> It doesn't matter about being born in a duckyard, as long as you are
> hatched from a swan's egg.
> > 'The Ugly Duckling' by Hans Christian Andersen, 1843

The last set of traits I want to conjure around is the idea of the 'wyrd'. 'Wyrd' is an Old English term, originally Norse, which has given rise to the modern word 'weird' although it does have other connotations. Wyrd was also a name for one of the 'norns', a triad of women responsible for overseeing human fate and destiny. Therefore 'wyrd' didn't originally just mean strange, odd, or different; it also implied destiny, magic and fate in a much more neutral, or even positive manner. It can therefore be interpreted to mean special or even exceptional.

Queer people have historically been different; it is the main element that groups myriad non-heterosexual identities and non-cisgender identities together, a shared experience of otherness. In being different we have been deemed dangerous, or people to be shunned at certain points in history, although in others we might be deemed a natural variation in humanity, or even as something powerful.

Myths and legends are often designed to illustrate certain ideas or laws in society. They can be teaching aids, or ways to explain complex and poorly understood ideas, from why the sun rises to why little girls shouldn't trust strange men in the forest. Rule breaking – both those rules enshrined in law and unofficial social norms – is almost always something deemed bad. In myths and legends, fairy tales and nursery rhymes we can see attempts to control and curb rule-breaking behaviour through moral narratives, particularly for young people and children.

Even mythical creatures are often bound up with at least one moral lesson or teaching. A mermaid might be a warning to sailors to watch out while at sea, or to be wary of beautiful women. It might also, depending on the story, symbolise for women the danger of vanity or the importance of virtue. Monsters are often by their nature transgressive. Medusa becomes a monster by breaking rules, even though this is outside her control. Werewolves and vampires are lessons against wild or lascivious behaviour and warnings of the dark consequences of giving in to these desires.

As queer people so often exist outside the laws of society, often breaking them by simply existing, we find ourselves in the same category as the demons and monstrosities of bestiaries and cautionary tales. The monsters in these stories can symbolise us, and by proxy we can begin to associate with them. Being wyrd, rather than weird, explains how we exist partly in folklore and partly in reality, naturally closer to the unicorn, the faerie and the succubus than other people, for better or for worse.

LGBTQ+ people also come from every stratum of society, but due to our identities and desires, irrespective of class, our lives are often lived at least partly in secret. We are therefore naturally drawn to secret places. These places might include venues which require a confidential handshake or door knock; they might be located in slums, ports, underground networks. These spaces are often frequented by sex workers, bohemians, foreigners, criminals and others deemed an underclass. Even wealthy, well-to-do queer folk might mix outside their station, in 'seedy' places where their white, heterosexual and cisgender cohort would not wish to be seen. To be queer historically is to mix with all kinds of other people who do not fit society's norms. It is no coincidence that the LGBTQ+ city centres of the world are often found around ports, or historically closely associated with migrant communities, particularly so-called Chinatowns, black neighbourhoods, red-light districts and jazz bars, all representing other differently marginalised communities. In the 1920s, known queer-friendly bars such as the Shim Sham Club or the Caravan Club in London would also attract sex workers and musicians of colour, these groups overlapping in establishments away from the judgemental eyes of the mainstream.

So this weirdness brings LGBTQ+ people into contact with other cultures, radical ideas, rebellious movements, activism and liberal politics. Such bohemian melting pots are therefore naturally fertile ground for creating art and culture that carries folklore.

In the foreword to this book, Joanne Harris says that folklore is often a way to 'speak truth to power'. It can be the stories that everyday people tell, the people who are otherwise downtrodden or without platforms. Queer people have often been closely connected with this, and can play an active part in constructing and preserving these voices.

This is not to say all queer people are intrinsically diverse, or down-to-earth, or revolutionary. Many do escape poverty through luck or circumstance, or were born with such privilege that they could live outside the 'wyrd' comfortably, and either escape persecution or repress their true selves. Not all, or even most, historic LGBTQ+ people were rebellious artists; they were every kind of person you can imagine. But the intrinsic weirdness and wyrdness that comes with being this kind of person can shift people's lives and perspectives towards alternative and transgressive ways of thinking. All of which is conducive to connecting with monstrous, strange and magical things.

THE END?

Every story needs an ending, and it is, I believe, often the hardest thing to write well. To complete the landing, and tie up all the many narrative strings into a neat, satisfying bow, is a true art form; even some of my favourite stories by incredible writers have terrible endings.

I cannot promise that this ending will succeed in satisfying fully, especially after the weird, messy journey we have taken together. But I hope in making it this far, you've taken something from looking at the tropes, characters and constructs in human storytelling through a decidedly queer lens. That you've seen the myriad perspectives that have helped construct some of the cornerstones of human mythology and legend. I hope that by laying this in front of you, story after story, monster after monster, trope after trope, you will see the same patterns and connections that I do. That even if you do not fully believe every assertion I have made, and think I am sometimes seeing shapes in clouds, that you do at least see the arc of the argument.

Queer people have been around since the dawn of time, and therefore you will find us everywhere in human history, if you care to look. But within folklore, mythology and legend, you will find our voices even more present, louder and woven more deeply into the very fabric of storytelling itself.

Next time you see a Pride parade, the crowd bedecked with devil's horns, mermaid scales and unicorn tank tops, I hope you'll look at these symbols differently. Not just as icons temporarily borrowed by a group of drunk adults with a childish fashion sense, but as symbols forged partly by and for people like them, but also different, who came before.

If you are yourself part of the parade, maybe this will encourage you to look at your own life and interests, and question where your particular passions have come from. Maybe you can see your own niche fascination or hobby as part of a great and complex lineage of story keepers between people, magic makers, time travellers and wyrd folk. I hope you find some beauty or meaning in that connection, or at least that it cements your right to claim these symbols as your own.

To writers of fiction and fantasy today, artists, poets, videogame designers and creators, I challenge you to carry this baton forward, and continue to find ways to tell new stories and reinvent old ones for queer people tomorrow.

As a final farewell, to my fellow witches, aliens, robots, fairies, werewolves, superheroes, ghosts, vampires, pirates, unicorns and mermaids . . . stay wyrd.

Notes

Author Notes: Mind Your She's and Q's

1 Fobister, Waawaate, *Nanabush A Trickster*, in O'Hara, Jean, *Two Spirit Acts: Queer Indigenous Performances*, Playwrights Canada Press (2014).

Chapter 1: A Twist in the Tail

1 Brook, Mitch, 'Why Luca Is An LGBTQ Story (Despite What Pixar Says)', Screen-Rant (2021).
2 Muller, Axel, Christopher Halls and Ben Williamson, *Mermaids: Art, Symbolism and Mythology*, University of Exeter Press (2022), p. 1.
3 Scribner, Vaughn, *Merpeople: A Human History*, Reaktion Books (2020).
4 Stewart, Peter, *The Polychrome Reconstruction of the Prima Porta Statue*, Frieze (2017).
5 Muller, Halls and Williamson, *Mermaids*, pp. 11–13.
6 Richter, Daniel S., 'Lucian of Samosata', Chapter 21 in Richter, Daniel S. and William A. Johnson (eds), *The Oxford Handbook of the Second Sophistic*, vol. 1, Oxford University Press (2017), pp. 328–9.
7 Moore, Lauren, 'Dying Gods, Syria and the Flood: A Study of Male Consorts and Syncretism in the Cult of Atargatis', *Historia Religionum: An International Journal*, 5 (2013), pp. 2035–6455.
8 Lightfoot, J. L., *On the Syrian Goddess*, Oxford University Press eBooks (2003).
9 Apuleius, *The Golden Ass*, translated by Walsh, P. G., Oxford University Press (2008).
10 Muller, Halls and Williamson, *Mermaids*, p. 24.
11 Barber, R. W. and Bodleian Library, *Bestiary: being an English version of the Bodleian Library, Oxford M.S. Bodley 764 with all the original miniatures reproduced in facsimile*, Boydell Press (2006).
12 Allinson, Francis G. and J. Loeb, *Menander, the Principal Fragments*, Harvard University Press (1970).
13 Mackenzie, C., *Extraordinary Women*, Faber & Faber (2009).

14 Scribner, *Merpeople*.
15 Wullschlager, Jackie, *Hans Christian Andersen: The Life of a Storyteller*, Penguin Books (2000).
16 Martin, Andrew, 'The Famous Phobic Chronic Masturbating Author Who Wouldn't Leave Charles Dickens' House', *Medium* (2021).
17 Wullschlager, *Hans Christian Andersen*, p. 155.
18 Wullschlager, *Hans Christian Andersen*, p. 1.
19 Andersen, Hans Christian, *The Little Mermaid*, Pushkin Children's Books (2020, original work published 1837).
20 Pells, Kelly, 'Bushey Artist Gets Egypt Bug', *Watford Observer*, 29 April 2016.
21 Holocaust Memorial Day Trust, '6 May 1933: Looting of the Institute of Sexology', Holocaust Memorial Day Trust (2023).

Chapter 2: Horn of Plenty

1 Pliny the Elder, *Natural History: A Selection*, translated by Healy, J. F., Penguin Books (2004).
2 Crompton, Louis, *Homosexuality and Civilization*, Harvard University Press (2006), p. 214.
3 Eschenbach, Wolfram von, *Parzival: A Knightly Epic (Complete)*, Library of Alexandria (1961).
4 Guido Cavalcanti, *The Metabolism of Desire: The Poetry of Guido Cavalcanti*, translated by Slavitt, D. R., AU Press (2012).
5 Rollinson, David, 'Rough Music' (1982), accessed via *LGBTQ+ History at Gloucestershire Archives*, Gloucestershire Archives.
6 Bell, K., 'The 18th-Century Dildo Found in a French Convent', *Medium* (2021, original work published 1706).
7 Sewell, Brian, 'The genius of Dürer', *Evening Standard* (5 April 2012).
8 Farber, Allen, 'Dürer: Excerpts from Primary Documents', State University of New York at Oneonta (n.d.).
9 Ross, R., *Aubrey Beardsley*, Books on Demand (2018, original work published 1907).
10 Ibid.
11 Laxman, S., 'Unicorn hunting: How bisexual women are fetishised on dating apps in India', *Vogue India* (February 2022).
12 Garcia, H., 'Ukraine's "unicorn" LGBTQ soldiers head for war', Reuters (2022).

Chapter 3: Radical Faeries

1 Suggs, Richard, *Fairies: A Dangerous History*, Reaktion Books (2018), p. 94.
2 Lind, E. and R. Werther, *Autobiography of an Androgyne*, Fredonia Books (2005).

3 Suggs, *Fairies: A Dangerous History*, pp. 17–18.

4 Kaufman, S., 'Ballets Russes, and the enduring dancing man', *Washington Post* (10 May 2013).

5 Zaczek, Ian, *Chronicles of the Celts*, Sterling Publishing Company Inc. (1996).

6 Taylor, Steve, *The Combat of Ferdiad and Cuchulain*, Vassar College (2019).

7 Lacey, Brian, *Terrible Queer Creatures: Homosexuality in Irish History*, Wordwell (2008), p. 51.

8 Klein, Naomi, *Doppelganger*, Knopf Canada (2023).

9 Suggs, *Fairies: A Dangerous History*, p. 101.

Chapter 4: Big Bad Wolves

1 Shoaf, J. P., *Bisclavret*, University of Florida (1996).

2 Atsma, Aaron J., 'Lycophron, Alexandra', Theoi Classical Texts Library, The Theoi Project (2000–2019).

3 Atsma, Aaron J., 'Lycaon (Lykaon) – Arcadian King of Greek Mythology', The Theoi Project (2000–2019).

4 Plutarch, *Plutarch's Lives, translated from the original Greek, with notes, critical and historical, and a life of Plutarch*, Derby & Jackson (1859).

5 Josephus, F. et al., 'Book XV – Chapter 1: Containing the Interval of 18 Years. From the Death of Antigonus to the finishing of the Temple by Herod', *Jewish Antiquities*, Harvard University Press (1998).

6 Ibid.

7 Unknown Scandinavian artist (1150–1200), Berserker Lewis Chess Piece, British Museum, ID: 1831,1101.125.

8 Moorhouse, Dan, *Egil's Saga: Icelandic Viking Saga* (full text), Schools History (n.d.).

9 Conner, Randy P., David Hatfield Sparks and Mariya Sparks, *Cassell's Encyclopedia of Queer Myth, Symbol and Spirit: Gay, Lesbian, Bisexual and Transgender Lore*, Continuum International Publishing Group (1997), p. 298, 'Seidr'.

10 Miguel, Muriel (2013), 'Hot 'n' soft: a lesbian retelling of the myth of Coyote and Fox', in, O'Hara, Jean, *Two Spirit Acts: Queer Indigenous Performances*, Playwrights Canada Press (2014).

11 Jenks, Albert Ernest, 'The Bear-Maiden. An Ojibwa Folk-Tale from Lac Courte Oreille Reservation, Wisconsin', *Journal of American Folklore*, vol. 15, no. 56 (1902), pp. 33–5.

12 Conner, Sparks and Sparks, *Cassell's Encyclopedia of Queer Myth, Symbol and Spirit*, p. 125, 'Double Woman'.

13 Ibid., p. 86, 'Bear'.

14 Prower, Tomás, *Queer Magic*, Llewellyn Publications (2021), p. 196.

15 Foster, Michael Dylan, *The Book of Yokai*, University of California Press (2015), p. 182.

16 Ashkenazi, Michael, 'The Fox and the Jewel: Shared and Private Meanings in Contemporary Japanese Inari Worship', *Journal of Japanese Studies*, vol. 26, no. 2 (2000), pp. 457–61.

17 Maring, Joel M. and Lillian E. Maring, 'Japanese Erotic Folksong: From Shunka to Karaoke', *Asian Music*, vol. 28, no. 2 (1997), pp. 27–49.

18 Foster, *The Book of Yokai*, p. 189.

19 Bellows, Henry Adams, *The Poetic Edda: Thrymskvitha*, Internet Sacred Text Archive (1936).

20 Perrault, C., R. Samber and H. Clarke, *The Fairy Tales of Charles Perrault*, DigiCat (2022).

21 Werewomaniac, *The Werewoman Handbook*, Big Closet (2011).

22 Rowling, J. K., *Harry Potter and the Half-Blood Prince*, Bloomsbury (2005), pp. 313–14.

23 Fur Science, 'Research findings: Sex, Relationships, Pornography', Orientation (2018).

Chapter 5: Children of the Night

1 Jackson, E. A. B., 'Least like saints: the vexed issue of Byron's sexuality', *Byron Journal*, vol. 38, no. 1 (2010).

2 Polidori, John, *The Vampyre*, CreateSpace Independent Publishing Platform (2012, original work published 1819), p. 8.

3 Beresford, Matthew, 'The Lord Byron/John Polidori relationship and the foundation of the early nineteenth-century literary vampire', University of Hertfordshire (2019).

4 Skal, David J., *Something in the Blood*, Liveright (2016), pp. 92–8.

5 Hacker, J. and A. M. Habermann, *The Alphabet of Ben Sira: Facsimile of the Constantinople 1519 edition*, Valmadonna Trust Library (1997).

6 Lesses, Rebecca, 'Lilith', *Halvi/Hyman Encyclopedia of Jewish Women*, Jewish Women's Archive (1999).

7 Le Fanu, S., *Carmilla*, Arcturus Publishing (2023).

8 Coleridge, S. T., *Christabel*, translated by Kalka, J., Ripperger & Kremers (2021).

9 Russo, Vito, *Celluloid Closet: Homosexuality in the Movies*, Harper and Row (1981).

10 Colangelo, B., 'Year of the vampire: *Dracula's Daughter* is the true queen of the Universal Monsters', Slashfilm (2022).

Chapter 6: Witch-hunts

1 Hedrick, Laura E., ' "Male and Female He created them": Counterfeit Masculinity and Gender Presentation as Social Structure in Scotland and England, c.1560–1707', *Journal of Irish and Scottish Studies*, vol. 6.2 (2013), pp. 138+viii.

2 Levack, B. P., *The Witch-hunt in Early Modern Europe*, Routledge (2016).

3 Human Rights Watch, 'Cameroon: Wave of Arrests, Abuse Against LGBT People' (2021).

4 Roxburgh, Shelagh, 'Homosexuality, Witchcraft, and Power: The Politics of *Ressentiment* in Cameroon', *African Studies Review*, vol. 62, no. 3 (2018), pp. 89–111.

5   Gaule, J., *Select cases of conscience touching witches and witchcraft* (1646).

6   Stevenson, Keira, 'Bridget Bishop', *New York Public Library*, Great Neck Publishing (2005).

7   Goodare, Julian, *The European Witch-Hunt,* Routledge (2016).

8   Shakespeare, William, *Macbeth*, Wordsworth Classics (1992).

9   Lejri, Selima, "'Are you a man?" Gender roles in Macbeth', *Représentations et Identités Sexuelles dans le Théâtre de Shakespeare*, Presses Universitaires de Rennes (2010).

10 Wedeck, Harry Ezekiel, *Pictorial History of Morals*, New York Philosophical Library (1964).

11 O'Hara, *Two Spirit Acts.*

12 Conner, Sparks and Sparks, *Cassell's Encyclopedia of Queer Myth, Symbol and Spirit.*

13 Roscoe, W., *The Zuni Man-Woman*, University of New Mexico Press (1996), p. 101.

14 Ibid.

15 Conner, Sparks and Sparks, *Cassell's Encyclopedia of Queer Myth, Symbol and Spirit.*

16 Conner, Randy P., 'Come, Hekate, I Call You to My Sacred Chants', Academia.edu. (2011).

17 Norton, Rictor, *Gay Heretics and Witches: A History of Homophobia* (2002, updated February 2011).

18 Hutton, Ronald, *The Witch – A History of Fear, from Ancient Times to the Present*, Yale University Press (2018), p. 142.

19 Ibid., p. 143.

20 Ibid., p. 141.

21 Ibid., p. 135.

22 Valiente, D., *The Charge of the Goddess – The Poetry of Doreen Valiente*, Centre for Pagan Studies Limited (2014).

23 Murphy, Carlyle, 'Lesbian, gay and bisexual Americans differ from general public in their religious affiliations', Pew Research Center (2015).

24 St. James, H., 'Elpha-Bi: Why *Wicked*'s green skinned heroine is a queer icon', The Theatrical Board (2018).

Chapter 7: Demon Twinks

1   Sunderland, Ty [@TySunderland], Twitter (31 July 2021).

2   Baker, Paul, *Polari – The Lost Language of Gay Men*, Routledge (2002).

3   Crowley, Aleister, *The Book of Goetia, Or the Lesser Key of Solomon the King [Clavicula Salomonis]*, Martino Fine Books (2010).

4   Beer, Robert, *The Handbook of Tibetan Buddhist Symbols*, Serindia Publications (2003).

5   Foster, Michael Dylan, *The Book of Yokai*, University of California Press (2015).

6   Brightman, Robert A., 'The Windigo in the Material World', *Ethnohistory*, vol. 35, no. 4, (1988), pp. 337–79.

7   Spier, Jeffrey, *Meet the Mesopotamian Demons*, Getty Museum (2021).

8   Anonymous, *Jewish Quarterly Review – October 1898 – The Testament of Solomon*, Read Books (2018).

9   Guiley, R., *The Encyclopedia of Demons and Demonology*, Infobase Publishing (2009).

10 Summers, M., *The Malleus Maleficarum of Heinrich Kramer and James Sprenger*, Courier Corporation (2012).

11 Asma, Stephen T., *On Monsters*, Oxford University Press (2009).

12 Gaster, M., *The Sword of Moses: An Ancient Book of Magic*, Literary Licensing, LLC (2014).

13 Kaczynski, Richard, *Perdurabo: The Life of Aleister Crowley*, North Atlantic Books (2002).

14 Anonymous, 'The Wickedest Man in The World', *John Bull*, Saturday 24 March 1923, p. 10.

15 Anonymous, 'A Man We'd Like to Hang', *John Bull*, Saturday 19 May 1923, p. 10.

16 Kaczynski, *Perdurabo*, p. 37.

17 Hedenborg White, M., 'Rethinking Aleister Crowley and Thelema', *Aries*, vol. 21, no. 1 (2020), pp. 1–11.

18 Herzig, T., 'The demons' reaction to sodomy: Witchcraft and homosexuality in Gianfrancesco Pico della Mirandola's "Strix"', *Sixteenth Century Journal*, vol. 34, no. 1 (2003), p. 53.

19 Mills, Robert, 'Seeing Sodomy in the "Bibles moralisées', *Speculum*, vol. 87, no. 2 (2012), pp. 413–68.

20 Mairobert, Mathieu François Pidanzat, *La nouvelle Sapho, ou histoire de la secte Anandryne*, P. F. Didot (1793).

21 Mendès, Catulle, *Méphistophéla*, Snuggly Books (2019, original work published 1889).

22 Vivien, Renée and Y. Quintin, *Sappho*, Erosonyx Éditions (2020, original work published 1903)

23 Ibid.

24 Ibid.

25 Rothwell, K., *Aristophanes' Wasps*, Oxford Greek and Latin College (2019).

26 Karras, Ruth Mazo, *Sexuality in Medieval Europe*, Routledge (2017), p.139.

27 Topsell, Edward, *The History of Four-Footed Beasts and Serpents*, Routledge (2013).

28 Keats, John, *The Complete Poems*, Penguin Books (1977).

29 Wu, Duncan, *30 Great Myths About the Romatics*, John Wiley & Sons, Ltd (2015).

30 Kimberly, C. E., 'Effeminacy, Masculinity, and Homosocial Bonds: The (Un)Intentional Queering of John Keats', *Romanticism on the Net* (2004), pp. 36–7.

31 Letter written 4 November 1820, printed in Gordon, George and Marchand, Leslie, *Byron's Letters and Journals*, Harvard University Press (1973).

32 Severn, Joseph, 'Joseph Severn Letters to Charles Brown', English History (1820).

33 Akinara, Ueda, *Tales of Moonlight and Rain*, translated by Chambers, Anthony H., Columbia University Press (2009).

34 Brown, J. C., *Immodest Acts: The Life of a Lesbian Nun in Renaissance Italy*, Oxford University Press (1986).

35 Vallese, Joe, *It Came from the Closet*, The Feminist Press (2022), pp. 11–13.

36 Peled, Ilan, 'Expelling the Demon of Effeminacy: Anniwiyani's Ritual and the Question of Homosexuality in Hittite Thought', *Journal of Ancient Near Eastern Religions*, vol. 10 (2010), pp. 69–81.

37 Ibid.

38 Bufford, R. K., *Counselling and the Demonic*, W Publishing Group (1988), pp. 105–6.

39 Dear, W., *The Dungeon Master: The Disappearance of James Dallas Egbert III*, Bloomsbury (1991).

40 Romano, A., 'The right's moral panic over "grooming" invokes age-old homophobia', Vox (2022).

Chapter 8: Queerly Departed

1 Hughes, William Richard, *Constance Naden*, Hansebooks (2017).

2 Pinto, Renato and Gretel Luciano, 'Transgendered Archaeology: The Galli and the Catterick Transvestite', *Theoretical Roman Archaeology Journal* (2013), p. 169.

3 Anonymous, 'Dig reveals Roman transvestite', BBC News, 21 May 2002.

4 Campbell, David, A. *Greek Lyric*, vol. v, *The New School of Poetry and Anonymous Songs and Hymns*, Harvard University Press (1993), p. 430.

5 Roscoe, W., 'Priests of the goddess: Gender transgression in ancient religion', *History of Religions*, vol. 35, no. 3 (1996), pp. 195–230.

6 Historic England Reconstruction portrait of a Roman gallus, based on the human remains and jet jewellery excavated from Grave 951 at Site 46, Bainesse Farm, Catterick (Roman Cataractonium), English Heritage, IC159/004c (2002).

7 Reeder, G., 'Same-sex desire, conjugal constructs, and the tomb of Niankhkhnum and Khnumhotep', *World Archaeology*, vol. 32 (2000), pp. 193–208.

8 Moilanen, U. et al., 'A Woman with a Sword? – Weapon Grave at Suontaka Vesitorninmäki, Finland', *European Journal of Archaeology*, vol. 25, no. 1 (2022), pp. 42–60.

9 Liang B., A. S. Cheung and B. J. Nolan, 'Clinical features and prevalence of Klinefelter syndrome in transgender individuals: A systematic review', *Clinical Endocrinology*, vol. 97, no. 1 (2022), pp. 3–12.

10 Balázs, Zsuzsanna, ' "What secret torture?": Normativity, Homoeros and the Will to Escape in Yeats's "The Land of Heart's Desire" and Edward Martyn's "The Heather Field" ', *Studi Irlandesi: A Journal of Irish Studies*, vol. 10, no. 10 (2020), pp. 23–41.

11 Farr, Florence, *The Dancing Faun*, Nabu Press (2010).

12 Yeats, William Butler, *The Speckled Bird*, McClelland & Stewart (1977).

13 Taylor, John H. and Daniel Antoine, *Ancient Lives New Discoveries: Eight Mummies, Eight Stories*, British Museum Press (2014), p. 311.

14 Forthcoming publication mentioned in email with Dr Rebecca Whiting from the British Museum.

15 Anonymous (pseudonym: Critic Fin de Siecle), 'What Is Fin de Siecle?', *The Art Critic*, vol. 1, no. 1 (1893), p. 9.

16 James, Henry, *The Turn of the Screw and The Lesson of the Master*, Prometheus Books (1996).

17 Gunter, Susan E. and Steven H. Jobe, *Dearly Beloved Friends: Henry James's Letters to Younger Men*, University of Michigan Press (2001).

18 Dupee, Frederick Wilcox, *Henry James: Autobiography*, Princeton University Press (1983, original work published 1956).

19 Davis, C. J., 'Love and Economics: Charlotte Perkins Gilman on "The Woman Question"', *American Transcendental Quarterly*, vol. 19 (2005), p. 243.

20 Lang, Andrew, 'Recollections of Robert Louis Stevenson', *North American Review*, vol. 160, no. 459, (1895), pp. 185–94.

21 Harman, Claire, *Robert Louis Stevenson: A Biography*, Harper Perennial (2006).

22 McGarry, M., *Ghosts of Futures Past: Spiritualism and the Cultural Politics of Nineteenth-century America*, University of California Press (2012), p. 154.

23 Guttierez, Cathy, *Handbook of Spiritualism and Channeling*, Brill (2015).

24 Adshead, W. P., M. Mould and Thomas Pallister Barkas, *Miss Wood in Derbyshire*, J. Burns (1879), p. 4.

25 Ibid., p. 18.

26 Robertson, Beth, A., 'Spirits of Transnationalism: Gender, Race and Cross-Correspondence in Early Twentieth-Century North America and Europe', *Gender and History*, vol. 27, no. 1 (2015), pp. 151–70.

27 Tromp, Marlene, 'Queering the Séance: Bodies, Bondage, and Touching in Victorian Spiritualism' in Guttierez, C. (ed.), *Handbook of Spiritualism and Channeling*, Brill (2015).

28 Marryat, Florence, *There is No Death*, David McKay (1917).

29 Hyun-Key Kim Hogarth in Howard, Keith (ed.), *Korean Shamanism: Revivals, Survivals and Change*, Royal Asiatic Society, Korea Branch, Seoul Press (1998).

30 Howard, *Korean Shamanism*.

31 Kim, Janice C. H. in Howard, ibid.

32 Kendall, Laurel, 'Of Gods and Men: Performance, Possession, and Flirtation in Korean Shaman Ritual', *Cahiers d'Extreme-Asie*, vol. 6, issues 45–63 (1991–2), pp. 113–28.

33 Kim, Tae-gon and Keith Howard in Howard, *Korean Shamanism*, p. 21.

34 Kendall, Laurel, *Shamans, Housewives, and other Restless Spirits: Women in Korean Ritual Life*, University of Hawaii Press (1985).

35 Kim and Howard in Howard, *Korean Shamanism*, p. 126.

36 Ibid.

37 Akinara, *Tales of Moonlight and Rain*, p. 85.

38 Ibid.

39 Owen, Wilfred, *The Poems of Wilfred Owen*, Wordsworth Editions (2014).

40 Rubenhold, Hallie, *The Five: The Untold Lives of the Women Killed by Jack the Ripper*, Mariner Books (2020), p. 15.

41 Brown, Robin, *All About History: Jack the Ripper*, Imagine Publishing (2015).

42 Robinson, Bruce, *They All Love Jack: Busting the Ripper*, 4th Estate (2016).

43 Gribton, Thomas, Police letter, 11 November 1888. From Thomas Gribton suggesting that policemen should dress up as women. National Archives. Document 5: reference HO 144/221 A49301C (1888), pp. 204–5.

44 Anonymous, 'A Foolish Joke', *Yorkshire Gazette*, 17 November 1888.

45 Anonymous, 'Man in Woman's Clothes', *Selby Times*, 18 October 1889.

46 Dowd, R., 'Transgender people over four times more likely than cisgender people to be victims of violent crime', Williams Institute (2021).

47 Brown, Howard and James Jeffrey Paul, 'In Search of Homosexual Rippers and Ripper Victims', forum messages from www.casebook.org (2002–3).

48 Berry-Dee, Christopher, *Talking with Serial Killers: World's Most Evil*, John Blake (2018).

49 Weller, Chris, 'Young women are the biggest true crime buffs – here's why', *Business Insider* (2016).

50 Suzuki, Kōji, *Ring*, translated by Rohmer, R. B. and Walley, Glynne, Vertical (2004).

51 Milton, Josh, '85% of gays are possessed by ghosts – according to a not-at-all ludicrous study', *PinkNews* (2022).

Chapter 9: Loving the Alien

1   Bowie, David, 'I went to buy some shoes – and I came back with Life On Mars', *MailOnline* (2008).

2   Crowe, Cameron, 'Playboy Interview: David Bowie', *Playboy* (1976).

3   Clay, Diskin, *Lucian: True History*, Oxford University Press (2021), pp. 76–7.

4   Ibid., p. 77.

5   Lucian, *Soloecista; Lucius or The Ass; Amores; Halcyon; Demosthenes; Podagra; Ocypus; Cyniscus; Philopatris; Charidemus; Nero*, translated by Macleod, M. D., Loeb Classical Library (1989).

6   Ibid.

7   Gilman, Charlotte Perkins, *Herland* (independently published 2020, original work published 1915).

8   Alexander, James B., *The Lunarian Professor*, Kessinger Publishing (2007, original work published 1909).

9   Ibid.

10 Wells, H. G., *The First Men in the Moon* (2005, original work published 1901).

11 Ibid.

12 Sharon, Avi, *Plato's Symposium*, Focus Publishing (1998), p. 36.

13 Ibid.

14 Ibid.

15 Jowett, Benjamin, *Plato's Symposium*, Massachusetts Institute of Technology: Classics Online (2019).

16 Ibid.

17 Aristophanes, *Birds; Lysistrata; Women at the Thesmophoria*, edited and translated by Henderson, Jeffrey, Loeb Classical Library (2015).

18 Carpenter, Edward, *The Complete Works of Edward Carpenter*, Shrine of Knowledge (1883).

19 Ulrichs, Karl, *Letters*, The British Library (1859).

20 Ibid., 22 September 1862 (Dear Sister).

21 Ibid.

22 Ibid., 28 November 1862 (To Wilhelm M., Gr., Luise, Ludewig, Ulrike, Uncle U., Aunt U., Wilhelm U.).

23 Ibid.

24 Birrell, A., *The Classic of Mountains and Seas*, Penguin Books (1999).

25 Crowley, Vivianne and Christopher Crowley, *Ancient Wisdom: Earth Traditions in the Twenty-First Century*, Carlton Books (2002), p. 195.

26 Skipper, Ben, 'HR Giger Dies: Quotes from the Surrealist Artist on Designing Alien', *International Business Times UK*, 13 May 2014.

27 Gallardo, Ximena C. and Jason C. Smith, *Alien Woman: The Making of Lt. Ripley*, Continuum (2004), p. 175.

28 Cameron, James, *Aliens*, 20th Century Fox (1986).

29 Abbott, Edwin A. and Ian Stewart, *Flatland: A Romance of Many Dimensions*, Dover Publications (1992), p. 70.

30 Ibid., p. 24.

31 Ibid.

32 Ibid., p. 25.

33 Mathews, Rupert, *Alien Encounters*, Arcturus Publishing (2007), pp. 117–18.

34 Ibid., p. 124.

35 Ibid., p. 162.

36 Ibid., p. 174.

37 Ibid., p. 177.

38 Strieber, Whitley, *Communion*, Beech Tree Books (1987).

39 Ibid., p. 83.

40 Marchant, Diane, 'A Fragment of Time', hosted on Fanfiction.net (1967).

41 Vallese, *It Came from the Closet*, p. 72.

Chapter 10: Rum, Bum and Concertina

1 Johnson, Charles, *A General History of Pirates*, King Solomon (2021, original work published 1724), p. 55.

2 Barker, Benjamin, *Blackbeard – or, The Pirate of Roanoke*, Biblio Bazaar (2008), p. 10.

3 Turley, Hans, *Rum, Sodomy, and the Lash*, New York University Press (1999), p. 2.

4 Burg, B. R., *Sodomy and the Pirate Tradition*, New York University Press (1995), p. xxxviii.

5 Ibid., p. 128.

6 Ibid., p. 129.

7 Headlam, Cecil (ed.), *America and West Indies: 12–20 June 1699, Calendar of State Papers Colonial, America and West Indies, vol. 17, 1699 and Addenda 1621–1698* (1908), pp. 283–91.

8 Johnson, *A General History of Pirates*, p. 132.

9 Burg, *Sodomy and the Pirate Tradition*, p. xxxix.

10 Ackerman, Rudolph, *Hand-coloured print of a cabin boy* (1799), Royal Museums Greenwich, PAF 4966.

11 Melville, H., *Moby-Dick*, Acclaim Books (1997, original work published 1851).

12 Ibid.

13 McMurray, Shane, *Sailors and sexuality: searching for LGBTQ+ histories in the Royal Navy*, Royal Museums Greenwich (2023).

14 Collins, F., *An Account of the Proceedings Against Capt. Edward Rigby, at the Sessions of Goal Delivery, Held at Justice-Hall in the Old-Bailey, on Wednesday the Seventh Day of December, 1698, for Intending to Commit the Abominable Sin of Sodomy, on the Body of One William Minton. Printed by Order of the Court* (1698).

15 Hacke, William, *A Collection of Original Voyages*, John Carter Brown Library by Scholars' Facsimiles & Reprints (1993, original work published 1699).

16 Gilbert, Arthur, N. 'Buggery and the British Navy, 1700–1861', *Journal of Social History*, vol. 10, no. 1 (1976), pp. 72–98.

17 Burg, *Sodomy and the Pirate Tradition*.

18 *Leondert Hussenlosch*, British Library (1726), p. 12.

19 Ibid., p. 13

20 Johnson, *A General History of Pirates*, p. 101.

21 Ibid.

22 Johnson, *A General History of Pirates*, p. 94.

23 Anonymous, *The Female Soldier*, CreateSpace Independent Publishing Platform (2014, original work published 1740), p. 25.

24 Ibid., p. 34.

25 Defoe, D., *The Life, Adventures, and Piracies of the Famous Captain Singleton*, CreateSpace Independent Publishing Platform (2014, original work published 1720).

26 Ibid.

27 Ibid.

28 Norton, Rictor (ed.), 'Daniel Defoe, On the Public Prosecution and Punishment of Sodomites, 1707', *Homosexuality in Eighteenth-Century England: A Sourcebook*, 8 August 2002, updated 15 June 2008.

Chapter 11: I'm Sorry, Dave

1 Kubrick, Stanley, *2001: A Space Odyssey*, Metro-Goldwyn-Mayer (1968).

2 Gelmis, Joseph, *The Film Director as Superstar*, Garden City, Doubleday and Company (1970).

3 Dery, Mark, *I Must Not Think Bad Thoughts*, University of Minnesota Press (2010).

4 Clarke, Arthur C., *2001: A Space Odyssey*, 50th ed, Orbit (1968), p. xiv.

5 Ibid., p. 99.

6 Hodges, Andrew, *The Enigma of Intelligence*, HarperCollins (1983), pp. 36–7.

7 Ibid., p. 47.

8 Turing, Alan, 'Can Digital Computers Think?', BBC Radio (1951).

9 Hodges, Andrew, *The Enigma of Intelligence*, HarperCollins (1983), p. 488.

10 Sharman, J., *The Rocky Horror Picture Show*, 20th Century Fox (1975).

11 Shelley, Mary Wollstonecraft (Godwin), *Frankenstein; or, the Modern Prometheus*, Project Gutenborg eBook of Frankenstein (1993, original work published 1818).

12 Marshall, Florence Ashton (ed.), *The Life and Letters of Mary Wollstonecraft Shelley: Volume II* (1970, original work published 1889), p. 273.

13 Stryker, Susan, 'My Words to Victor Frankenstein above the Village of Chamounix: Performing Transgender Rage', *GLQ: A Journal of Lesbian and Gay Studies*, vol. 1, no. 3 (1994), pp. 237–54.

14 Lagerlöf, Selma, 'Slåtterkarlarna på Ekolsund', Project Runeberg (1912).

15 Reichardt, Jasia, *Robots: Fact, Fiction and Prediction*, Penguin Books (1978), p. 7.

16 King, Jack, 'M3GAN was factory made to be an LGBTQ+ cult icon', *GQ*, Condé Nast (11 January 2023).

17 Strachey, Chris, 'The "Thinking" Machine', *Encounter*, October (1954), pp. 25–31.

Chapter 12: Ex-Men

1 Davisson, Zack, *The First Superhero – The Golden Bat?*, Comics Bulletin (2010).

2 Unknown Neo-Assyrian engraver (circa 700 BCE), clay tablet with cuneiform script recording part of *The Epic of Gilgamesh*, The British Museum. ID: K.3375.

3 *The Epic of Gilgamesh*, translated by George, Andrew, Penguin Books (2016).

4 Fry, Stephen, *Troy*, Chronicle Books (2021).

5 Atsma, Aaron J., 'Dares of Phrygia's History of the Fall of Troy', The Theoi Project (2000–2019).

6 Ptolemaeus Chennus and Ptolemaeus Hephaestion (100–138 BCE), *New History*, The Tertullian project.

7 Homer, *The Iliad*, translated by Hammond, Martin, Penguin Books (1987)

8 Atsma, Aaron J., 'Aeschylus, Fragments 57–154: The Memnôn: Fragment 64' (2000–2019).

9   Shakespeare, William, *Troilus and Cressida*, Penguin Shakespeare (2006).

10 Symonds, John Addington, *A Problem in Greek Ethics: Being an inquiry into the phenomenon of sexual inversion, addressed especially to medical psychologists and jurists*, Good Press (2012, original work published 1893).

11 Ibid., p. iv.

12 Mayor, Adrienne, *The Amazons: Lives and Legends of Warrior Women Across the Ancient World*, Princeton University Press (2016), p. 11.

13 Ibid., p.136.

14 Tsvetaeva, Marina, *Letter to the Amazon*, Ugly Duckling Presse (2016).

15 Mayor, *The Amazon*, p. 1.

16 Lepore, Jill, 'The Surprising Origin Story of Wonder Woman', *Smithsonian Magazine* (October 2014).

17 Marston, William Moulton, *Wonder Woman: The Golden Age*, vol. 2, DC Comics (2018).

18 Smith, Roland, R. R., *Antinous: Boy Made God*, Ashmolean Museum (2018).

19 Curtius Rufus, *Histories of Alexander the Great, Book 10*, Oxford University Press (2009).

20 Lee, Stan, 'Marvel Comics unveils gay gunslinger', CNN (13 December 2002).

21 Wachowski, Lily, 'The Matrix is a "trans metaphor", Lilly Wachowski says', BBC News (7 August 2020).

Chapter 13: Five Magic Beans

1   Latva, O. and Leskelä-Kärki, M., *Meri ja Tove: Elämää Saaristossa*, Helsinki: John Nurmisen Säätiö (2022).

2   Prower, Tomas, *Queer Magic: LGBT+ Spirituality and Culture from Around the World*, Llewellyn Publications (2018), p. 13.

3   Kirby, J., 'A new group-selection model for the evolution of homosexuality', *Biology & Philosophy*, vol. 18 (2003), pp. 683–94.

4   Jubber, Nicholas, *The Fairy Tellers: A Journey into the Secret History of Fairy Tales*, John Murray (2022).

References

Abbott, Edwin A., and Ian Stewart, *Flatland: A romance of many dimensions*, Dover Publications, 1992.

Ackerman, Rudolph, *Hand-coloured print of a cabin boy*, Image ID: PAF4966, Royal Museums Greenwich, www.rmg.co.uk/collections/objects/rmgc-object-129101

Adshead, W. P., M. Mould and Thomas Pallister Barkas, *Miss Wood in Derbyshire*, J. Burns, 1879.

Akinara, Ueda (translated by Anthony H. Chambers), *Tales of Moonlight and Rain*, Columbia University Press, 2009.

Alexander, James B., *The Lunarian Professor*, Kessinger Publishing, 2007 (original work published 1909).

Al-Khadi, Amrou, *My Life as a Unicorn*, Fourth Estate, 2019.

Allinson, Francis. G. and J. Loeb, *Menander, the Principal Fragments*, Harvard University Press, 1970.

Andersen, Hans Christian, *Complete Andersen's Fairy Tales*, Wordsworth Editions, 2009 (original work published 1843).

Andersen, Hans Christian, *The Little Mermaid*, Pushkin Children's Books, 2020 (original work published 1837).

Anonymous, 'Errores Gazariorum', ed. Julian Goodare, Rita Voltmer and Liv Helene Willumsen, *Demonology and Witch-Hunting in Early Modern Europe*, Routledge, 2020.

Anonymous, *The Female Soldier,* CreateSpace Independent Publishing, 2014 (original work published 1740).

Anonymous, 'A Foolish Joke', *Yorkshire Gazette*, 17 November 1888.

Anonymous, 'Man in Woman's Clothes', *Selby Times*, 18 October 1889.

Anonymous, 'The Wickedest Man in the World', *John Bull*, 24 March 1923, p. 10, British Newspaper Archive, www.britishnewspaperarchive.co.uk/viewer/bl/0003234/1923 0324/041/0010

Anonymous, 'A Man We'd Like to Hang', *John Bull*, 19 May 1923, p. 10, British Newspaper Archive, www.britishnewspaperarchive.co.uk/viewer/bl/0003234/19230519/048/0010

Anonymous, *The Female Soldier*, CreateSpace Independent Publishing, 2014 (original work published 1750).

Anonymous, 'The Testament of Solomon', *The Jewish Quarterly Review (October, 1898)*, Read Books Ltd, 2018.

Anonymous, 'Notes on the Fin de Siècle Movement in Parisian Art and Literature', *Art Critic*, vol. 1, no. 1, 1893, pp. 4–9, www.jstor.org/stable/20494208

Apuleius, translated by P. G. Walsh, *The Golden Ass*, Oxford University Press, 2008.

Aristophanes, ed. Jeffrey Henderson, *Birds. Lysistrata. Women at the Thesmophoria*, Loeb Classical Library, 2015.

Ashkenazi, Michael, 'The Fox and the Jewel: Shared and Private Meanings in Contemporary Japanese Inari Worship', *Journal of Japanese Studies*, vol. 26, no. 2, 2000, pp. 457–61.

Asma, Stephen. T., *On Monsters*, Oxford University Press, 2009.

Atsma, Aaron J., 'The Memnôn: Fragment 64', Aeschylus, Fragments 57–154, www.theoi.com/Text/AeschylusFragments2.html

Atsma, Aaron J., 'Dares Phrygius', The Theoi Project, www.theoi.com/Text/DaresPhrygius.html#:~:text=DARES%20OF%20PHRYGIA's%20History%20of,of%20Hephaestus%20in%20the%20Iliad

Atsma, Aaron J., 'Lykaon', The Theoi Project, www.theoi.com/Heros/Lykaon.html

Atsma, Aaron J., 'Lycophron, Alexandra', The Theoi Project, www.theoi.com/Text/LycophronAlexandra.html

Baker, Paul, *Polari – The Lost Language of Gay Men*, Routledge, 2002.

Balázs, Zsuzsanna, ' "What secret torture?": Normativity, Homoeros and the Will to Escape in Yeats's "The Land of Heart's Desire" and Edward Martyn's "The Heather Field" ', *Studi Irlandesi: A Journal of Irish Studies*, vol. 10, no. 10, 2020, pp. 23–41.

Barber, R. W. and Bodleian Library, *Bestiary: being an English version of the Bodleian Library, Oxford M.S. Bodley 764 with all the original miniatures reproduced in facsimile*, Boydell Press, 2006.

Barker, Benjamin, *Blackbeard – or, The Pirate of Roanoke*, Biblio Bazaar, 2008.

BBC News, 'The Matrix is a "trans metaphor", Lilly Wachowski says', 7 Aug 2020, www.bbc.co.uk/news/newsbeat-53692435

BBC News, 'Dig reveals Roman transvestite', 21 May 2002, news.bbc.co.uk/1/hi/england/1999734.stm

Beer, Robert, *The Handbook of Tibetan Buddhist Symbols*, Serindia Publications, 2003.

Bellows, Henry Adams, *The Poetic Edda: Thrymskvitha*, Internet Sacred Text Archive, 1936, www.sacred-texts.com/neu/poe/poe11.htm

Berry-Dee, Christopher, *Talking with Serial Killers: World's Most Evil*, John Blake, 2018.

Birrell, A., *The Classic of Mountains and Seas*, Penguin Books, 1999.

Bowie, David, 'Loving the Alien', *Tonight*, EMI America, 1984.

Bowie, David, 'I went to buy some shoes – and I came back with Life On Mars', *MailOnline,* 2008.

Boyer, P. and S. Nissenbaum, *The Salem Witchcraft Papers*, Da Capo Press Inc., 1977.

Brightman, Robert A., 'The Windigo in the Material World', *Ethnohistory*, vol. 35, no. 4, 1988, pp. 337–79.

Brook, Mitch, 'Why Luca Is An LGBTQ Story (Despite What Pixar Says)', *ScreenRant*, 19 June 2021, screenrant.com/luca-gay-lgbtq-queer-story-why-pixar/

Brown, Howard and James Jeffrey Paul, 'In Search of Homosexual Rippers and Ripper Victims', Casebook, 2002–2003, https://www.casebook.org/forum1998/messages/1/47414a74.html?1041660213

Brown, J. C., *Immodest Acts: The Life of a Lesbian Nun in Renaissance Italy*, Oxford University Press, 1986.

Brown, Robin, *All About History: Jack the Ripper*, Imagine Publishing Ltd, 2015.

Bufford, R. K., *Counseling and the Demonic*, W Publishing Group, 1988.

Burg, R. R., *Sodomy and the Pirate Tradition*, New York University Press, 1995.

Butler, S., and Sir Charles Sedley, *Dildoides. A burlesque poem.*, Gale ECCO, Print Editions, 2010 (original work published 1706).

Cameron, James, *Aliens*, 20th Century Fox Studios, 1986.

Campbell, David A., *Greek Lyric, Volume V: The New School of Poetry and Anonymous Songs and Hymns*, Harvard University Press, 1993.

Carol, Lewis, *Alice's Adventures in Wonderland*, Macmillan Collector's Library, 2016.

Carpenter, Edward, *The Complete Works of Edward Carpenter*, Shrine of Knowledge, 1883.

Cavalcanti, Guido and D. R. Slavitt, *The Metabolism of Desire: The Poetry of Guido Cavalcanti*, Au Press, 2012.

Chennus, Ptolemaeus, & Hephaestion, Ptolemaeus, *New History*, The Tertullian Project, www.tertullian.org/fathers/photius_copyright/photius_05bibliotheca.htm

Clarke, Arthur C., *2001: A Space Odyssey (50th Edition)*, Orbit, 1968.

Clay, Diskin, *Lucian: True History*, Oxford University Press, 2021.

Clements, Ron and John Musker, *The Little Mermaid*, Walt Disney Pictures, 1989.

Colangelo, B., 'Year Of The Vampire: Dracula's Daughter Is The True Queen Of The Universal Monsters', *Slash Film*, 2022, www.slashfilm.com/773968/year-of-the-vampire-draculas-daughter-is-the-true-queen-of-the-universal-monsters/

Coleridge, S.T. and J. Kalka, *Christabel*, Ripperger & Kremers, 2021.

Collins, F., *An Account of the Proceedings Against Capt. Edward Rigby, at the Sessions of Goal Delivery, Held at Justice-Hall in the Old-Bailey, on Wednesday the Seventh Day of December, 1698, for Intending to Commit the Abominable Sin of Sodomy, on the Body of One William Minton. Printed by Order of the Court.* University of Michigan, 1698, quod.lib.umich.edu/e/eebo2/A25634.0001.001/1:1?rgn=div1;view=fulltext

Conner, Randy P., David Sparks and Mariya Sparks, *Cassell's Encyclopedia of Queer Myth, Symbol and Spirit*, Continuum International Publishing Group, 1997.

Conner, Randy P., *Come, Hekate, I Call You to My Sacred Chants*, Academia.edu, 2011, www.academia.edu/4005066/Come_Hekate_I_Call_You_to_My_Sacred_Chants

Crowe, Cameron, 'Playboy Interview: David Bowie', *Playboy* (1976).

Crowley, Aleister, *The Book of Goetia, Or the Lesser Key of Solomon the King*, Martino Fine Books, 2010.

Crowley, Vivianne and Christopher Crowley, *Ancient Wisdom: Earth Traditions in the Twenty-First Century*, Carlton Books Ltd, 2002.

Dahl, Roald, *The Minpins*, Puffin, 2013.

Daniel, Rod, *Teen Wolf*, Atlantic Entertainment Group, 1985.

Darkshire, Oliver, *Queercoded: Transcendentally Gay Villains for Dungeons and Dragons*, Dungeon Masters Guild, 2021.

Davis, C. J., 'Love and economics: Charlotte Perkins Gilman on "the Woman Question"', *American Transcendental Quarterly*, vol. 19, no. 4, 2005.

Davisson, Zack, 'The First Superhero: The Golden Bat?', SuperHeroHype, 2010, forums.superherohype.com/threads/the-first-superhero.350006/

Dear, W., *The Dungeon Master: The Disappearance of James Dallas Egbert III*, Bloomsbury, 1991.

Defoe, D., *The Life, Adventures, and Piracies of the Famous Captain Singleton*, CreateSpace, 2014 (original work published 1903).

Dery, Mark, *I Must Not Think Bad Thoughts*, University of Minnesota Press, 2012.

Dowd, R., 'Transgender people over four times more likely than cisgender people to be victims of violent crime', UCLA Williams Institute, 2021, williamsinstitute.law.ucla.edu/press/ncvs-trans-press-release/

Dupee, Frederick Wilcox, *Henry James: Autobiography*, Princeton University Press, 1983 (original work published 1956).

Eschenbach, Wolfram von, *Parzival: A Knightly Epic (Complete)*, Library of Alexandria, 1961.

Esquenazi, Deborah, *Southwest of Salem: The Story of the San Antonio Four*, Sam Tabet Pictures, Motto Pictures & Naked Edge Films, 2016.

Fanu, S. L., *Carmilla*, Arcturus Publishing Ltd., 2023.

Farber, Allen, 'Albrecht Dürer: Excerpts from Primary Documents', State University of New York at Oneonta, employees.oneonta.edu/farberas/arth/arth200/artist/durer_primary_docs.html

Farr, Florence, *Dancing Faun*, Nabu Press, 2010.

Faxneld, Per, *Satanic Feminism: Lucifer as the Liberator of Woman in Nineteenth-Century Culture*, Oxford University Press, 2017.

Foster, Michael Dylan, *The Book of Yokai*, University of California Press, 2015.

Fry, Stephen, *Troy*, Chronicle, 2021.

Fur Science, *Sex, Relationships, Pornography*, 5.1: Orientation, 2018, furscience.com/research-findings/sex-relationships-pornography/5-1-orientation/

Gallardo, Ximena C. and Jason C. Smith, *Alien Woman: The Making of Lt. Ripley*, Continuum, 2004.

Garcia, H., 'Ukraine's "unicorn" LGBTQ soldiers head for war', Reuters, 31 May 2022, www.reuters.com/world/europe/ukraines-unicorn-lgbtq-soldiers-head-war-2022-05-31/

Garside, Emily, *Gay Aliens and Queer Folk*, Calon, 2023.

Gaster, M., *The Sword of Moses: An Ancient Book of Magic*, Literary Licensing, LLC, 2014.

Gaule, J., *Select cases of conscience touching witches and witchcraft*, University of Michigan Library, 1646, quod.lib.umich.edu/cgi/t/text/text-idx?c=eebo;idno=A85867. 0001.001

Gelmis, Joseph, *The Film Director as Superstar*, Doubleday, 1970.

George, Andrew (tr.), *The Epic of Gilgamesh*, Penguin Classics, 2016.

Gilbert, Arthur, N., 'Buggery and the British Navy, 1700–1861', *Journal of Social History*, vol. 10, no. 1 (1976), pp. 72–98.

Gilman, Charlotte Perkins, *Herland*, independently published 2020 (original published 1915).

Gloc-9, 'Sirena', *MKNM: Mga Kwento Ng Makata*, Universal Records Philippines, 2012.

Goodare, Julian, *The European Witch-Hunt*, Routledge, 2016.

Gordon, George and Leslie Marchand, *Byron's Letters and Journals*, Harvard University Press, 1973.

Gribton, Thomas, police letter from 'Thomas Gribton suggesting that policemen should dress up as women', National Archives, Document 5, Reference HO 144/221 A49301C, 11 Nov 1888, pp. 204–5.

Guiley, R., *The Encyclopedia of Demons and Demonology*, Infobase Publishing, 2009.

Gunter, Susan E. and Steven H. Jobe, *Dearly Beloved Friends: Henry James's Letters to Younger Men*, University of Michigan Press, 2001.

Guttierez, Cathy, *Handbook of Spiritualism and Channelling*, Brill, 2015.

Hacke, William, *A Collection of Original Voyages*, John Carter Brown Library, 1993 (original work published 1699).

Hacker, J. and A. M. Habermann, *The Alphabet of Ben Sira: facsimile of the Constantinople 1519 edition*, Valmadonna Trust Library, 1997.

Hall, Radcliffe, *The Well of Loneliness*, Penguin Modern Classics, 2015.

Harman, Claire, *Robert Louis Stevenson: A Biography*, Harper Perennial, 2006.

Headlam, Cecil, 'America and West Indies: June 1699', *Calendar of State Papers Colonial, America and West Indies*, vol. 17, 1908, pp. 283–91, British History Online, www.british-history.ac.uk/cal-state-papers/colonial/america-west-indies/vol17/pp283-291

Hedrick, Laura E., ' "Male and Female He created them": Counterfeit Masculinity and Gender Presentation as Social Structure in Scotland and England, c.1560 – 1707', *Journal of Irish and Scottish Studies*, vol. 6, no. 2, 2013, pp. 115–136.

Herzig, T., 'The demons' reaction to sodomy: Witchcraft and homosexuality in Gianfrancesco Pico della Mirandola's Strix', *Sixteenth Century Journal*, vol. 34, 2003, p. 53.

Hillyer, L. (dir.), *Dracula's Daughter*, Universal Pictures, 1936.

Historic England, *Reconstruction portrait of a Roman gallus, based on the human remains and jet jewellery excavated from Grave 951 at Site 46, Bainesse Farm, Catterick (Roman Cataractonium)*, English Heritage, 2002, historicengland.org.uk/images-books/photos/item/IC159/004

Hodges, Andrew, *The Enigma of Intelligence*, Harper Collins, 1983.

Holocaust Memorial Day Trust, '6 May 1933: Looting of the Institute of Sexology', Holocaust Memorial Day Trust, 2023, www.hmd.org.uk/resource/6-may-1933-looting-of-the-institute-of-sexology/

Homer, Martin Hammond (tr.), *The Iliad*, Penguin Classics, 1987.

Housman, C., *The Were-Wolf*, 1stworld Publishing, 2005.

Howard, Keith, *Korean Shamanism: Revivals, Survivals and Change*, Royal Asiatic Society, Seoul Press, 1998.

Hughes, William Richard, *Constance Naden*, Hansebooks, 2017.

Human Rights Watch, 'Cameroon: Wave of Arrests, Abuse Against LGBT People', 2021, www.hrw.org/news/2021/04/14/cameroon-wave-arrests-abuse-against-lgbt-people

Hussenlosch, Leondert, 'Untold Lives', British Library.

Hutton, Ronald, *The Witch: A History of Fear, from Ancient Times to the Present*, Yale University Press, 2018.

Jackson, E. A. B., 'Least like saints: the vexed issue of Byron's sexuality', *Byron Journal*, vol. 38, 2010.

James, H., 'Elpha-Bi: Why *Wicked*'s green skinned heroine is a queer icon', The Theatrical Board, 2018, www.thetheatricalboard.com/editorials/hayleybi

James, Henry, *The Turn of the Screw: The Lesson of the Master*, Prometheus Books, 1996.

Jenks, Albert Ernest, 'The Bear-Maiden. An Ojibwa Folk-Tale from Lac Courte Oreille Reservation, Wisconsin', *The Journal of American Folklore*, vol. 15, no. 56, 1902, pp.33–5.

Johnson, Charles, *A General History of Pirates*, King Solomon, 2021 (original work published 1724).

Josephus, F. et al., 'Book XV, Chapter 1: Containing the Interval of 18 Years. From the Death of Antigonus to the finishing of the Temple by Herod', *Jewish Antiquities*, Harvard University Press, 1998.

Jowett, Benjamin, *Plato's Symposium*, Massachusetts Institute for Technology: Classics Online, 2019, classics.mit.edu/Plato/symposium.html

Kaczynski, Richard, *Perdurabo: The Life of Aleister Crowley*, North Atlantic Books, 2002.

Karras, Ruth Mazzo, *Sexuality in Medieval Europe*, Routledge, 2017.

Kaufman, S., 'Ballets Russes, and the enduring dancing man', *Washington Post*, 2013, www.washingtonpost.com/entertainment/museums/ballets-russes-and-the-enduring-dancing-man/2013/05/09/0d367e1c-b7ef-11e2-b94c-b684dda07add_story.html

Keats, John, *The Complete Poems*, Penguin, 1977.

Kendall, Laurel, *Shamans, Housewives, and other Restless Spirits: Women in Korean Ritual Life*, University of Hawaii Press, 1985.

Kendall, Laurel, 'Of Gods and Men: Performance, Possession, and Flirtation in Korean Shaman Ritual', *Cahiers d'Extreme-Asie*, vol. 6, 1991–2, pp. 45–63.

Kimberly, C. E., 'Effeminacy, Masculinity, and Homosocial Bonds: The (Un)Intentional Queering of John Keats', *Romanticism on the Net*, 2004.

King, Jack, 'M3GAN was factory made to be an LGBTQ+ cult icon', *GQ*, Condé Nast, 11 Jan 2023, www.gq-magazine.co.uk/culture/article/megan-movie-lgbtq-icon

Kirby, J., 'A new group-selection model for the evolution of homosexuality', *Biology & Philosophy*, vol. 18, 2003, pp. 683–94.

Kōji Suzuki, Rohmer, R. B. and Glynne Walley, *Ring*, Vertical, 2004.

Kubrick, Stanley, *2001: A Space Odyssey*, Metro-Goldwyn-Mayer, 1968.

Lacey, Brian, *Terrible Queer Creatures: Homosexuality in Irish History*, Wordwell, 2008.

Lagerlöf, Selma, *Slåtterkarlarna på Ekolsund*, Project Runeberg, 1912, runeberg.org/trollı/ekolsund.html

Lang, Andrew, 'Recollections of Robert Louis Stevenson', *North American Review*, vol. 160, no. 459, 1895, pp. 185–94.

Lang, Andrew, *The Arabian Nights Entertainments*, Biblioteca Virtual Universal, 1918, biblioteca.org.ar/libros/167042.pdf

Latva, O. and M. Leskelä-Kärki, *Meri ja Tove: Elämää Saaristossa*, Helsinki: John Nurmisen Säätiö, 2022.

Laxman, S., 'Unicorn hunting: How bisexual women are fetishised on dating apps in India', *Vogue India*, 22 Feb 2022, www.vogue.in/culture-and-living/content/unicorn-hunting-how-bisexual-women-are-fetishised-on-dating-apps-in-india

Lee, Stan, 'Marvel Comics unveils gay gunslinger', CNN, 13 Dec 2002, cnn.com/2002/ALLPOLITICS/12/13/cf.opinion.rawhide.kid/

Lejri, Selima, ' "Are you a man?" Gender roles in Macbeth', *Représentations et identités sexuelles dans le théâtre de Shakespeare*, Presses Universitaires de Rennes, 2010.

Levack, B. P., *The Witch-Hunt in Early Modern Europe*, Routledge, 2016.

Lepore, Jill, 'The Surprising Origin Story of Wonder Woman', *Smithsonian Magazine*, October 2014, www.smithsonianmag.com/arts-culture/origin-story-wonder-woman-180952710/?no-ist

Lesses, Rebecca, 'Lilith', *Halvi/Hyman Encyclopedia of Jewish Women*, Jewish Women's Archive, 1999, jwa.org/encyclopedia/article/lilith

Liang B., A. S. Cheung and B. J. Nolan, 'Clinical features and prevalence of Klinefelter syndrome in transgender individuals: A systematic review', *Clinical Endocrinology*, vol. 97, 2022, p.3–12.

Lightfoot, J. L., *On the Syrian Goddess*, Oxford University Press, 2003.

Lind, E. and R. Werther, *Autobiography of an Androgyne*, Fredonia Books, 2005.

Loizou, Polis, *A Good Year*, Fairlight Moderns, 2022.

Lucian (translated by M. D. Macleod), *Dialogues of the Dead; Dialogues of the Sea-Gods; Dialogues of the Gods; Dialogues of the Courtesans*, Loeb Classical Library, 1989.

Lucian (translated by M. D. Macleod), *Soloecista; Lucius or The Ass; Amores; Halcyon; Demosthenes; Podagra; Ocypus; Cyniscus; Philopatris; Charidemus; Nero*, Loeb Classical Library, 1989.

Machard, A., *The Wolf Man*, Thorton Butterworth, 1934.

MacCarthy, F., *Byron: Life and Legend*, Farrar, Straus and Giroux, 2004.

Mackenzie, C., *Extraordinary Women*, Faber & Faber, 2009.

Mairobert, Mathieu François Pidanzat, *La nouvelle Sapho, ou histoire de la secte Anandryne*, P. F. Didot, 1793.

Marchant, Diane, *A Fragment of Time*, Fanfiction.net, www.fanfiction.net/s/7989303/1/A-fragment-in-time

Maring, Joel M. and Lillian E. Maring, 'Japanese Erotic Folksong: From Shunka to Karaoke', *Asian Music*, vol. 28, no. 2, 1997, pp. 27–49.

Marryat, Florence, *There Is No Death*, David McKay, 1917.

Marryatt, Frederick, *The White Wolf of the Hartz Mountains*, Fantasy and Horror Classics, 2011.

Marshall, Rob, *The Little Mermaid*, Walt Disney Pictures, 2023.

Marston, William Moulton, *Wonder Woman: The Golden Age, Vol. 2*, DC Comics, 2018.

Martin, Andrew, 'The Famous Phobic Chronic Masturbating Author Who Wouldn't Leave Charles Dickens' House', *Medium*, 17 Oct 2021, historianandrew.medium. com/the-famous-phobic-chronic-masturbating-author-who-wouldnt-leave-charles-dickens-house-aa3c937a80a0

Mathews, Rupert, *Alien Encounters*, Arcturus Publishing, 2007.

Mayor, Adrienne, *The Amazons: Lives and Legends of Warrior Women Across the Ancient World*, Princeton University Press, 2016.

McGarry, M., *Ghosts of Futures Past: Spiritualism and the Cultural Politics of Nineteenth-century America*, University of California Press, 2012.

McMurray, Shane, 'Sailors and sexuality: searching for LGBTQ+ histories in the Royal Navy', Royal Museums Greenwich, 1 Feb 2023, www.rmg.co.uk/stories/blog/library-archive/sailors-sexuality-searching-lgbtq-histories-royal-navy

Melville, H., *Moby Dick*, Acclaim Books, 1997 (original work published 1851).

Mendès, Catulle, *Mephistophela*, Snuggly Books, 2019.

Miller, Arthur, *The Crucible*, Penguin Classics, 2000 (original work published 1953).

Mills, Robert, 'Seeing Sodomy in the "Bibles moralisées"', *Speculum*, vol. 87, no. 2, 2012, pp. 413–68.

Milton, Josh, '85% of gays are possessed by ghosts – according to a not-at-all ludicrous study', *PinkNews,* 2022.

Moilanen, U. et al., 'A Woman with a Sword? – Weapon Grave at Suontaka Vesitornin-mäki, Finland', *European Journal of Archaeology*, vol. 25, 2022, pp. 42–60.

Moore, Lauren, 'Dying Gods, Syria and the Flood: A Study of Male Consorts and Syncretism in the Cult of Atargatis', *Historia Religionum: An International Journal*, vol. 5, 2013.

Moorhouse, Dan (n.d.), *Egil's Saga: Icelandic Viking Saga (Full Text)*, Schools History, schoolshistory.org.uk/topics/primary-history/source-material-the-vikings/egils-saga-icelandic-viking-saga-full-text/

Muller, Axel, Christopher Halls and Ben Williamson, *Mermaids: Art, Symbolism and Mythology*, University of Exeter Press, 2022.

Murphy, Caryle, 'Lesbian, gay and bisexual Americans differ from general public in their religious affiliations', *Pew Research Centre*, 26 May 2015.

Norton, Rictor, 'Daniel Defoe: On the Public Prosecution and Punishment of Sodomites, 1707', *Homosexuality in Eighteenth-Century England: A Sourcebook*, 8 Aug 2002, updated 15 Jun 2008, rictornorton.co.uk/eighteen/defoe.htm

Norton, Rictor, 'Gay Heretics and Witches', *A History of Homophobia*, 2002, updated 18 Feb 2011, rictornorton.co.uk/homoph04.htm

Owen, Wilfred, *The Poems of Wilfred Owen*, Wordsworth Editions Ltd., 2002.

O'Hara, Jean, *Two Spirit Acts: Queer Indigenous Performances*, Playwrights Canada Press, 2014.

Peled, Ilan, 'Expelling the Demon of Effeminacy: Anniwiyani's Ritual and the Question of Homosexuality in Hittite Thought', *Journal of Ancient Near Eastern Religions*, vol. 10, 2010, pp. 69–81.

Pells, Kelly, 'Bushey Artist Gets Egypt Bug', *Watford Observer*, 29 April 2016, www.watfordobserver.co.uk/news/14461427.bushey-artist-gets-egypt-bug/

Perrault, C., R. Samber and H. Clarke, *The Fairy Tales of Charles Perrault*, DigiCat, 2022.

Pflugfelder, G. M., *Cartographies of Desire: Male-male sexuality in Japanese discourse, 1600-1950*, University of California Press, 2007.

Pinto, Renato and Gretel Luciano, 'Transgendered Archaeology: The Galli and the Catterick Transvestite', *Theoretical Roman Archaeology Journal*, 2013.

Pliny, The Elder, J. F. Healy (ed.), *Natural History: A Selection*, Penguin Classics, 2004.

Plutarch, *Plutarch's Lives: Translated from the Original Greek, with Notes, Critical and Historical, and a Life of Plutarch*, Derby & Jackson, 1859.

Polidori, John, *The Vampyre*, CreateSpace, 2012 (original work published 1819).

Prower, Tomás, *Queer Magic*, Llewellyn Publications, 2021.

Quintus Curtius Rufus, J. E. Atkinson and J. Yardley (tr.), *Histories of Alexander the Great: Book 10*, Oxford University Press, 2009.

Reeder, G. 'Same-Sex Desire, Conjugal Constructs, and the Tomb of Niankhkhnum and Khnumhotep', *World Archaeology*, vol. 32, 2000, pp. 193–208.

Reichardt, Jasia, *Robots: Fact, Fiction and Prediction*, Penguin, 1978.

Richter, Daniel S., 'Chapter 21: Lucian of Samosata', *Oxford Handbook of the Second Sophistic*, Daniel S. Richter and William A. Johnson (eds.), Oxford University Press, vol. 1, 2017.

Robertson, Beth A., 'Spirits of Transnationalism: Gender, Race and Cross-Correspondence in Early Twentieth-Century North America and Europe', *Gender and History*, vol. 27, 2015, pp. 151–70.

Robinson, Bruce, *They All Love Jack: Busting the Ripper*, Fourth Estate, 2016.

Roelens, Jonas, 'A Woman Like Any Other: Female Sodomy, Hermaphroditism and Witchcraft in Seventeenth-Century Bruges', *Journal of Women's History*, vol. 29, no. 4, 2017, pp. 11–34.

Romano, A., 'The right's moral panic over "grooming" invokes age-old homophobia', *Vox*, 21 April 2022, www.vox.com/culture/23025505/leftist-groomers-homophobia-satanic-panic-explained

Roscoe, W., 'Priests of the goddess: Gender transgression in ancient religion', *History of Religions*, vol. 35, no. 3, pp. 195–230, 1996, doi.org/10.1086/463425

Roscoe, W., *The Zuni Man-Woman*, University of New Mexico Press, 1996.

Ross, R., *Aubrey Beardsley*, Books on Demand, 2018 (original work published 1907).

Rothwell, K., *Aristophanes' Wasps*, Oxford Greek and Latin College, 2019.

Rowling, J. K., *Harry Potter and the Half-Blood Prince*, Bloomsbury, 2005.

Roxburgh, Shelagh, 'Homosexuality, Witchcraft, and Power: the Politics of Ressentiment in Cameroon', *African Studies Review*, vol. 62, 2018, pp. 89-111.

Rubenhold, Hallie, *The Five: The Untold Lives of the Women Killed by Jack the Ripper*, Mariner Books, 2020.

Ruberg, Bonnie, *Video Games Have Always Been Queer*, New York University Press, 2019.

Sappho, Renée Vivien and Y. Quintin, *Sappho*, Erosonyx Éditions, 2020 (original work published 1903).

Scott, Ridley, *Alien*, Brandywine Productions, 1979.

Scribner, Vaughn, *Merpeople: A Human History*, Reaktion Books, 2020.

Severn, Joseph, *Joseph Severn Letters To Charles Brown 1820*, English History, englishhistory.net/keats/letters/john-keats-letters-joseph-severn-to-charles-brown/

Sewell, Brian, 'The genius of Durer', *The Standard*, 5 Apr 2012, www.standard.co.uk/showbiz/celebrity-news/the-genius-of-durer-7428306.html

Shakespeare, William, *Macbeth*, Wordsworth Classics, 1992.

Shakespeare, William, *Troilus and Cressida*, Penguin Shakespeare, 2006.

Sharman, J., *The Rocky Horror Picture Show*, 20th Century Studios, 1975.

Sharon, Avi, *Plato's Symposium*, Focus Publishing, 1998.

Shelley, Mary, *Frankenstein,* Gutenberg, 1818, www.gutenberg.org/files/84/84-h/84-h.htm

Shoaf, J. P., *Bisclavret*, University of Florida, 1996, people.clas.ufl.edu/jshoaf/files/bisclavret.pdf

Skal, David. J., *Something in the Blood*, Liveright, 2016.

Skipper, Ben, 'H. R. Giger Dies: Quotes From the Surrealist Artist on Designing Alien', *International Business Times*, 13 May 2014, www.ibtimes.co.uk/hr-giger-dies-quotes-surrealist-artist-designing-alien-1448365

Smith, Roland, R. R., *Antinous: Boy Made God*, Ashmolean Museum, 2018.

Spier, Jeffrey, 'Meet the Mesopotamian Demons', *Getty Museum*, 2021, www.getty.edu/news/meet-the-mesopotamian-demons/

Stewart, Peter, 'The Polychrome Reconstruction of the Prima Porta Statue', *Frieze*, 1 Oct 2017, www.frieze.com/article/polychrome-reconstruction-prima-porta-statue

Strachey, Chris, 'The "Thinking" Machine', *Encounter*, October 1954, pp. 25–31.

Strieber, Whitley, *Communion*, Beech Tree Books, 1987.

Strudwick, Nigel, *Masterpieces of Ancient Egypt*, British Museum Press, 2006.

Stryker, Susan, 'My Words to Victor Frankenstein above the Village of Chamounix: Performing Transgender Rage', *GLQ: A Journal of Lesbian and Gay Studies*, vol. 1, 1994, pp. 237–54.

Suggs, Richard, *Fairies: A Dangerous History*, Reaktion Books, 2018.

Summers, M., *The Malleus Maleficarum of Heinrich Kramer and James Sprenger*, Courier Corporation, 2012.

Sunderland, Ty [@TySunderland], Twitter, 31 July 2021, twitter.com/TySunderland/status/1421541705799569408?s=20

Symonds, John Addington, *A Problem in Greek Ethics: Being an inquiry into the phenomenon of sexual inversion, addressed especially to medical psychologists and jurists,* Good Press, 2021 (original work published 1893).

Taylor, John H. and Daniel Antoine, *Ancient Lives, New Discoveries: Eight Mummies, Eight Stories*, British Museum Press, 2014.

Taylor, Steve, *Combat of Ferdiad and Cuchulain*, Vassar College, 2019, adminstaff.vassar.edu/sttaylor/Cooley/Ferdiad.html

Tom Robinson Band, 'Cabin Boy', *War Baby: Hope and Glory*, Castaway Northwest, 1984.

Topsell, Edward, *The History of Four-Footed Beasts and Serpents and Insects*, Routledge, 2013.

Turing, Alan, *Can Digital Computers Think?*, BBC Radio, 1951.

Turley, Hans, *Rum, Sodomy and The Lash*, New York University Press, 1999.

TSvetaeva, Marina, *Letter to the Amazon*, Ugly Duckling Presse, 2016.

Ulrichs, Karl, 'Letters', British Library, 1859.

Unknown Neo-Assyrian engraver (circa 700 BCE), 'The Gilgamesh Tablet', Clay tablet with cuneiform script recording part of *The Epic of Gilgamesh*, British Museum, ID: K.3375, online artefact record: www.britishmuseum.org/collection/object/W_K-3375

Unknown Scandinavian artist (1150–1200), 'Chess-piece', Berserker Lewis Chess Piece, British Museum. ID: 1831,1101.125, online artefact record: www.britishmuseum.org/collection/object/H_1831-1101-125

Valiente, D., *The Charge of the Goddess – The Poetry of Doreen Valiente*, Centre for Pagan Studies Limited, 2014.

Vallese, Joe, *It Came From The Closet: Queer Reflections on Horror*, Feminist Press, 2022.

Wedeck, Harry Ezekiel, *Pictorial History of Morals*, New York Philosophical Library, 1964.

Weller, Chris, 'Young women are the biggest true crime buffs – here's why', *Business Insider*, 2016.

Wells, H.G., *The First Men in The Moon*, 2005, (original work published 1901).

Werewomaniac, *The Werewoman Handbook*, Big Closet, 2011.

White, M. Hedenborg, 'Rethinking Aleister Crowley and Thelema', *Aries*, Brill, 2020.

Wilde, O. and W. Goldsmith, *The Canterville Ghost*, GenNext Publication, 2023.

Wu, D., *30 Great Myths about the Romantics*, John Wiley & Sons, 2015.

Wullschlager, Jackie, *Hans Christian Andersen: The Life of a Storyteller*, Penguin, 2001.

Yeats, William Butler, *The Speckled Bird*, McClelland & Stewart, 1977.

Yeats, William Butler, *The Collected Poems*, Vintage Classics, 1970.

Zaczek, Ian, *Chronicles of the Celts*, Sterling Publishing Company Inc., 1996.

Image Sources

Page 6: *Smoking Lesbian Mermaid* by George Leonnec, 1926
© La Vie Parisienne n°2, 1926 / HPrints

Page 8: Portion of a tapestry, featuring Sirinx as described by Rafael. Peru, 1680–1720
© Victoria and Albert Museum, London

Page 18: *Little Mermaid* by Edmund Dulac
© Archivart / Alamy Stock Photo

Page 21: *Merman Reaching Up* by Myrtle Broome
© Bushey Museum and Art Gallery

Page 22: Costume Ball at the Institute for Sexual Science in Berlin, before 1928
© Magnus-Hirschfeld-Gesellschaft e.V., Berlin

Page 29: A bestiary featuring a unicorn
© Getty Images

Page 33: *The Abduction of Proserpine on a Unicorn* by Albrecht Dürer, 1516
© Art Collection 4 / Alamy Stock Photo

Page 43: Costume design by Leon Bakst (1866–1924) for Carabosse, the wicked fairy godmother in *The Sleeping Beauty*
© World History Archive / Alamy Stock Photo

Page 45: Maude Adams as Peter Pan, 1905
© Picryl

Page 50: A group of Radical Faeries gather for an Equinox ritual in London, 2017
© Mike Kear / Alamy Stock Photo

Page 57: *Jupiter in the Guise of Diana Seducing Callisto* by Jacob Adriaensz Backer
© ART Collection / Alamy Stock Photo

Page 65: *The Fox's Wedding*, 1800
© Penta Springs Limited / Alamy Stock Photo

Page 83: An engraving from the gothic novel *Carmilla* by Sheridan Le Fanu, 1872
© Pictorial Press Ltd / Alamy Stock Photo

Page 85: A promotional poster for *Dracula's Daughter*, 1936
© Wikimedia Commons

Page 97: A woodcut of Hermaphroditus: the male-female principle of alchemic transmutation straddling the winged globe of chaos, 1625
© Historical Picture Archive / Alamy Stock Photo

Page 103: A marble statuette of Hecate
© Penta Springs Limited / Alamy Stock Photo

Page 104: *Witches Going to Their Sabbath* by Luis Ricardo Falero, 1878
© The Picture Art Collection / Alamy Stock Photo

Page 105: *The Night-Hag Visiting Lapland Witches* by Henry Fuseli, 1796
© IanDagnall Computing / Alamy Stock Photo

Page 119: Marginalia drawing by Aleister Crowley from his personal copy of *The Goetia: The Lesser Key of Solomon the King* (Foyers, UK: Society for the Propagation of Religious Truth, 1904), Warburg Institute, University of London
© Ordo Templi Orientis

Page 126: A depiction of Lamia
© Wikimedia Commons / Wellcome Collection

Page 145: Human mummy, name unknown (British Museum: EA6704)
© The Trustees of the British Museum

Page 150: A photograph of a woman exuding ectoplasm
© Chronicle / Alamy Stock Photo

Page 165: David Bowie as The Man Who Fell to Earth, 1976
© Mary Evans / Studiocanal Films Ltd / Alamy Stock Photo

Page 179: *Alien* artwork by H. R. Giger, 1978
© Maximum Film / Alamy Stock Photo

Page 193: *Cabin Boy* by Thomas Rowlandson, 1799
© The Print Collector / Alamy Stock Photo

Page 199: An engraving of Anne Bonny and Mary Read
© Lebrecht Music & Arts / Alamy Stock Photo

Page 202: An engraving of Hannah Snell, 1854
© Old Paper Studios / Alamy Stock Photo

Page 206: Crew of *USS Saratoga* dressed up for a 'Crossing the Line' ceremony
© Aviation History Collection / Alamy Stock Photo

Page 218: *The Nymph Salmacis and Hermaphroditus* by Michel de Marolles, 1655
© The Print Collector / Alamy Stock Photo

Page 230: A basalt carving depicting Gilgamesh and Enkido fighting Humbaba
© Zev Radovan / Alamy Stock Photo

Acknowledgements

Every good mythical beast is some kind of hybrid, formed from bits and pieces of other creatures mashed together. That is the nature of this book also. But a book isn't made from body parts, it's made from people: people who have supported me in ways they may, or may not, realise.

The fierce brave heart of the beast is my husband, Dan. He's the one that's kept the blood flowing and the ventricles pulsing. Without him there'd be no book. But from the heart flow the major veins and arteries: Alex Hay, Anneka Holden, Amy Klein, Fran Darvill and Sheldon K. Goodman are their names. They've allowed the beast to stay alive, drawn energy from its breath and occasionally kept its pulse in check.

The face of the beast, the part with eyes that leads it through the scary world of publishing to either enthral or terrorise, is made up of my agent Carrie Kania, my development editor Hayley Shepherd, and the publication team at Unbound including Aliya Gulamani and Flo Garnett. But the twitching ears and flared nostrils, those sensitive parts are Jay Hulme and Ben Paites, ensuring the beast doesn't lumber into a wall of stereotypes or fly headlong into a quagmire of problematic misrepresentation or historical misinformation!

My monster also has three sturdy limbs; it is a mismatched tripod! One oozing tentacle is the National Maritime Museum, where I cut my teeth in museum work and fleshed out my mermaid fascination. The carved wooden talon on the other side is the Museum of London, which accidentally inspired the title for this book. And the last limb, a strange insectile appendage, is the British Museum, which despite many critiques of provenance, is also an entire world, alive with historic wonders and mythological oddities.

Then there are the wings, one on each side, which give our shambling oddity flight, allowing it to take off. One is Robert Berg, who opened the doors to the Disney story, and the other is Amber Butchart, who suggested I write a book in the first place (Amber this is your fault!).

The beast is also glam, très chic! It has two fabulous horns: my mum, Suzan Swale, and dad, Robert Coward, who have always stood by their strange gay son and supported him every step of the way.

But it's also a fearsome beast, with stabbing tusks, wicked-sharp but ornately carved: Katherine McAlpine and Nick Coveney, who have always fought for me and my ideas even when I haven't been able to myself.

Finally there are the feathers, scales, hairs and quills, the skin and exoskeleton that cover the beast. These are people I've never met, but whose YouTube videos, books and articles I have consumed and been inspired by: Caelan Conrad for their work on *What Is A Groomer?*, Rowan Ellis's reflections on nonbinary aliens, Harry Brewis for his exploration of H. P. Lovecraft, Natalie Wynn's discussions around the philosophy of gender, and Princess Weekes's and Sarah Z's deconstructions of fandom and queerbaiting to name a few.

Also Chris Carpineti: you'll get your demonology books back at some point, promise!

In truth, every cell, neuron and fibre of this misshapen monster is a person or an experience. Many of them you will find acknowledged at the back of this book, most are not. To all of you, named and unnamed: thank you.

Index

Unbound is the world's first crowdfunding publisher, established in 2011.

We believe that wonderful things can happen when you clear a path for people who share a passion. That's why we've built a platform that brings together readers and authors to crowdfund books they believe in – and give fresh ideas that don't fit the traditional mould the chance they deserve.

This book is in your hands because readers made it possible. Everyone who pledged their support is listed below. Join them by visiting unbound. com and supporting a book today.

Jonathan Baldock
Chris Baldwin
Ryan Balgobin
David Ball
Deborah J Ballantyne
Rose Bamber
Andrea Bandelli
Adam-Thomas Bane
Alasdair Barclay
G. B. Bard
Richard Barker
Angharad Barlow
Greg Barnes
Connor Barr
Sara Barratt
Chris 'Boo Boo' Barrett
Chris Barrett-Molloy
Daniel Bartlett
Rob Bassett
Matt Bates
TJ Batok
Rachel E. Bauer
Julie Baugh
Matt Baume
Julianna Bautista
Emma Bayliss
Vikki Bayman
John Beattie
Tatyana Beck
Anton Becker
Avery Becker
Tyler Behrens
Kieran Bell
Patrick Bell
Kevin Benham
Stuart Bennett
Olivier J. M. Béquignon
Ian Beresford
Oliver Berger
Swinda Berghoef
Donna & Fraser Berry
Matthew Bess
Nadia Betkouchar

Mathew Bevan
Jack Bibby
James Bicaldo & Mark
    Street
Roxane Bicker
Jon Biggs
Kari Birchman
Stewart Birnie
Scott Birrell
Evelyn Bishop
Sage Bishop
Graeme Black
Ryan Blackburn
Owen and Jenny
    Blacker
Vladimir Blagoderov
Fran Bleach
Jessica Blye
Ryan Boczar
Jacob Bogart
Timothy Bolduc
Colby Bomberowitz
Emmanuelle
    Bonnefond
Clare Boothby
Alexander Borg
Sam Bosbach
Ed Boulter-Comer
Sam Bowers
Luke Bowyer
Andrew Boyer
Julie Bozza
Michael Bramham
James Brandon
Nadine Brandt
Thomas Brandt
Gerette Braunsdorf
Mikey Brett-McStay
Emma Britton
Dario Brocchini
Miklos Brodersen
Angela Brooks
Ross Brooks

Rob Browatzke
Ash Brown
Isabella Brown
Jack & Orville Brown
Jane S Brown
Quinn Brown
Ryan Brown
Brian Browne
Jonathan Bruce
Bryan
Jesse Bryce
Seán Bryceland
Anwen Bullen
Georgia Bullock
Rakesh Bungar
Peter Bunzl
James Burgon
Kevin Burke
Sarah Burrough
James Burt
Philip Bußmann
Tony Butchart-Kelly
Jacob Butler
Jamie Butler
John Butler
Kevin C
Matthew C
Myla C
Pia C
Tre C
Matt Cain
Eric Calamari
Regina Caldart
Alex 'Bert' Call
Joseph Callow
Peter Camba-Alvarez
Eric Cameron
Dorian Campbell
Lizzy Campbell
Kathryn Campbell-
    Kibler
Tomàs Canet
Elizabeth Card

Sheena Carmichael
Alfredo Carpineti
Robert Carrasco
Wayne Carringer
Laura Carter
Carter
Minnow Carty
Martin Casey
Brad Cassidy
Charles Castleberry
Luke Cavalli
Bertrand Cavayé
Karin Celestine
Brianda Cepeda
Rafael Ugarte Chacón
Shadie Chahine
Jenny Chamarette
Brandon Chamberlain
David Lars
   Chamberlain
Justin Chang
Corinne Chapman
KJ Charles
Amber Chester
Antonio Chew
Kacey Chilvers
Joanne Chittenden
Jon Choy
Daniel Church
Gary Clark
Scott H. A. Clark
Sonja Clark
Thom Clark
Edward Clarke
Rob Clarke
Roger Clarke
Trevor Clarke
James Claverley
Rosie Claverton,
   Excalibur Bascom
Peter Clayton
Leon Clement
Stephen Clifford

David Clover
Lindsey Cobb
Jonathan Cockeram
Daniel Cohen
Dylan Coldwater
Emma Coleman
Lauren Coleman
Michael Collins
Amanda Comet
Vanessa Compagnoni
Sinead Conneely
Dan Connolly
Caelan Conrad
Gareth Conroy-
   Edwards
Jonathan Coombes
Alex Cooper
Carly Cooper
John 'Cooper'
Lian Cooper
Martin Cooper
Andy Corrigan
Peter Corrigan
James Couldry
Steven Coultate
Angela Coveney, Nick
   Coveney
Karen Coverett
Richard Coxon
Fiona Craig
Peter Craske-Phillips
Kay Crawford
Red-Elisabeth Craze
Susan Crites
Charlie Croissant
Marion Cromb
James Cronin
JP Cross
David Crowe
Julia Croyden
Rebekah-Jayne Crozier
Crystal Lake
   Managment

Alex Cunningham
Gordon Cunningham
Tallulah Cunningham
Ewan Cushan
Stefanie Cuthbert
Michael Cutts
Gary Daly
Marc John Bordier Dam
Janet Danks
Francesca Darvill
Raven Todd DaSilva
Colin Davey
Charlotte Davies
Chris Davies
Dai Davies
Katrina Davies
Matt Davies
Matthew Davies
Mattie Davies
Phil Davies
Robert Davies
Chris Davis
Alexandra Dawe
Ginny Dawe-Woodings
Stuart Day
Jerry Daykin
Nick de Figueiredo
David De La Rosa
Michael De La Torre
Luan Eloy de Lima
Helmut De Nardi
Carolina De Vivo
Emily Deans
Heather Deeming
Christina Delzenero
David Demchuk
Phoebe Demeger
Jen Denison
Kat Denvir
Emma Dermott
Matt Dexter
Arjun Dhanjal
Geri Diorio

Craig Dixon
Katherine Dixon-
    Warren
DJG
Mark Dodyk
Ian Doherty
George Doji
Sara Domanski
Damien Donnelly
Martyn Dore
Russell Dornan
Ryan Doyle
Matthew Drapper
Jorrit Drewes
Kate Drinane
Jon Dryden Taylor
Ellie Dudgeon
Simon Duncan
Caitlyn Dunn
Sara K Dunn
Hayley Dunning
Dan Early
Matthew Eastman
Jason Eddy
Nick Ede
Ceri Edwards
Carolin Eichhorn
Hatem Elerwi
Anthony Ellaby
Ashley Elliott
Oliver Ellis
Philip Ellis
Holly Elms
Imogen Ely
Susanne Emde
Aron Estaver
Cat Evans
Daniel Evans
Dave (Shinty) Evans
Johnathen Evans
Lauren Evans
Matt Evans
Richard G. Evans

Victoria Evans
    (WhovianMummah)
Aleks Fagelman
Nicky Fahey
Duncan Falk
Pondy-Upton Family
Timothy Farmer
William Farnworth
Mike Farquhar
Louise Farquharson
Laine Farrell
Brian Farrey-Latz
Steven Faulkner
A J de la Fe Guedes
Dave Fearon
Conaugh Feehan
Jakob Feldtfos
    Christensen
Abi Fellows
Conor Fenton
Ashley Ferguson
Craig Ferguson
Rowan Ferreira
Edward Ficklin
Fidget
Matt Fitzgerald
Ian Fitzpatrick
James Fitzpatrick
Jamie Flack
Molly Flatt
Victoria Fletcher
Will Fletcher
Kerry Flinn
Willem Fokkenrood
Mary Foley
Vladimíra Fonfarova
Guy Foord-Kelcey
For Silin Razza-Baril
Stuart Forbes
Christine Ford
Amy Forster-Smith
Douglas Forsyth
Liam Forsyth

Michaeljon Fosker
Amy Foulds
Joanne Foxton
Lena Frain-Atallah
Paul Fraine
Esther Frankort
Milane Frantz
Jake Freeman
Christopher French
Liam French Robinson
Isobel Freyley
Thiago Froio and
    Harmish Mehta
Brian Fuchs
Becca Fulkerson
James Fuller
Niall Fulton
Diane Furlong
Jo G
Joan G
Johnny G
Gajendran
Monica C. Gallo
Ander Luque García
Chris Garland
Graham Garner
Christine Garretson-
    Persans
Laura Gavinelli
Christoph Gebhard
Amro Gebreel
Jacqueline Geller
Ricky Gellissen
Umber Ghauri
Christopher
    Giannoukos
Suzanne Gibbs
Thomas Gibbs
Alison Giles
Jonathan Gill
Nigel Gilmore-Cook
Christopher Gilpatrick
Simon Gilson

Richard Girvan
Ryan Glasby
Edward Glauser
Matthew Glenn
Craig Glennie
Chris Glinski
Douglas Glynn
Geneviève Godin
David Godwin
Rain Gomez
Rebeca Gómez Morilla
Rupert Good
Grant Goodwin
Jay Gordon
Sarah Gorringe
Christopher Gorry
Danny Gottleib
Marie-Claire Gould
Jo Gower
Chad Gowler
Joe Grant
Elyse M Grasso
Amelia Gray
Michael Graysmark
Marcus Green
Suraj Gregory-Kumar
James Gregory-Monk
Erlend Magnus
    Greibesland Stark
Chris Griffin
Sarah Griffin
Oscar A. Torres
    Grimaldo
Martin Grimm
Dominic Grindle
Darrell Grizzle
Ante Grković
Heather Groves
Morgane Grummert
Paul Guest
Margarita Guidos
Aliya Gulamani
Richard Gush

Babs Guthrie
Kathryn Gynn
Will Haden
Henrik Hafstad
Garry Haining
Kristóf Hajós
Andrew Hall
Joanne Hall
Marie Hall
Oli Hall
Will Hall
Jeremy Hallstrom
George Halstead
Meg Halstead
Bess Hambleton
Ryan Hamill
Jozef Hamilton
Kristof Hamilton
Marc Hamilton
Robert Hamilton
Joe Hammond
Stephan Hampton
Rob Harcombe
James Hardcastle
Lucas Hardy
Paul Harfleet
Patrick Harkin
Alastair Harris
Chelsea Harris
Jess Harris
Joe Harris
Sophie Harris
Isaac Hartmann
Tricia Harvey
Stephen Haskins
Peter Hasted
Marshall Hatley
Simon Hawthorn
Alex Hay
Gavin Hayes
Rae Haylock
Lucy Heard
Callum Heath

Sebastian Hendra
Lewis Henshall
Frazer Heritage
Thomas Hescott
Jeff Hess
Martin Hetherington
Hannah Hethmon
Nos Hexe
James Hickmott
Harriet Hicks
David Higgins
Loch Hightower
Neal P Hill
Mary Jo Hinson
Joe Hinson, Mary Jo
    Hinson
Alan Hitchin
Ondrej Hoberla
Emily Hodder
Claire Hodges
Jack Hodgkiss
Holly Hodson
Matthew Hodson
Stephen Hogg
Anneka Holden
Kirk Holland
Keith Hollenkamp
Simon Holloway
Brian Holmes
Kote Holmes
Michael Holt
Kerenza Hood
James Hope
Sam Hope
Elizabeth Hopkinson
Maxwell Hopkinson
Edward Howe
Nathan Howell
Mark Howie
Dara Howley
Victoria Hoyle
Lesley Hoyles
Shunping Rick Huang

Heather Huber
Lisa Hughes
Robert Hughes
Donita Hulme
Ben Humphrys
The Hunhoffs
Jamie Hunt
Stefan Patrik
    Hüttenmoser
Jacek Hutyra
Lizzie Huxley-Jones
Pauline Inglis
Stuart Innes
Ben Ioannou
Farah Ismail
Robyn Jackson
Sam Jackson
Briony Jackson-
    Newbold
Saffa Jan
Peter Jasperse
Jakub Jazdzewski
Jane Jeans
Eirnin Jefford Franks
Patrick Jeffries
Laura Jellicoe
Serena Jenkins
Tom Jenkins
Brett Jensen
Tyler Jerrom
Marjorie Johns
Be Johnson
Michael Johnson
Paul Johnson
Alun Jones
Darren Jones
Helen Jones
Matthew Jones
Nina Jones
Rhiannon Jones
Thomas Jones
Tim Owen Jones
Mary Jordan-Smith

Ronan Jouffe
Alex Jump
Christopher June
Piotr Jung
Mike Jury
Ste K
Malvina K.
Kafeïa
Constance Kaine
Joanne Kakuda
Michal Kaminski
Carrie Kania
Kadir Karababa
Spenser Kash
Stephen Kay
Kat Kellermeyer
Jack Kelley
Kevin Kelly
Sarah-Louise Kelly
Jamie Kelsey
David Keltie-
    Armstrong
Sam Kemp
Jonathan Kennedy
Andrew Kenrick
Matt Kerlogue
Emma Kernahan
Nathan Kerr
Hazel Kerrison
Kestrell
Thomas Keyton
Dom Khayat
Christopher Killerby
Chloe Kincaid
Toby 'Merpola' King
Marcus Kingi
Stephen Kirk
Laura Klein
Gareth Klose
Cate Kneale
Guinevere Knight
James Knight
Sebastian Kola-Bankole

Hayley Korczynski
Pshem Kowalczyk
Aaron Kraemer
Helene Kreysa
Stevie Kroft
Gregory Kroll
Keith B. Krum
Fabrice Kutting
Phillip L.
Mae L.-Jensen
Terryn Laird
Cameron Lam
Laura Lamb
Dan Lambden
Alex Lambert
Orphée Lamotte
Simon Landmine
Michael Langan
Sam Langford
Gemma Larkin
Léon Larkings
P. E. 'Beef' Larsen
Benjamin Last
Andy Lau
Frankie Laufer
Jessica Law
Ben Lawrence
Rhys Lawton
Richard L. Lawyer
Michael Lax
SF Layzell
Andrew Le Breton
Lindon Le Lai
Graeme Lea-Ross
Ben Leach
Bill Leal
Steven Learmonth
Andrew Leicester
James Leigh
Rachel Leigh
Daniel Lennox
Marina Leoni
Ellen Grace Lesser

Rob Lewington
Jessica Lewis
Otti Lewis
E. Lewy
Andrew Leyland
Lianvis
Mike Licudi
Taryn Lindhorst
Lucas Lixinski
Eve Lizie
Lottie Llewelyn-Wells
Salvador Lloret-Fariña
George Lloyd
Robert Lock
Nick Lodge
Camille Lofters
Polis Loizou
Rosie Loveridge
David Lowbridge-
　Ellis
William Lowther
Samuel Ludford
Heiko Ludwig
Alannah Luide-Brown
Joshua Lurie
Kathryn Luznicky
Richard Lyle
Mike Lynch
Richard Lynn
James Lyon
Kyle Lysher
Adelai M
Andrew M-N
Chiara Mac
Richard Mace
Willie Mackenzie
Drew Mackie
Andrew MacKinnon
John Maclean
Eilidh Macpherson
Adam Macqueen
Mark Maczko
Madame Earl Grey

Jannat Majeed
Ali Majid
Catt** Makin
Katherine Maldonado
Marcin Malinow
Andy Malone
Han Malyn
Navjot Mangat
Natasha Mangion
Nico Mara-McKay
Joshua Marchant
Lady Margaret
Benito Marino
Keith Marks
Simon Marks, Amy
　Maidment
Inga Markstrom
Kevin Marnell
Christopher Marsland
Deborah Martin
Will Martin
Mikayel Martirosyan
Ian Massa-Harris-
　McFeely
Phillip Mathis
Devin Matlock
Anthony Matthews
Jenna Matthews
Brian Mattucci
Ric Mauger
Indigo Maughn
Sean Tobias May
Melissa Maynard
Justin Mays
Graeme McAllister
Katherine McAlpine
Eoghan McArdle
Andrew McArthur
Danni McAuley
Rob McClenaghan-
　Harrop
Conor McCormack
Wesley McCraw

Drew McCray
Mike McCulloch
Katelyn McDade
Conway McDermott
Reed McDonough
Greg McDougall
Katie McDowell
Robert McDowell
Josh McElravy
Jenna McElroy
Constance McEntee
MH McFerren
Frank McGee
Kevin McGee
Ferdiad McGowan
Meghan McGrath
Adam McGreggor
Josie McGregor
Joe McIntyre
Bob McKay
Anthony McKee
Devlin McKee
Faye McKeever
Kevin McKenna
Neil McKenna
James McKeon
Andrew McKeown-
　Henshall
Danny McKeown-
　Henshall
Duncan McLaren
Lesley McLarnon
Frankie McLaughlan
David McMaster
Parami McMillan
Dan McNeil
Gregg McWhirk
Ryan McWilliams
Claire Mead
Andrew Medlyn
Richard Medoff
Samuel & Edward
　Meeks

Al Meggs
Ross Meikle
Jaime Mercado
Phil Mercer
Luke Meredith
Meredith
Caroline Mersey
Edith Mewis
Tanaka Mhishi
Mufseen Miah
Shannen Michaelsen
Callum Michie
Margaret Middleton
Alex Mildenhall
Ellie Miles
Sean Millar
Gunnar Miller
Scott Millman
Hereward Mills
Jennifer Mills
Marinos Miltiadous,
    Dean Cowper
Dale Miracle
Missne
Jacob Mitchell
Jake Mitchell
Fran Moldaschl
Ken Monaghan
Beth Montague-Hellen
Brandon Montenegro
Theodore Montgomery
Andrew Moore
Martin Moore
Michael Moore
Sarah Moore
Katy Moran
Amy Louise Morgan
Cat Morgan
Jon Morgan
Charlotte Morris
Fionnuala Morris
Rob Morris
Rebecca Morris-Buck

David Morrison
Kate Morrison
Sarah Morrison
Clemmie Moule
Emily Mount
Guillaume A. Mueller
Carlton Mullis
Ruaidhrí Mulveen
Lauren Mulville
Demetrio Muñoz
Cara Murphy
Niall Murray
Darcie Nadel
Claire Nally
Nomi Naomi
Carlo Navato
Chris Needham
John Neil
Antony Nelson
Niamh Nestor
Benjamin Nevius
Dean Newby
Steve Newby
E. E. Newell
Amy Newton
Sophie Newton
Jack Ng
Sean Ngai
Matt Nicholls
Morgan Duna Nichs
Nina Nicole
Mike Niedzwiecki
Jake Niemeyer
Jake NightRaven2365
Nikolay
Gordon Nixon
Jenni Nock
Michael Nolan
Sally Noonan
Robyn Norfolk
Simon Norman
Annie Norman (Bad
    Squiddo Games)

Alexandra Norrish
Jenny Northeast
Daniel Northover
Alice Norton
Willow Norton
Isaac Núñez Hernández
Andrew Nunn
Tomás Ó Cinnéide
Cathal Ó Ruaidh
Megan O'Donnell
Adam O'Farrell
Jade Elizabeth O'Neil
Karen O'Sullivan
Dean Tāne O'Rafferty
David Ogden
Florence Okoye
Mark Oldroyd
John Oliver
Olly loves Matt
Conor Olmstead
Christopher Olsen
James Olsen
Ondřej
Alicia Orellana
Benedicto Orevillio
Orla
Jemma Orme
Carlos Ors
Robert Orzalli
Joe Osborne
Gabrielle Osrin
Adam Ostrowski
Olivette Otele
Watt Otter
Catherine Owen
Martin Page
Tashya Page
Tom Page
Leigh Pain
Ben Paites
Kylie Pan
Chris Park
Marcia Louise Parks

James Parnell-Mooney
Ruby Parnham-Cope
Benjamin Parsons
Neil Parsons
Kaizad Patel
David Patterson
Teo Patty
Jonathan Payne
John Peach
Greg Pearson
Evelina Pecciarini
Richard Peck
Claire Peet
David Peet
Dr. Andrew Joseph
   Pegoda
Aneirin Pendragon
Katrina Penn
Mike Pennell
Caroline and James
   Pennock
Tomas Persson
Shelley W. Peterson
Bobbie Petford
Mark Phifer
Neil Philip
Amanda Phillipson
Robb Pickard
Kathryn Picken
Klaus Piechocki-Brown
Karen F. Pierce
Eddie Pile
Scott Pilkington
Danielle Pines
Katrina Pitt
Emil Pohl
JR Poklemba
Lewis Pollard
Tracey Pollard
Rodolfo Ponce
Steve Pont
MIchael Lee Porter
Anabel Portillo

Sophie Potter
Bryanne Pouncy
Luke Povey
Rosanne Powell
Chris Power
Adam Powers
Brian Pozun
Rhianna Pratchett
Kyle Prati
Rebecca Prentice
Michael Pretty
Lee Prosser, Gogi
   Macjcenovic, Derek
   Craig
Michel Provost
Russell Pryce
Gavin Pugh
Mike Pugh
Ally Putvin
Erin Quan
Georgia Quarry
Rory Queripel
Andrew J Quinn
Scott Quinn
Nicky Quint
Saúl Quirós
Laurena R
Kira R.
Andrew Radford
Paul Rahl
Jon Rainford
Amanda Ramsay
Mark Rance
Jason Ranville
Claudia Rapp
Ben Rattigan
Audacia Ray
Jonathan Ray
Alejandro Rebon
   Portillo
El Redman
Bethan Rees
Lydian Reeves

Eric Reithel
Melissa Relfe
Alex Rendall
Jonny Rex
Danny Reynolds
Mark Reynolds
Robbie Reynolds
Chris Rhodes
Jon Rice
Wallie Rice
Mark Rich
Iona Edward
   Richardson
Lukas Richter
Eric Riddler
Suzanne Ridealgh
Justin Ridley
Luc Riesbeck
Eric Riley
Anthony Rimmer
Jamie Rimmer and
   James Fuller
Pamela Ritchie
Kate Roberts
Rhodri Roberts
Chris Robson Day
Elfi Rodatos
Martina Astrid Rodda
Jim & Luke Rodden
Zach Rodriguez
Nicholas Roethlisberger
Lynsey Rogers
Phoenicia Rogerson
Ian Rohde-Bell
Alex Romanos
Stephen Rooney
Sam Roots
Mark & Nicholas
   Rosado
Eva Rose
Sarah Rose
Virginia Rounds
Niall Rowe

Paul Rowell
Jon Rowlands
Des Rowlinson
Daniel Rucky
Aud Ruge Stokka
Bonnie Russell
Daniel Russell
Stuart Russell
Cal Rydzinski
Lauren, Dan, Char &
    Linc Sabo-Crawford
Charlotte Sachs
Waldorf Salad
Daniel James Salas-
    Escabillas
Ben Salter
Lí Samhain
Guido Sanchez
Alexander Sanderson
Adam Sandham
Nafi Sanou
Matthew Saunderson
Chris Scales
Kevin Scannell
Florence Schechter
Oskar Schmidt-Hansen
Jennifer Schofield
Christopher Schubert
Johanna Schuepbach
Jenny Schwarz
Fabienne Schwizer
Gemma Scott
Grace Scott
Lorna Scott
River Scott
Sarah Scott
Will Scott
Lisa Scott-Thacker
Phil Scully
Jeff Seddon
Icy Sedgwick
Sam Segrest-Suessmith
Jill Seidenstein

Katherine Sellar
Candi Servatius
Benjamin Seward
Madeleine Sexton
Aaron Shanks
Rogan Shannon
Kailen Shantz
Sabine Sharp
Erin Sharpe
Steven Shaw
Glenn Sheard
Michael Sheldon
C.R. Shelidon
Dean Shelley
Clare Shepherd
Emma Shepherd
Martin Sherlock
Steven Shiel
William Shockley-
    Temple
Etai Shofel
Pete Shorney
Bryony Shuter
Pol Siligardos
Jorge Silva
Marlon Simeon
Jeffrey Simons
Brian Simpson
Coleman Simpson
Charles Andrew Singh
    Saini
Charlotte Emily
    Skardon
Aisling Skeet
Ian Skinnari
Benjamin Skinner
Craig Skinner
Ezra Slack
Lindy Smart
Markéta Šmídová
Amelia Smith
Anika Smith
Brian Smith

Caroline Smith
Eddie Smith
J Tyler Smith
Kii Smith
Rachel-anne Smith
Sam Smith
Simon Smith
Steve Smith
Tristan Smith
Zan Smith
John Smoleskis
Kate So
Mary Solano
Iskandar Solmaz
Elena Soper
Alison Souter
Andrew Southern
Meredith Spies
Stephen Spillane
Harald Sprengel
Megan Springate
Jeremy Sprinkle
Martijn Spruit
Pierrette Squires
Sr Belladonna in Gloire
    de Marengo
Jenny Staff
Martin Stafford
Catherine Stahl
Thom Stanbury
Alex Stanley
Andrew Stark
Charlotte Stark
Emily Starling
Jaime Starr
Jonathan Stephen
Marina Stern
Ruth Stevens
Paul Stevenson
Ronnie Stewart
Gwilym Stone
Lois Stone
Louie Stowell

Pamela Strachman
Andrew Strange
Zoë Strange-Gould
Carly Straughan
Rich Strickland
Sacha Stronach
Kaelan Strouse
Wiktor Struk
Adam Stuart
Pendragon Stuart
Pippa Stubbs
Sarah Stupak
Ben Rhys Sturrock
Christine Styrnau
Charlotte Suckling
Damon Suede
Ed Sum
Ken Summers
Nicholas Surges
Michael Swafford
Mary Swainson
Suzan Swale
Laura Sweeney
Sam Swindell
Avi Syme
Mark Syson-Harvey
Ashley Szczerbaniwicz
Kim T
Rob T
Sean Tai
Ian Tallis
William Tanski IV
Mermaid Tay
Al Taylor
Deb Taylor
JT Taylor
Lize Taylor
Jane Teather
Ezra Tellington
Curtis Tenney
Grisly Terror
Laura Terry
Conner Tervit

Marianna Terzakis
Jack Theobald
Barry Theodore
Emma Thimbleby
Aisling Third
Aurelien Thomas
Gavin J Thomas
George Thomas
Ian Thomas
Steven Thomas
Danielle Thompson
Liz Thompson
Nicholas Thompson
Ian Thompson-Corr
Amelia Thorp
Thomas Tilbey
Chloe Timms
Joanna Tindall
andrew tobert
Laura Tobin
Robert Tompkins
Damia Torhagen
Joshua R. Torres
Will Tosh
David Rodriguez Tovar
Billy Tran
Roxanne Tran
Kaitlin Tremblay
John Tresadern
Katherine Truax
Cyril Paul Trudgian
Soen Trueman
Richard Truscott
Christie Tucker
Sian Tukiainen
Robert Tunmore
Jamie-Lee Turner
Max Turner
James Turowski
Tzigi
Lee Underwood
Will Ung
Matt Valenti

Gothic Valley WI
William van Assen
Joost van den Ossenblok
Clark Gillian Van
    Herrewege
Davy Van Obbergen
Roeland van Zeijst
Robert Vaughan
VELA
Deco Verri
Love, Vic
Pierre Vienne
Nicolas Vigneron
Kalle Vikman
Kristian Villalobos
Jo Violet
Vicky Vladic
Laura von Holt
Veronica Wagner
Olivia Wakefield
Lainey Grace Wakeman
Peter Waldron
Kevin Walker
Josie Wall
Eric Wallace
Robert Wallace
Sara Walls
Raye Walsh
Dylan Walters
Abi Walton
Carole-Ann Warburton
Steve Wardlaw
Ashley Warren
Sarah Warren
Rory Wasylyk
Louise Waters
Rocky Waters
Scott Waterson
Tara Watkin
Ric Watts
Wil Watts
Fi Weatherwax
Chris Webb

David Lee Webb
Robert Webb
Kimberley Wegner
Julie Weir
Chris Wells
Connie Wells
Scott Wells
Mark Wentworth
Bradley West
Caroline West
Lizzie Westbrook
Anthony James
   Weston
Jack Wetherill
Jaz Weyer Brown
Michael & Nigel
   Whaley-Stephens
Ben Wheare
Christopher Wheeler
Doreen Wheeler
Laura White
Stuart White
Benji Whitehouse
Susan Whitehouse
Alex Whitmarsh

Chris Whyte
Steven Whyte
David Widenmaier-
   Smith
Lara Wilde Moon
Scarlett Wilkie
Rachel Wilkinson
Carwyn Williams
Huw Williams
LJ Williams
Russell Williams
Steven Williams
Jasmine Williamson
Rich Williamson
Rob Willoughby
Alan Wilson
James Wilson
Johanna Wilson
Tom Wiltshire
Beatrice Wing
Liam Winning
Mat Winser
Q Wirtz
Julia Wolfe
Carol Wood

Gemma Wood
Jim Woodall
Tom woodland
Robert Charles
   Wootton
Callum M Wright
Daniel Wright
Dorian A Wright
Mike and Alan Wright
Brett Wrightbrook
Don Yarman
Gayle Yeomans
Svetoslav Yordanov
Toprak Yörük
Martin Young
Richard Young
Teagan Young
Steven Yull
Thomas Zachariason
Frederick Zennor
Aleks Zglińska and
   Thea Cochrane
Marcy Zimmerly
Evan Ziolkowski
Anna Zschokke

A Note on the Author

Sacha Coward is a researcher, historian and public speaker. He has worked in museums and heritage for fifteen years, running tours focused on LGBTQ+ history for museums, cemeteries, archives and cities all around the world. Sacha has featured on a variety of television, radio and podcast shows and written articles on topics as varied as Turing's Law, the rainbow flag, Caravaggio's paintings and Viking burials. *Queer as Folklore* is his first book.

A Note on the Type

The text of this book is set in Adobe Garamond Pro. Released in 1989, it is a digital adaptation of the roman types of Claude Garamond and the italic types of Robert Granjon. It's one of several versions of Garamond. It is believed that Garamond based his font on Bembo, cut in 1495 by Francesco Griffo in collaboration with the Italian printer Aldus Manutuis. Garamond types were first used in printed books in Paris around 1532.